DICTIONARY
OF
CONSERVATIVE QUOTATIONS

DICTIONARY
OF
CONSERVATIVE QUOTATIONS

Edited by
IAIN DALE

First published in Great Britain 1999
by Politico's Publishing
8 Artillery Row, London, SW1P 1RZ, England

Tel 0171 931 0090
Email politicos@artillery-row.demon.co.uk
Website http://www.politicos.co.uk

A catalogue record for this book is available from the British Library

ISBN 1 90230 115 3

Printed and bound in Great Britain by St Edmundsbury Press.
Cover Design by Ad Vantage.

CONTENTS

FOREWORD
by
Rt Hon. William Hague

When Conservative Prime Minister Benjamin Disraeli commented that: 'The wisdom of the wise and the experience of the ages are perpetuated by quotations', he was, more than likely, envisaging a collection selected from his own prodigious output. It is true, however, that dictionaries of historical quotations are an ideal way to discover the personalities which have dominated our political landscape, both past and present. To know that Burke is an important conservative thinker is not the same as understanding what he meant by saying: 'liberty must be limited in order to be possessed'.

Quotations allow those of us who do not have time to pore over multiple learned tomes to access the thoughts of many brilliant, important, observant or just plain eccentric minds and to learn how the world looked through their eyes.

In the often frenzied environment that the modern politician inhabits, crammed with back-to-back appointments and three-minute interviews, it is hard to remember that words are never entirely spontaneous or disposable. Like particles of pure energy, words assume many different forms and can be turned to suit any purpose the moment demands, yet, as a consequence of being drawn on time and again, they accumulate their own histories and a wide range of meanings.

A word like 'conservative' has been around long enough for people to understand very different things by it—just ask Edward Heath or Margaret Thatcher! Occasionally, famous quotations will be rewarded by inclusion in popular idiom. Harold Macmillan's comment about the 'wind of change' in South Africa is an obvious example. Most political words will, it is true, be quickly forgotten but all remain available to be excavated and rediscovered by future generations. Dictionaries of quotations are, in many respects, exercises in political archaeology.

What is particularly pleasing to me about a specialist Conservative dictionary of quotations is how it illustrates the breadth and depth of conservatism as a political tradition. Indeed, it has a proud pedigree, counting among its numbers thinkers of the calibre of John Locke, Edmund Burke and Michael Oakeshott; great wartime leaders, including Pitt the Younger and Winston Churchill; radical economic reformers like Robert Peel and Margaret Thatcher, and oratorical geniuses such as the Elder Pitt and Ronald Reagan. Less eminent, although no less conservative, are colourful characters like Edwina Currie, the might-have-beens like Barry Goldwater, or the forgotten—who can recall the key events of Henry Addington's Premiership? Finally, there are those, like Alan Clark, whose wit can be savage but who can make us laugh.

What, if anything, do these conservative figures have in common? In consulting quotations from Aristotle (we claim him!) to Margaret Thatcher, from Abraham Lincoln to Karl Popper, certain themes recur: a suspicion of state intervention; an admiration for the traditional institutions of social and political life and a belief in the virtue of individual liberty—so far as it does not undermine these institutions. The pleasure of a book such as this lies in exploring the diversity of ways in which Conservatives have thought about these and a vast array of other questions. I certainly do not agree with all of the quotations in this book. Some, such as Abraham Lincoln's views on race before he became president, make for quite difficult reading. Conservatives, unfortunately, are no different from other kinds of people in falling prey to the prejudices of the day. They are perhaps a little better than some at maintaining a healthy scepticism towards passing political fads.

Any political organisation as old as the Conservative Party inevitably has its historical fault lines. The modern party which, to use John Major's words, believes in a 'classless society', was once led by Lord Salisbury, to whom democracy meant 'simple despotism'. Neither have Tories always been advocates of free trade, as Robert Peel learned to his cost.

Whatever the particular view expressed, I like to think that, on the whole, the quotations in this book show that conservatism is a political tradition alive with ideas and enriched by many thoughtful, intelligent and funny people. I can't deny that sometimes they have got it wrong, but I still have no doubt in saying that were Disraeli alive today, he would amend one of his quotations to read: 'The wisdom of the wise and the experience of the ages are perpetuated by *Conservative* quotations!'

William Hague
Leader of the Conservative Party

FOREWORD
by
Michael Brown

Quotations are the pepper and salt, the garnish and the sauce of the politician's stock-in-trade. They are also the foundation stones for the writer, the biographer and the political journalist. They illustrate, they entertain, they embarrass, they insult and they often define the character of those who use them.

Many quotations, written by others, are often borrowed by politicians to enhance an argument or a principle. Usually this is because the quotation is already well known and, having stood the test of time, withstands constant repetition. But their use can sometimes come back, like a boomerang, to haunt those who fail to live up to the expectation of the quotation selected. An example of the latter, most observers would probably agree, was the use by Margaret Thatcher, as she stood on the threshold of power outside 10 Downing Street in 1979, of the lines written by Saint Francis of Assisi. 'Where there is discord may we bring harmony' presaged the promise of tranquillity which was hardly the best description of Mrs Thatcher's eleven and a half years in office. I yield to no-one in my admiration of the great Lady's achievements, but as she set about breaking up the post-war socialist consensus, which had been based on a cosy cross-party harmony, there was a necessary discord throughout her Premiership as she took on a host of enemies at home and abroad. Her use of the quotation was to be hurled back at her throughout her years in Downing Street.

Margaret Thatcher became far more quotable as a result of the things she said, usually about herself, rather than for the quotations she borrowed from others. Quotations by others, about her, also helped to reinforce her style and character. No-one will ever forget her famous line: 'you turn if you want to; the Lady's not for turning', during the 1980 Conservative Party conference. The Conservatives had been in power for just eighteen months and the monetarist policies were taking their toll on unemployment. A huge trade union protest march outside the conference hall had even encouraged 'wet' Young Conservatives to hand over their security passes to some of the protestors who gained unauthorised entry into the hall in order to heckle the Prime Minister during her speech. But the heckling and the doubts within the party—not least among several Cabinet ministers –were soon forgotten. That single phrase was a defining moment in establishing the character of Margaret Thatcher as determined, strong and unbending. Her reputation for resolution of purpose was firmly established by those eleven words in the eyes of journalists, commentators and, above all, the general public. Like her or loathe her, that sentence was to be the memorial to all her subsequent achievements. At moments of great national crisis, such as the Falklands conflict and the miners' strike, everyone referred back to that original quotation and did not expect Margaret Thatcher to waver until she had defeated her aggressors.

Some quotations, by others, about Margaret Thatcher helped, unwittingly, at an early stage to reinforce her image of power and strength. Shortly after she became Conservative Party leader her tough stance against the Soviet Union led to her being dubbed, in the Soviet Magazine *Red Star,* as the 'Iron Lady'. The term was meant to be derogatory in its tone but Mrs Thatcher, seizing on the quotation, embraced its implication and milked it to her advantage for all its worth. 'The Iron Lady of the Western World? Me, a cold war warrior? Well, yes …' Those old Communists in Moscow did more, by that description, for Margaret Thatcher's reputation than any spin doctor or advertising agency.

One of the joys of referring to quotations from the past is to see how arguments which have exercised our forebears still rage today. No issue illustrates the case better than the governance of Europe. Back in 1876, Otto von Bismarck noted that: 'whoever speaks of Europe is wrong. It is a geographical concept'. Quotations about a German desire to conquer and control Europe exercised British ministers then as it does Conservative politicians now. The late Nicholas Ridley reminded us, in 1990, of a variation of Bismarck's quotation when he said during an interview with The *Spectator:* 'This [European Monetary Union] is a German racket designed to take over the whole of Europe.' Poor Mr Ridley paid for his observation by resigning from the Cabinet, but few doubted that he was speaking for Margaret Thatcher who remained nervous of German reunification after the Berlin Wall came down. I remember dining with Enoch Powell when he upbraided me as I talked loosely about 'Europe', and failed to define my idea of the concept. His riposte cut me down to size when he also echoed Bismarck with the put-down, 'Europe is nothing except a line on a map'. He ordered me to refer to what, he assumed, I meant to say: namely 'the Common Market'. Ever after, I have always referred to the EEC, subsequently re-styled the EC and now known as the EU, as 'the Common Market'. Dennis Skinner, the Labour MP for Bolsover, continues to do the same.

On the other side of the European debate, which continues to rage to this day within the Conservative Party, we can see the early seeds of pro-European Conservatism which were sown in quotations from Lord Salisbury over a century ago. He would be standing shoulder to shoulder with Michael Heseltine and Kenneth Clarke, if he were alive today. His credentials were established in 1888 when he said: 'we are part of the community of Europe and we must do our duty as such'. Even the dreaded word 'federalism' was alive and well in 1897, when he said: 'the federated action of Europe is our sole hope of escaping from the constant terror and calamity of war'.

Quotations from politicians bring out their cruelty and no-one gets greater applause or opprobrium, usually in equal measure, than Norman Tebbit when in full cry with the downright rude or unkind put-down. His 'on your bike' (mis)-quotation is set in context in this book, but even he may now regret his call in the Commons, to Tom Litterick, a Labour MP during the 1970s, to: 'go and have another heart attack'. Mr Litterick, who had been seriously ill, died of a heart attack shortly afterwards. Mr (now Lord) Tebbit wore, as a badge of pride, the epithet of a 'semi-house trained pole-cat' which Harold Wilson used to describe him.

As the mists of time enveloped some famous quotations, their authors ran the risk of being mis-quoted. Accuracy is sometimes difficult to achieve when the original quotations are re-told by others, and myths, along with journalistic poetic licence, enter the world of quotations. Much effort has gone into this anthology to achieve accuracy and I am delighted to see famous quotes correctly set out in full in their original context. Good examples of these are Harold Macmillan's 'you've never had it so good' comment in 1957. In fact, the original quotation was much more circumspect. 'Indeed, let's be frank about it—some of our people have never had it so good'. Margaret Thatcher was popularly supposed to have said 'rejoice, rejoice' at the conclusion of the Falklands conflict, and had the remark thrown back in her face when it subsequently went wrong. What she actually said after the first stage of the war, the recapture of South Georgia, was: 'just rejoice at the news and congratulate our armed forces and the Marines. Rejoice!'

The following pages offer a goldmine of varieties of conservative philosophy and thought and rightly provide a decent helping of quotations from our free-enterprise brethren in the United States of America. Some of the best originators of our modern-day Conservative principles of thrift, small government, capitalism and freedom built their careers serving as Presidents of the United States.

Even in 1776, the year the American Constitution was signed, John Adams, who became America's second President, hit on the phrase beloved of most Thatcherite Conservatives when he confronted the challenge posed today by Tony Blair's attempts to find a 'Third Way' in politics. Mr Adams noted that: 'in politics the middle way is none at all', and should be a useful reference point to all in the Conservative Party who feel that there can be no compromise between the power of the state and the power of the individual.

Many quotations are provided by Ronald Reagan, who, though much derided by the liberal intelligentsia in Britain as well as America, looks like taking his place as one of the great American Presidents in upholding the principles of conservative philosophy. His inability to control the Federal budget deficit did not undermine his understanding of the need to do so and a selection of his many quotes in favour of reducing public expenditure are rightly reproduced. Mr Reagan's simple messages of strong defence and minimalist government made him a hero to conservatives in America as Margaret Thatcher was in Britain. Although an American, Mr Reagan was also capable of using the richness of the English language and gave the lie to the old adage that America and England are two countries separated by a common language. My favourite Reagan quotation, uttered during a time of national tragedy, was his beautiful tribute to those who died in the *Challenger* space disaster, in 1986: 'they slipped the surly bonds of earth [to] touch the face of God'. Who knows whether they were the words of a speech-writer or not? I daresay that many of the quotations recorded here had one or two helping hands, but those that say them take the credit—or endure the responsibility. Who knows whether it was a speech-writer or George Bush who wrote the line in his 1988 speech: 'Read my lips: no new taxes'. The six words guaranteed his election as President but were to be his undoing four years later when he lost to Bill 'it's the economy, stupid' Clinton.

As one who tried in vain, during eighteen years as an MP, to say something vaguely memorable, I only seemed to utter comments which were always quoted against me. Now I earn my living hanging on to politicians' every utterances in the hope that I can get a 'good quote'. This book contains the best of the 'good quotes' spoken down the ages of Conservative history.

Michael Brown
Conservative MP 1979–97
Parliamentary sketch-writer, The Independent *1998–*

INTRODUCTION

This book has been an absolute pleasure to compile. One cannot fail to learn from the words of wisdom or fail to be amused, entertained or informed. But the trouble with compiling a book of quotations is that one inevitably leaves out some obvious favourites. I am sure I have been guilty of that in this volume. Quotations have fascinated me all my adult life. Whether writing articles or making speeches they are invaluable for politicians of every hue.

I am indebted to my colleagues at Politico's for aiding and abetting me in this endeavour, particularly Sam Griffiths for his sterling efforts. I am also grateful to Mery Cave of the *Salisbury Review* for her assistance.

I have purposely omitted quotes by non-conservative politicians on their criticism or definition of Conservatism. I might include them in the second edition. If you have enjoyed this volume but know of quotations you think should have been included, please feel free to write to me, as we intend to publish new editions of this book in the future.

The quotes have been selected according to a number of criteria but as with all books of quotations, the selection is somewhat coloured by my own choices. Where possible I have included the subject's biographical details. Please forgive any omissions or feel free to send me corrections. It has not been possible to source every quote, but in my view it is better to include a good quote than exclude it purely on the basis of lack of provenance. No doubt some quotations may have been attributed wrongly or have been printed in a slightly different form to the original. No doubt readers may puzzle over the exclusion of a particular favourite quotation. Please feel free to write to me with any corrections or suggestions for a new edition.

I would like to acknowledge other volumes of quotations which have been especially helpful in compiling this book. They include the *Oxford Dictionary of Political Quotations, Right Thinking* by Edward Leigh, Andrew Roth's *Parliamentary Profiles, Scorn & Read my Lips* by Matthew Parris among others.

I would like to thank Duncan Brack, the series editor for this three-volume series of quotations books. His combination of patience, calmness and tenacity have made him a pleasure to work with—which has enabled me to forgive his support for the Liberal Democrats! Despite several efforts on my part I have sadly failed to persuade him that today's Conservative Party is the true inheritor of the Liberal tradition. But there is still time …

My thanks (as editor and publisher) are also due to Chris Youd at AdVantage, not just for their splendid work on the design of the cover for this book, but also for their work on all the books published by Politico's Publishing over the last twelve months.

The eagle-eyed reader might spot that I have drawn heavily from my previous published book, *As I Said to Denis: The Book of Margaret Thatcher Quotations,* published by Robson Books. I make no apology for the fact that there are a large number of quotes from Margaret Thatcher and Ronald Reagan. These two politicians shaped the world we live in today, no matter how much others might decry the fact. The world is a safer place and a more prosperous place thanks to them and let us never forget it.

William Hague has a tough act to follow. I hope he can draw solace and encouragement from this book in the exciting task which he faces—that of restoring the Conservative Party to its natural position—that of government.

August 1999   *Iain Dale*

CONSERVATIVE
QUOTATIONS

For Margaret Thatcher
—whose vision inspires us

Earl of Aberdeen

1784–1860; Prime Minister 1852–1855

I consider war to be the greatest folly, if not the greatest crime, of which a country could be guilty, if lightly entered into. If a proof were wanted of the deep and thorough corruption of human nature, we should find it in the fact that war itself was sometimes justifiable.

> Speech in the House of Lords, 4 April 1845

I think it clear that all government in these times must be a government of progress, conservative progress, if you please; but we can no more be stationary, than reactionary.

> Letter to Henry Goulburn, 2 September 1852

As we are drifting fast towards war, I should think the Cabinet ought to see where they are going.

> Letter to the Earl of Clarendon on the Crimean War, 7 June 1853

Lord Acton

1834–1902; Historian

Liberty alone demands for its realisation the limitation of the public authority, for liberty is the only object which benefits all alike, and provokes no sincere opposition.

> The Home and Foreign Review, 1862

The man who prefers his country before any other duty shows the same spirit as the man who surrenders right to the state. They both deny that right is superior to authority.

> Ibid.

Patriotism is in political life what faith is in religion.

> Nationality, 1862

The danger is not that a particular class is unfit to govern. Every class is unfit to govern.

> Letter to Mary Gladstone, 1881

The law of liberty tends to abolish the reign of race over race, of faith over faith, of class over class. It is not the realisation of a political ideal: it is the discharge of a moral obligation.

> Ibid.

Power, like a desolating pestilence
Pollutes what'er it touches; and obedience,
Bane of all genius, virtue, freedom, truth,
Makes slaves of men and of the human frame
A mechanised automation,
Power tends to corrupt and absolute power absolutely

> 1887

Great men are almost always bad men even when they exercise influence and not authority.

> 1887

The one pervading evil of democracy is the tyranny of the majority, or rather of that party, not always the majority that succeeds, by force or fraud, in carrying elections.

> History of Freedom & Other Essays (1907)

Liberty is not the means to a higher political end. It is itself the highest political end.

> Ibid.

The great question is to discover, not what governments prescribe, but what they ought to prescribe; for no prescription is valid against the conscience of mankind. Before God, there is neither Greek nor Barbarian, neither rich nor poor, and the slave is as good as his master, for by birth all men are free; they are citizens of that universal commonwealth which embraces all the world, brethren of one family, and children of God. The true guide of our conduct is no outward authority, but the voice of God, who comes to dwell in our souls, who knows all our thoughts, to who we are owing all the truth we know, and all the good we do; for vice is voluntary, and virtue comes from the grace of the heavenly spirit within.

Ibid.

John Adams

1735–1826; American President 1796–1800

The judicial power ought to be distinct from both the legislative and executive, and independent upon both, so that it may be a check against both, so that it may be a check upon both.

Thoughts on Government, 1776

Liberty cannot be preserved without a general knowledge among the people, who have a right and a desire to know; but besides this, they have a right, an indisputable, unalienable, indefeasible, divine right to that most dreaded and envied kind of knowledge, I mean of the characters and conduct of their rulers.

An Essay on the Canon and the Feudal Law, 1765

The jaws of power are always opened to devour, and her arm is always stretched out, if possible, to destroy the freedom of thinking, speaking and writing.

Ibid.

I agree with you that in politics the middle way is none at all.

1776

Democracy never lasts long. It soon wastes, exhausts, and murders itself. There never was a democracy that did not commit suicide.

1814

Fear is the foundation of most governments.

1776

The happiness of society is the end of government

1776

Phelp Adams

Capitalism and communism stand at opposite poles. Their essential difference is this: The communist, seeing the rich man and his fine home, says: No man should have so much. The capitalist, seeing the same thing, says: All men should have as much.

Samuel Adams

1722–1803; Leader in the American Revolution

If ye love wealth greater than liberty, the tranquillity of servitude greater than the animating contest for freedom, go home from us in peace. We seek not your counsel, nor your arms.

Crouch down and lick the hand that feeds you; May your chains set lightly upon you, and may posterity forget that ye were our countrymen.
Let us contemplate our forefathers, and posterity, and resolve to maintain the rights bequeathed to us by the former, for the sake of the latter.
> 1771

We cannot make events. Our business is wisely to improve them. Mankind are governed more by their feelings than by reason. Events which excite those feelings will produce wonderful effects

Lord Addington
1757–1844; Prime Minister 1801–1804

In youth the absence of pleasure is pain. In old age the absence of pain is pleasure.

The burden [of income tax] should not be left to rest on the shoulders of the public in time of peace because it should be reserved for the important occasions which, I trust, will not soon recur.

Konrad Adenauer
1876–1967; German Chancellor

A thick skin is a gift from God.
> *New York Times,* 1959

Aeschyslus
c. 5th century BC; Playwright

Every ruler is harsh whose rule is new.
> *Prometheus Bound*

Aesop
c. 550 BC

United we stand, divided we fall.
> *The Four Oxen and the Lion*

Little by little does the trick.
> *Crow and the Pitcher*

It is easy to despise what you cannot get.
> *The Fox and the Grapes*

Be content with your lot, one cannot be first in everything.
> *The Peacock and Juno*

Spiro Agnew
1918–96; US Vice President 1969–73

If you've seen one city slum, you've seen 'em all.
> Detroit, 1968

A spirit of national masochism prevails, encouraged by the effete corps of impudent snobs, who characterise themselves as intellectuals.
> New Orleans, 1969

Yippies, hippies, yahoos, Black Panthers, lions and tigers alike—I'd swap the whole damn zoo for the kind of young Americans I saw in Vietnam.

Jonathan Aitken
1942–; Conservative MP 1974–97

I wouldn't say she was open-minded on the Middle East so much as empty-headed. For instance, she probably thinks that Sinai is the plural of sinus.
> On Margaret Thatcher's views on the Middle East

Hervey Allen

Every new generation is a fresh invasion of savages.

William Barclay Allen

1944– ; Afro-American Political Scientist

This is a way of proceeding our country which leads to disaster … People are in the habit of thinking in terms of race, or gender-anything except of being an American. Until we learn once again to use the language of American freedom in an appropriate way that embraces all of us, we're going to continue to harm this country.
> C-Span, 1992

It is misleading to call affirmative action reverse discrimination, as we often do. There is no such thing, any more than the opposite of injustice, for example is reverse injustice.
> American Enterprise Institute, 1985

James Madison thought that the most important test of American freedom would be the ability of our political system to guarantee the rights of minorities without exceptional provisions for their protection. Affirmative action is incompatible with that constitutional design. Whoever calls for affirmative action declares at the same time that constitutional design has failed and that we can no longer live with our constitution.
> Ibid.

Leo Amery

1873–1955; Conservative MP

For twenty years he has held a season ticket on the line of least resistance, and has gone wherever the train of events has carried him, lucidly justifying his position at whatever point he has happened to find himself.
> On H. H. Asquith, speech in the House of Commons, 1916

Speak for England, Arthur!
> To Arthur Greenwood in the House of Commons, 2 September 1939

You have sat here too long for any good you have been doing. In the name of God, go!
> To Neville Chamberlain, quoting Cromwell, 7 May 1940

Conservatism recognises that individual effort, the individual desire to excel, the will for individual achievement and recognition will always remain the indispensable vitamins of human society. But the individuals it has in mind are also citizens. The qualities of co-operation, of public duty, of willingness to sacrifice personal interest and even life itself for the common cause are essential elements in the individuality we would strive to foster.
> The *Ashridge Journal*, 1943

David Amess

1952–; Conservative MP, 1983–

I am interested in everything and expert in nothing.

I do not believe in the equality of men and women ... If I were pressed I would say that women are superior to men.

I would pull the lever.
On hanging

Michael Ancram

Conservative MP

I have not 'singled out' Lothian—I have singled out *four* local councils.
As Junior Scottish Office minister, on the sale of council houses, 1987

Thomas Aquinas

1227–74; Theologian

Because the aim of a good life on this earth is blessedness in heaven, it is the king's duty to promote the welfare of the community.
On Princely Rule

Reason in man is rather like God in the world.
Opuscule II De Regno

Jeffrey Archer

1940–; Conservative MP 1970–74

She'll be Prime Minister until the middle of next century.
On Margaret Thatcher, 1989

Hannah Arendt

1906–75; American philosopher

The most radical revolutionary will become a conservative on the day after the revolution.
New Yorker, 1970

The third World is not a reality, but an ideology.

Aristophanes

c.450–385BC; Greek dramatist

A horrible voice, bad breath and a vulgar manner—the characteristics of a popular politician.

Aristotle

384–322 BC; Greek philosopher

Democracy arose from men's thinking that if they are equal in any respect they are equal absolutely.
Politics

Good laws, if they are not obeyed, do not constitute good government.
Ibid.

Those who think that all virtue is to be found in their own party principles push matters to extremes; they do not consider that disproportion destroys a state.
Ibid.

Sometimes the demagogues, in order to curry favour with the people, wrong the notables.
Ibid.

'Even when laws have been written down they ought not always to remain unaltered.' But the law has no power to command obedience except that of habit which can only be given by time, so that a readiness to change from the old to new laws enfeebles the power of the law.
Ibid.

The most perfect political community is one in which the middle class is in control and outnumbers both of the other classes.

Ibid.

Poverty is the parent of revolution and crime.

Ibid.

… he who is unable to live in society, or has no need because he is sufficient for himself, must either be a beast or a god.

Ibid.

The male is by nature superior and the female inferior; one rules and the other is ruled.

Ibid.

Democracy [as literal majority rule] … arises out of the notion that those who are equal in any respect are equal in all respects; because men are equally free, they claim to be absolutely equal.

Ibid.

We make war that we may live in peace.

Nicomachean Ethics

Virtue, like art, constantly deals with what is hard to do, and the harder the task the better the success.

Ibid.

No tyrant need fear till men begin to feel confident in each other.

Ibid.

The generality of men are naturally apt to by swayed by fear rather than by reverence, and to refrain from evil, rather because of the punishment that it brings, than because of its own foulness.

Ibid.

It is best that laws should be so constructed as to leave as little as possible to the decision of those who judge.

Rhetoric, 1

Dick Armey

US Congressman

Governments punish success and reward failure.

Know that euphemisms for restricting trade are created by those who benefit from restrictions.

February 1993

Be sceptical of gloomy prognostications from people who are in the business of peddling more government.

Ibid.

Mathew Arnold

1822–1888; Poet and Educationalist

The world is forwarded by having its
    attention fixed on the best things
Fullness of life and power of feeling, ye
Are for the happy, for the soul at ease,
Who dwell on a firm basis of content!
But he, who has outlived his prosperous
    days—
But he, whose youth fell on a different
    world
From that on which his exiled age is
    thrown—
Whose mind was fed on other food, was
    train'd
By other rules than are in vogue to-
    day—
Whose habit of thought is fixed, who
    will not change,
But, in a world he loves not, must subsist
In ceaseless opposition, be the guard

Of his own breast, fettered to what he
    guards,
That the world win no mastery over
    him—
From Empedocles on Etna 1852

… what a man seeks through his
education is to get to know himself
and the world.
A speech at Eton

Raymond Claude Ferdinand Aron

1905–1983; French philosopher

The intellectual who no longer feels
attached to anything is not satisfied
with opinions merely; he wants certainty, he wants a system. The Revolution provides him with his opium.
The Opium of the Intellectuals, 1995

Communist faith justifies the means.
Communist faith forbids the fact that
there are many roads towards the
Kingdom of God.
Ibid.

Far from being the … philosophy of
the Proletariat, Communism merely
makes use of … pseudo–science in
order to attain its own end, the seizure
of power.
Ibid.

Nancy Astor

1879–1964; Conservative MP

Astor: Winston, if I were your wife I
    would put poison in your coffee.
Churchill: Nancy, if I were your hus-
    band I would drink it.
At Blenheim Palace, 1912

Nobody wants me as a Cabinet Minister and they are perfectly right. I am an
agitator, not an administrator.

Sir Humphrey Atkins

1922–98; Conservative MP 1955–87

Jim Prior is his own man. We all are.
On Prior's resignation as Secretary of
State for Northern Ireland, 1984

Sir Francis Bacon

1561–1626; Lawyer and essayist

Alonso of Aragon was wont to say in
commendation of age, that age appears
to be best in four things—old wood
best to burn, old wine to drink, old
friends to trust and old authors to read.
Apothegus, 1624

In government, change is suspected
through to the better.

The best governments are always subject
to be like the fairest crystals, where
every icicle and grain is seen, which in a
fouler stone is never perceived.

To worship the people is to be worshipped.

Nay, the number of armies importeth
not much, where the people is of
weak courage; for as Virgil saith, It
never troubles the wolf how many the
sheep be.
Essays, 1625.

The four pillars of government …
religion, justice, counsel, treasure.
Essays of Seditions

There be three things which make a
nation great and prosperous, a fertile

soil, busy workshops, easy conveyance for men and goods from place to place. New nobility is but the act of power, but ancient nobility is the act of time.

Of Nobility, 1625

It is a strange desire to seek power and to lose liberty.

Of Great Place, 1625

Walter Bagehot

1826–77; Essayist

In such constitutions [as England's] there are two parts. First, those which excite and preserve the reverence of the population—the dignified parts. And next, the efficient parts—those by which it, in fact, works and rules.

The English Constitution, 1867

It has been said that England invented the phrase 'Her Majesty's Opposition'; that it was the first government which made a criticism of administration as much a part of the polity as administration itself. This critical opposition is the consequence of cabinet government.

Ibid.

The natural impulse of the English people is to resist authority.

Ibid.

An opposition, on coming to power, is often like a speculate merchant whose bills become due. Ministers have to make good their promises, and they find difficulty in doing so.

Ibid.

It is often said that men are ruled by their imaginations; but it would be truer to say that they are governed by the weaknesses of their imaginations.

Ibid.

The finest brute votes in Europe.

Ibid.

In happy states, the Conservative Party must rule upon the whole a much longer time than their adversaries. In well-framed politics, innovation—great innovation that is—can only be occasional. If you are always altering your house, it is a sign either that you have a bad house, or that you have an excessively restless disposition—there is something wrong somewhere.

1874

A constitutional statesman is in general a man of common opinion and uncommon abilities.

National Review, 1856

The cure for admiring the Lords is to go and look at it.

The most influential of constitutional statesmen is the one who most felicitously expresses the creed of the moment, who administers it, who embodies it in laws and institutions, who gives it the highest life it is capable of, who induces the average man to think: I could not have done it any better if I had had time myself.

National Review, 1856

No real English gentleman, in his secret soul, was ever sorry for the death of a political economist.

One of the greatest pains to human nature is the pain of a new idea.

Physics & Politics, 1869

The electorate is the jury writ large.
Parliamentary Reform

Dullness in matters of government is a good sign, and not a bad one. In particular, dullness in parliamentary government is a test of its excellence, and indication of its success.
1856

There is no method by which men can be both free and equal.
The *Economist,* 1863

When great questions end, little parties begin.

The best reason why monarchy is a strong government is that it is an intelligible government. The mass of mankind understands it, and they hardly anywhere in the world understand any other.
The English Constitution, 1872

Kenneth Baker

1934–; Conservative MP 1968–97, Cabinet Minister 1985–92

Crime is always on the news. Crime prevention doesn't feature so often in the headlines but in the last ten years, and in the last five particularly, we have put crime prevention on the agenda for every police force, every local authority, every housing association, every car manufacturer and insurer, and on the personal agenda of many millions of ordinary people.
As Home Secretary, 1991

No Conservative government has ever accepted that parts of our inner cities might become no-go areas for the rule of law.
As Home Secretary, 1991

It's no use peddling the idea that unemployment and crime are the Government's fault and opportunities are restricted by, for instance, lack of child care or racism. I see the growth of a so-called underclass as the most formidable challenge to a secure and civilised way of life throughout the developed world.
As Home Secretary, 1992

Socialists make the mistake of confusing individual worth with success. They believe you cannot allow people to succeed in case those who fail feel worthless.

We have so reduced the power of the courts to lock up children—for basically good reasons—we now have a handful of young people we cannot really cope with.
As Home Secretary, 1993

Mrs Thatcher categorised her Ministers into those she could put down, those she could break down and those she could wear down.
The *Independent,* 11 September 1993

Was I ever one of us?
To Charles Powell, BBC TV, September 1993

Stanley Baldwin

1867–1947; Prime Minister 1923, 1924–9, 1935–7

A lot of hard-faced men who look as if they had done very well out of the war.
Referring to the first House of Commons elected after the First World War.

Four words, of one syllable each, are words which contain salvation for this country, and for the whole world. They are 'faith', 'hope', 'love' and 'work'.

Speech in the House of Commons, 16 February 1923

A platitude is simply a truth repeated until people get tired of hearing it.

29 May 1924

There are three classes which need sanctuary more than others—birds, wild flowers and Prime Ministers.

Observer, 24 May 1925

Safety First does not mean a smug self-satisfaction with everything as it is. It is a warning to all persons who are going to cross a road in dangerous circumstances.

1929

The papers conducted by Lord Rothermere and Lord Beaverbrook are not newspapers in the ordinary accept-ance of the term. They are engines of propaganda, for the constantly chang-ing policies, desires, personal wishes, personal likes and dislikes of two men … What the proprietorship of these papers is aiming at is power, and power without responsibility—the prerogative of the harlot throughout the ages.

17 March 1931

Had the employers of past generations all of them dealt fairly with their men there would have been no unions.

1931

There are three groups that no British Prime Minister should provoke: the Vatican, the Treasury and the miners.

I think it is well also for the man in the street to realise that there is no power on earth that can protect him from being bombed. Whatever people may tell him, the bomber will always get through … The only defence is offence, which means that you have to kill more women and children more quickly than the enemy if you want to save yourselves.

10 November 1932

Let us never forget this; since the day of the air, the old frontiers are gone. When you think of the defence of England you no longer think of the chalk cliffs of Dover, you think of the Rhine.

30 July 1934

He spent his whole life in plastering together the true and the false and therefrom manufacturing the plausible.

On Lloyd George

I give you my word there will be no great armaments.

To the International Peace Society, 1935

If there is going to be a war—and no one can say that there is not—we must keep him fresh to be our war Prime Minister.

On the main reason for excluding Winston Churchill from his Cabinet, November 1935

You will find in politics that you are much exposed to the attribution of false motive. Never complain and never explain.

Quoted by Harold Nicolson

The intelligent are to the intelligentsia what a gentleman is to a gent.

Arthur Balfour

1848–1930; Prime Minister 1902–1905

Conservative prejudices are rooted in a great past and Liberal ones in an imaginary future.

It is unfortunate, considering that enthusiasm moves the world, that so few enthusiasts can be trusted to speak the truth.
19 May 1891

I am a Conservative because I am absolutely certain that no community in this world has ever flourished, or could ever flourish, if it was faithless to its own past.

The energies of our system will decay, the glory of the sun will be dimmed, and the earth, tideless and inert, will no longer tolerate the race which, for a moment disturbed its solitude. Man will go down into the pit, and all his thoughts will perish.
The Foundations of Belief, 1895

I thought he was a young man of promise but it turns out he was a young man of promises.
On Winston Churchill, 1899

World Crisis—Winston has written four volumes about himself and called it World Crisis.

Biography should be written by an acute enemy.
1927

I never forgive but I always forget.

Douglas Bandow

1957– ; Aide to Ronald Reagan

… the most interesting form of welfare institution in the West, at least to those concerned about individual liberty and personal independence, is collective self-help, or mutual aid as it is more commonly called.
Welfare Reform has become a Forgotten Issue, 1992

Claude Frederic Bastiat

1801–1850; French statesman and economist

Try to imagine a regulation of labour imposed by force that is not a violation of liberty; a transfer of wealth imposed by force that is not a violation of property. If you cannot reconcile these contradictions, then you must conclude that the law cannot organise labour and industry without organising injustice.
Ibid.

Lord Beaverbrook

1879–1964; Newspaper magnate and Conservative MP

Mr Baldwin, a well-meaning man of indifferent judgement who, whether he did right or wrong, was always sustained by a belief that he was acting for the best.
1931

His [Stanley Baldwin] successive attempts to find a policy remind me of a chorus of a third-rate review. His evasions reappear in different scenes and in new dresses, and every time they dance with renewed and despairing vigour. But it is the same old jig. He didn't care in which direction the car was travelling, so long as he remained in the driver's seat.
On Lloyd George

Daniel Bell

1919– ; American Sociologist

… equality of opportunity is a zero-sum game in which individuals can win in different ways. But equality of result, or redistributive polices, essentially is a zero-sum game, in which there are distinct losers and winners. And inevitably these conditions lead to more open political competition and conflict.

The Winding Passage, 1980

Distributive justice is one of the oldest and thorniest problems for political theory. What has been happening in recent years is that entitlement, equity, and equality have become confused with one another, and the source of rancorous political debate. Yet they are also the central value issues of the time.

Ibid.

William Bennett

1943–; American Republican Politician

It is bad enough that so much of what passes for art and entertainment these days is the rampant promiscuity and the casual cruelty of our popular culture. To ask us to pay for it is to add insult to injury. We will not be intimidated by our cultural guardians into accepting either the insult or the injury.

It is hard to fight a war when you've got to debate the worthiness of fighting it.

CNN, December 16, 1989

Discrimination on the basis of race is illegal, immoral, and unconstitutional, inherently wrong and destructive of democratic society.

Counting by Race, 1979

All real education is the architecture of the soul.

If we believe that good art, good music and good books will elevate taste and improve the sensibilities of the young—which they most certainly do—then we must also believe that bad music and bad books will degrade. As a society, as communities, as policy makers, we must come to grips with the truth.

The Devaluing of America, 1992

Conservatism as I understand it is not essentially theoretical or ideological, but is rather a practical matter of experience. It seeks to conserve the best elements of the past.

Ibid.

Conservatives are interested in pursuing policies that will better reinforce and encourage the best of our people's common culture, habits and beliefs.

Ibid.

Conservatism … is based on the belief that the social order rests upon a moral base, and that what ties us together as a people … is in constant need of support.

Ibid.

The problem is that some people tend to regard anyone who would pronounce a definitive judgement as an unsophisticated Philistine or a closed-minded 'elitist' trying to impose his view on everybody else.

Ibid.

Arthur Benson

1862–1922

Land of Hope and Glory, mother of
   the free,
How shall we extol thee, who are born
   of thee?
Wider still and wider shall they bounds
   be set,
God, who made thee mighty, make
   thee mightier yet.
> *Land of Hope and Glory*

Brigette Berger

1928–; American Sociologist

[T]he family, and specifically the
bourgeois family, is the necessary social
context for the emergence of autonomous individual who are the empirical
foundation of political democracy. This
has been so historically. There is every
reason to think that it continues to be
so today.
> *The War Over the Family*

No amount of legislation and court
decisions can produce in the individual such basic moral ideas as the
inviolability of human rights, the
willing assent to legal norms, or the
notion that contractual agreements
must be respected.
> Ibid.

… the bourgeois family has been
particularly effective in providing a
haven of stability in a rapidly changing
society. The tensions of modernisation,
even under relatively benign circumstances, are trying for the individual;
the family is the most important
institution in which the child is prepared to withstand these tensions …
> Ibid.

Public policy with regard to the family
should primarily be concerned with
the family's capacity to take care of its
children, its sick and handicapped, and
its aged. The basic principle here
should be that, whenever possible,
these needs are best taken care of *within*
the family, *any family* … regardless of
social or cultural type. This means that
the overriding concern of public
policy should be to provide support for
the family to discharge these caring
tasks, rather than to relieve the family
of these tasks.
> Ibid.

[I]f one wants to foster the bourgeois
family, the best course to take is to give
people freedom of choice. Most of
them will whose bourgeois values and
bourgeois life-styles—especially people
in the 'targeted' groups of the poor and
disadvantaged.
> Ibid.

Peter Berger

1929–; American political philosopher

Modern capitalism … has been a
liberating force. The market in and of
itself liberates people from the old
confines of subsistence economies.
> *The Capitalist Revolution*, 1986

Kapitalistische luft macht frei [the air of
capitalism liberates]
> Adaptation of traditional German
> adage: 'the city air liberates'; Ibid.

[The liberating qualities of capitalism] is the empirical justification of the ideological position that there is an intrinsic connection between the economic freedom and all other liberties ... However, it does not follow from this that their liberating forces of capitalism are inevitable or irreversible.
>Ibid.

Isaiah Berlin

1909–1998; Philosopher

Liberty is liberty, not equality or fairness or justice or human happiness or a quiet conscience.
>*Two Concepts of Liberty,* 1958

The fundamental sense of freedom is freedom from chains, from imprisonment, from enslavement by others. The rest is extension of this sense, or else metaphor.
>*Four Essays on Liberty,* 1969

The Bible

In the sweat of thy face shall thy cut bread.
>Genesis 3:10

Eye for Eye, tooth for tooth, hand for hand, foot for foot.
>Exodus, 21:24

He that smiteth a man, so that he die, shall be surely put to death.
>Exodus, 23:20

Neither shalt thou favour a poor man in his cause.
>Exodus, 23:12

Thou art a God ready to pardon, gracious and merciful, slow to anger and of great kindness.
>Nehemiah

Where your treasure is, there shall your heart be also.
>Matthew, 6:21

John Biffen

1930– ; Conservative MP, Cabinet Minister, 1979–87

She was a tigress surrounded by hamsters.
>On Margaret Thatcher, December 1990

He was the sewer and not the sewage.
>On Bernard Ingham

John Biggs-Davison

1918–88; Conservative MP 1955–88

I have never conceived it my duty as a Member of Parliament to seek to amend the Ten Commandments.
>November 1976

Nigel Birch

1906–81; Conservative MP

My God, they've shot our fox!
>On hearing of the Chancellor, Hugh Dalton's, resignation in 1947

For the second time the Prime Minister has got rid of a Chancellor of the Exchequer who tried to get expenditure under control. Once is more than enough.
>Following Macmillan's replacement of Selwyn Lloyd with Reginald Maudling, 1963

Lord Birkenhead (F E Smith)

1872–1930; Conservative MP 1906–18,
Cabinet Minister 1915–1923, 1924–28

Austen always played the game and
always lost it.
On Austen Chamberlain.

I think Baldwin has gone mad. He
simply takes one jump in the dark;
looks round; and then takes another.
1923

Otto von Bismarck

1815–98; German Chancellor

The less people know about how
sausages and laws are made, the better
they'll sleep at night.

Politics is not an exact science.

Whoever speaks of Europe is wrong. It
is a geographical concept.
1876

I have always found the word Europe
on the lips of those politicians who
wanted something from other Powers
which they dared not demand in their
own names.
1878

Politics is the art of the possible.
1867

The politician has not to revenge what
has happened but to ensure that it does
not happen again.
1867

A lath of wood painted to look like
iron.
On Lord Salisbury at the Congress of
Berlin, 1878

The old Jew! That is the man
On Disraeli at the Congress of Berlin,
1878

If reactionary measures are to be
carried, the Liberal Party takes the
rudder, from the correct assumption
that it will not overstep the necessary
limits; if liberal measures are to be
carried, the Conservative Party takes
office in its turn for the same consideration.

William Blackstone

1723–80; Lawyer

And, lastly, to vindicate these rights,
when actually violated and attacked,
the subjects of England are entitled, in
the first place, to the regular administration and free course of justice in the
courts of law; next to the right of
petitioning the king and parliament for
redress of grievances; and, lastly, to the
right of having and using arms for self-
preservation and defence.
Commentaries on the Laws of England
(1765–9)

That the king can do no wrong is a
necessary and fundamental principle of
the English constitution.
Ibid.

The royal navy of England hath ever
been its greatest defence and arma-
ment; it is its ancient and natural
strength; the floating bulwark of our
island.
Ibid.

It is better that ten guilty persons
escape than one innocent one suffer.
Ibid.

Lord (Robert) Blake

1916–; Historian

It is too often said that Thatcherism is a departure from Conservative tradition. She proclaims herself to be radical. In one sense she is; but in another sense she is harking back to an older set of policies. After all, for most of the time since 1846 Conservatives have been in favour of low taxation, an enterprise culture, a stable currency, and minimal state intervention; and, apart from a curious aberration by Disraeli, have viewed what was quaintly called the trade union movement with a frosty eye.

The *Times*, 1989

Allen Bloom

1930–1992; American political philosopher

Affirmative action now institutionalises the worst aspects of separatism.

On black militancy in American Universities; *The Closing of the American Mind,* 1987

Democratic society cannot accept any principle of achievement other than merit.

Ibid.

David Boaz

1953– ; Libertarian

A key point to keep in mind is that non-government schools, which have to offer a better product to stay in business, do a better job of educating children.

Liberating Schools, 1991

Henry St John, Viscount Bolingbroke

1678–1751; High Tory

The constitution will be reverenced by him [the patriot king] as the law of God and of man; the force of which binds the king as much as the meanest subject, and the reason of which binds him much more.

Napoleon Bonaparte

1769–1821; Emperor of the French 1804–15

A form of government that is not the result of a long sequence of shared experiences, effort and endeavours, can never take root.

1803

He who saves his country violates no law.
Maxims

My maxim was, *la carrière est ouverte aux talents,* without distinction of birth or fortune.

1817

Andrew Bonar Law

1858–1923; Prime Minister 1922–1923

If, therefore, war should ever come between these two countries [Britain and Germany], which Heaven forbid! It will not, I think be due to irresistible natural laws, it will be due to want of human wisdom.

House of Commons, 27 November 1911

If I am a great man then a good many great men of history are frauds.

In a letter to Max Aitken, 13 November 1911

A man with the vision of an eagle but with a blind spot in his eye.

> On F. E. Smith, Lord Birkenhead, 1917

I am afraid I shall have to show myself very vicious, Mr Asquith, this session. I hope you will understand.

> To Asquith at the beginning of the 1912 session of Parliament

They [the Liberal Government] have turned the House of Commons into an exchange where everything is bought and sold. In order to retain for a little longer the ascendancy of their Party, to remain a few months longer in office, they have sold the Constitution, they have sold themselves.

> Speech in Belfast

I can imagine no length of resistance to which Ulster can go in which I should not be prepared to support them, and in which, in my belief, they would not be supported by the overwhelming majority of the British people.

> Speech in Blenheim Palace

In war it is necessary not only to be active but to seem active.

> 1916

I must follow them. I am their leader.

Christopher Booker

1937– ; Journalist

In the life of any government, however safe its majority, there comes a moment when the social movements of which it had once been the expression, turn inexorably against it. After that mo-

ment, every mistake it makes becomes magnified; indeed blunders multiply as if feeding on themselves; and both outwardly and inwardly the Government appears to be at the mercy of every wind.

> The Neophiliacs, 1969

Our government has recently unleashed the greatest avalanche of regulations in peacetime history; and wherever we examine their working we see that they are using a sledgehammer to miss a nut.

> 1995

Daniel Boorstin

1914–; American Historian

[W]e must abandon the prevalent belief in the superior wisdom of the ignorant. Unless we give up the voguish reverence for youth and for the 'culturally deprived,' unless we cease to look to the vulgar community as arbiters of our art and literature, and of all our culture, we will never have the will to de-provincialise our minds.

> Democracy and its Discontents, 1971

Education is learning what you didn't even know you knew.

> Ibid.

We must recognise that many of the acts committed in the name of equal opportunity are in fact acts of discrimination.

> Ibid.

We must not allow ourselves to become the Quota States of America.

> On the tendency for minority education agendas; Ibid.

Robert Bork

1927– ; US Judge

In a constitutional democracy the moral content of law must be given by the morality of the framer or legislator, never by the morality of the judge.
American Enterprise Institute, 1977

Those who made and endorsed our Constitution knew man's nature, and it is to their ideas rather than to the temptations of utopia, that we must ask that our judges adhere.
The Tempting of America, 1990

Peter Bottomley

1944–; Conservative MP 1975–

When [The IRA] plant such bombs, it proves they can scare people, it proves they can kill people, it proves nothing.
1990

Virginia Bottomley

1948– ; Conservative MP 1984– , Cabinet Minister 1992–97

Suicide is a real threat to health in a modern society.
As Health Secretary, 1993

Smoking is a dying habit
As Health Secretary, 1993

Edward Boyle

1923–81; Conservative MP

Nothing in politics is ever as good or bad as it first appears.
Quoted in the *Whitelaw Memoirs*

Rhodes Boyson

Conservative MP

Politically there is no record of the continuance of political freedoms when economic freedoms have died.

The militants in Liverpool spend money as if it came from outer space.
1987

Lord Brabazon of Tara

Make no mistake about it, the repercussions of this new invention [television] are going to be ... very wholesome because they tend to keep the home together ... It does mean that people stay at home.
1950

Sir Leon Brittan

1939–; Conservative MP 1974–88. Cabinet Minister, 1983–86, European Commissioner 1988–99

The two offences of which people of all ages are most fearful are violent street crimes and burglary. Efforts against these two crimes must be targeted to make the best possible use of the available intelligence and skilled detective powers.
As Home Secretary, 1985

D. W. Brogan

1900–74; Historian

Political corruption breeds infection. The best safeguard is the fresh air of publicity.
The Free State

Peter Brooke

1934–; Conservative MP 1977–, Cabinet
Minister, 1987–94

Clearly, the future is still to come.
    1986

Warren Brookes

1929–; American Journalist and Economist

[T]he whole notion of using the tax
system as a method of redistributing
wealth rests on a fallacy—namely
that wealth is money, and that all one
has to do to transfer wealth is transfer
money. The trouble with that hy-
pothesis is that money is nothing
more than a medium of exchange.
Real wealth is the total productive
output of the economy in the form
of services and goods, which are in
turn the products of the energy,
resources and talents of the people
who produce them. Thus merely
passing money around does little to
change a nation's real productive
output or wealth, nor does it change
the inherent 'wealth capacity' of
individual citizens. All it does is to
reduce the real value of the money
itself through inflation.
    The Economy in Mind, 1982

The attempt to redistribute wealth by
redistributing money through the
progressive tax tables only winds up
keeping the poor, the rich, and the
middle classes struggling even harder to
keep up with taxation.
    Ibid.

In [America], it is still safe to say that
80%–90% of the new jobs and economic growth is contributed by the
efforts, imagination, energy and initiative of less than 5%-10% of all individuals
    Ibid.

In the process [of wealth creation, the]
top 5%-10% has become very rich, and
not always very nice; but genius seldom
seems to equate with meekness and
charity.
    Ibid.

… without those well-rewarded
individuals who often have risked
everything to create the one new
enterprise in ten that succeeds, our
economy would become stagnant and
trickle-down would quickly be replaced by dole-out as it has in Poland,
Russia, China, Cuba, or even England.
    Ibid.

Inflation itself has its fundamental roots
in the politics of envy.
    Ibid.

Is it really any wonder that that the
money they print is *green*?
        On the use of inflationary measures
        to pay for wealth redistribution; Ibid.

Instead of genuine breakthroughs, we
are seeing more and more in consumer
products what we have seen on television shows: safe spin offs, frequent rip-
offs, and modest variations on past
success models.
        On the dangers of Corporations
        losing their entrepreneurial touch;
        Ibid.

Lord Brookeborough

Conservative MP

If it weren't for these troubles, Ireland would be a very happy place.
> As Ulster Minister with special responsibility for tourism, 1970

Michael Brotherton

Conservative MP 1979–84

Social security scroungers should be made to give a pint of blood every six months.
> 1979

Lord Brougham

1778–1868; Lord Chancellor

What is valuable is not new, and what is new is not valuable.
> *Edinburgh Review,* 1880

Education makes a people easy to lead, but difficult to drive; easy to govern, but impossible to enslave.

Andrew Brown

Thatcherism is not an ideology, but a political style: a trick of presenting reasonable, rather pedestrian ideas in a way that drives reasonable men into a frothing rage.
> The *Spectator,* 1984

Michael Brown

1951–; Conservative MP 1979–97, Sketch Writer, The *Independent* 1998–

It was like losing my mother. My mother is still alive but one day she won't be, and when that occurs it will, I suspect, be exactly like the day that Margaret Thatcher resigned.
> *Daily Telegraph,* 25 October 1993

Angela Browning

Conservative MP

The idea that there are women who run perfect homes and have delightful children who never get chickenpox without giving a month's notice is unrealistic.

Patrick Buchanan

American Republican Politician

And from the ancient forests of Oregon, to the Inland Empire of California, America's great middle class has got to start standing up to the environmental extremists who put insects, rats and birds ahead of families, workers and jobs.
> Republican Convention speech, August 17 1992

William Buckley, Jr.

1925– ; Journalist

Knee-jerk liberals and all the certified saints of sanctified humanism are quick to condemn this great and much-maligned Transylvanian statesman.
> On Vlad the Impaler

I mean to live my life an obedient man, but obedient to God, subservient to the wisdom of my political ancestors; never to the authority of political truths arrived at yesterday at the voting booth.
> *Up From Liberalism,* 1959

The state is a divine institution. Without it we have anarchy, and the lawlessness of anarchy is counter to the national law; so we abjure all political theories which view the state as inherently and necessary evil. But it is the state which has been in history the principal instrument of abuse of the people, and so it is central to the conservative program to keep the state from accumulating any but the most necessary powers.

The Catholic World

What was wrong with communism wasn't aberrant leadership, it was communism.

June 30 1995

Ivor Bulmer-Thomas

1905–93; Conservative MP

If he ever went to school without any boots it was because he was too big for them.

On Harold Wilson, Conservative Party Conference 1949

Julie Burchill

1959–; Journalist

Despite the Right-On hysteria, Mrs Thatcher has never been an old-fashioned girl. Voting for her was like buying a Vera Lynn LP, getting it home and finding 'Never Mind the Bollocks' inside the red white and blue sleeve … She basically doesn't believe that sex is such a big deal; this is why she has proved such a disappointment to Whitehouse, Gillick, Anderton and the sperm-ridden minds of the Right who wanted moral rearmament and got a 2p in the pound tax cut instead.

From the article 'Margaret Thatcher'

Mrs Thatcher is not trying to drag this country kicking and screaming into the nineteenth century. She's a brutal futurist, a Conservative with no interest in conserving, especially ye olde England and its ye olde industries.

Ibid.

[Mrs Thatcher] is an internationalist—unlike Labour, who lash themselves into a sentimental tizzy every time Johnny Foreigner puts in a bid for a British sweet factory.

Ibid.

What people forget is that it was not easy, until very recently, being Margaret Thatcher. She is one of those strange socio-economic mutations, like Morrisey, who have nowhere to go but the top. She is the misfit who made it …

Ibid.

[Mrs Thatcher] has always had to take stick for being a woman; from the drunken Tory who asked her at a Number 10 luncheon while she was Edward Heath's Education Minister if there was any truth in the rumour that she was a woman, to the caring, anti-sexist Labour Party and their Ditch the Bitch campaign of 1983. (How would they react to a black Conservative leader—Dump the Coon?)

Ibid.

Mrs Thatcher is not uncaring or cruel, but she is naïve. She can't comprehend how many absolutely useless, helpless

and hopeless a good many people are and is cursed with an incredible optimism and romanticism as to what the individual is capable of. If she kicks away the crutches, it's because she really does believe that everybody has the ability to walk without them.
Ibid.

Like Kennedy, Roosevelt and Stalin, [Mrs Thatcher] has reached that place between holiness and hologram where no one seriously expects the policies to work but no one can shake the symbolism and what it means to their sense of the nation.
Ibid.

Because we won our little war, no-one will be tortured in Argentina tonight. We are no longer a joke.
Ibid.

I don't believe in Thatcherism but I do believe in Thatcher, given the options. It is to her, not her discredited policies, that there really is no alternative. Send her victorious, happy and glorious. Because it's either that or getting excited about making runner-up in the Eurovision Song Contest.
Ibid.

Edmund Burke

1729–1797; Statesman and political philosopher

The laws reach but a very little way. Constitute government how you please, infinitely the greater part of it must depend upon the exercise of powers which are left at large the prudence and uprightness of the ministers of the State. Even all the use and potency of the laws depend on them. Without them, your commonwealth is no better than a scheme upon paper; not a living active, effective constitution.
Thoughts on the Causes of the Present Discontents, 1770

When bad men combine, the good must associate; else they will fall, one by one, on an unpitied sacrifice in a contemptible struggle.
Ibid.

The greater the power, the more dangerous the abuse.
Speech on the Middlesex election, 1774

To tax and to please, no more than to love and be wise, is not given to men.
Bristol, October 13 1774

Your representative owes you, not his industry only, but his judgement; and he betrays instead of serving you if he sacrifices it to your opinion.
Speech to the electors of Bristol, November 1774

All government indeed, every human benefit and enjoyment, every virtue and every prudent act is founded on compromise and barter.
Second Speech on Conciliation with America: The Thirteen Resolutions, March 22 1775

It is not what a lawyer tells me I may do; but what humanity, reason, and justice tell me I ought to do.
Ibid.

The concessions of the weak are the concessions of fear.
Ibid.

Abstract liberty, like other mere abstractions, is not to be found.
Ibid.

Freedom and not servitude is the cure of anarchy; as religion and not atheism, is the true remedy for superstition.
Ibid.

The use of force alone is but temporary; it may subdue for a moment; but it does not remove the necessity of subduing again: and a nation is not governed which is perpetually to be conquered.
Ibid.

I do not know the method of drawing up an indictment against a whole people. Magnanimity in politics is not seldom the truest wisdom; and a great empire and little minds go ill together.
Ibid.

The power of perpetuating our property in our families is one of the most valuable and interesting circumstances belonging to it, and that which tends the most to the perpetuation of society itself.

History is a preceptor of prudence, not of principles. The principles of true politics are those of morality enlarged; and I neither now do, nor ever will admit of any other.

Liberty must be limited in order to be possessed.
1777

There is a boundary to men's passions when they act from feelings; but none when they are under the influence of imagination.

Whenever a separation is made between liberty and justice, neither, in my opinion, is safe.

You can never plan the future by the past.

We are afraid to put men to live and trade each upon his own private stock of reason; because we suspect that the stock in each man is small, and that the individuals would do better to avail themselves to the general bank and capital of nations and of ages … Prejudice is of ready application in the emergency, it previously engages the mind in steady course of wisdom, and virtue, and does not leave the man hesitating in the moment of decision, sceptical, puzzled and unresolved. Prejudice renders a man's virtue his habit; and not a series of unconnected acts. Through just prejudice, his duty becomes part of his nature.
Reflections on the Revolution in France, 1790

Government is a contrivance of human wisdom to provide for human wants. Men have a right that these wants should be provided for by this wisdom.
Ibid.

To make us love our country, our country ought to be lovely.
Ibid.

People will not look forwards to posterity who never look backward to their ancestors.
Ibid.

A state without the means of change is without the means of conservation.
Ibid.

A nation is not an idea only of local extent and individual momentary aggregation, but it is an idea of continuity, which extends in time as well as in numbers and in space. By the unbridled facility of changing the state as often and as much and in as many ways as their floating fancies or fashions, the whole chain and continuity of the commonwealth would be broken. No generation could link with the other. Men would become little better than the flies of a summer.
> Ibid.

To be attached to the subdivision, to love the little platoon we belong to in society, is the first principle of public affections. It is the first link in the series by which we proceed towards a love of our country and mankind.
> Ibid.

Manners are more important than laws. Upon them, in great measure, the law depends,
> Ibid.

Party division, whether on the whole operating for good or evil, are things inseparable from free government.
> Ibid.

He was not merely a chip off the old block, but the old block itself.
> On William Pitt the Younger

There is but one law for all, namely that law that governs all law, the law of our Creator, the law of humanity, justice, equity, the law of nature and nations.
> Trial of Warren Hastings, 1794

A thing may look specious in theory, and yet be ruinous in practice; a thing may look evil in theory, and yet be in practice excellent.
> Ibid.

All that is necessary for the triumph of evil is that good men do nothing.
> Attrib. 1795

Mere parsimony is not true economy … Expense and great expense, may be an essential part of true economy.
> Letter to a Noble Lad, 1796

George Bush

1924– ; American President 1988—92

Giving peace a chance does not mean taking a chance with peace.
> August 1990

The power of America rests in a stirring but simple idea—that people will do great things if you only set them free.

Drug dealers need to understand a simple fact. You shoot a cop and you're going to be severely punished—fast. And if I had my way, with your life.
> Washington Post, March 10 1989

Not all spending initiatives were designed to be immortal.
> February 9 1989

Much good can come from the prudent use of power.
> January 1992

Read my lips: no new taxes.
> Republican National Convention, 1988

When I need a little free advice on Saddam Hussein I turn to country music.

Boy, they were big crematoriums weren't they?
>On a visit to Auschwitz

Use power to help people. For we are given power not to advance our own purposes, not to make a real show in the world, nor a name. There is but one just use of power and it is to serve the people.

We are a nation of communities, of tens and tens of thousands of ethnic, religious, social, business, labour unions, neighbourhoods, regional and other organisations, all of them varied, voluntary and unique … a brilliant diversity spread like stars, like a thousand points of light in a broad and peaceful sky.
>Republican National Convention, 1988

I don't want to run the risk of ruining what is a lovely recession.
>(Meaning 'reception'), 1992

John Butcher

1946–; Conservative MP 1979–97

We can beat them in the 1980s and 1990s. We have beaten them in other respects and we can do it again.
>As junior Trade and Industry Minister, on Japan, 1984

R A Butler

1902–82; Conservative MP 1932–66, Cabinet Minister 1941–5, 1951–64

Politics is the art of the possible.

The civil service machine is a bit like a Rolls Royce. You know it's the best machine in the world, but you're not quite sure what to do with it.

In politics you must always keep running with the pack. The moment that you falter and they sense that you are injured, the rest will turn on you like wolves.
>Quoted by Dennis Walters

I think a Prime Minister has to be a butcher and know the joints. That is perhaps where I have not been quite competent—in knowing all the ways that you can cut up the carcass.
>1966

Politics is largely a matter of the heart.

Stewart Butler & Anna Kondra

The secret to making real progress against poverty and distress is to realise that it will come from a 'bottom up' and not a 'top down' process … Rather than try to stamp out diversity in an effort to find the unitary solution to welfare and social problems, we should be nurturing diversity, recognising that it is the key to success and progress in all fields.
>*Out of the Poverty Trap,* 1987

Albert Camus

1913–60; French novelist

A free press can, of course, be good or bad, but most certainly, without freedom it will never be anything but bad … Freedom is nothing else but a chance to be better, whereas enslavement is a certainty of the worst.
>*Resistance, Rebellion & Death,* 1960

What is a rebel? A man who says no.
>1951

George Canning

1770–1827; Prime Minister 1827

The happiness of constant occupation is infinite.
> Letter to Lord Boringdon, 1796

I do not think it would be politic or for the interests of the country to have this House quite subject to popular control.
> 1810

Away with the cant of 'measures not men' the idle supposition that it is the harness and not the horses that draw the chariot along. No, Sir, if the comparison must be made, if the distinction must be taken, men are everything, measures comparatively nothing.
> Speech in the House of Commons attacking the Addington government, 1802

I am compelled to confess that, in the conduct of public affairs, the good object of my contemplation is the interest of England … intimately connected as we are with the system of Europe, it does not follow that we are therefore called upon to mix ourselves on every occasion, with a restless and meddling activity, in the concerns of the nations which surround us.
> Speech at Plymouth, 1823

I consider it to be the duty of a British statesman in internal as well as external affairs, to hold a middle course between extremes; avoiding alike extravagancies of despotism or the licentiousness of unbridled freedom.
> Speech in the House of Commons, 1826

The whips' duty is to make a House and keep a House and cheer the Minister.

Thomas Carlyle

1795–1881; Historian

Truth and justice alone are capable of being 'conserved' and preserved. The thing which is unjust, which is not according to God's law, will you in a God's universe try to conserve that? It is so old, say you? Yes, and the hotter haste ought you of all others to be in to let it grow no older! If but the faintest whisper in your hearts intimate to you that it is not fair—hasten, for the sake of Conservatism itself, to probe it rigorously, to cast it forth at once and for ever if guilty.

All work, even cotton spinning, is noble; work is alone noble.

Not what I have, but what I do is my kingdom.
> *Sator Resartus*

The great law of culture is: Let each become all that he was created capable of being.
> *Critical and Miscellaneous Essays*, 1827

Adversity is sometimes hard upon a man; but for one man who can stand prosperity, there are a hundred that will stand adversity.
> *Heroes and Hero Worship*, 1841

The history of the world is but the biography of great men.
> Ibid.

Andrew Carnegie

1835–1919; American Industrialist and philanthropist

Surplus wealth is a sacred trust which its possessor is bound to administer in his lifetime for the good of the community.
> *Wealth,* 1889

Upon the sacredness of property civilisation itself depends—the right of the labourer to his hundred dollars in the savings bank, and the right of the millionaire to his millions.
> Ibid.

Lord Carrington

1919–; Cabinet Minister 1970–74, 1979–82

If you're at the summit, you're trying to climb a mountain.
> Former foreign secretary on the finer points of international diplomacy, 1986

Lewis Carroll

1832–98; Author

If everybody minded their own business, the Duchess said in a hoarse growl, the world would go round a deal faster than it does.
> *Alice in Wonderland*

The rule is, jam tomorrow and jam yesterday, but never jam today.
> *Through the Looking Glass*

Dame Barbara Cartland

Novelist

If you vote for Kinnock, you are voting against Christ.
> 1992

Thomas Nixon Carver

American Conservative

The trouble with radicals is that they only read radical literature, and the trouble with conservatives is that they don't read anything.
> Quoted by J. K. Galbraith

Cato

234–149 BC

He approaches nearest to the gods who knows how to be silent even though he knows he is right.

By Liberty I understand the power which every man has over his own actions, and his right to enjoy the fruits of his labour, art, and industry, as far as by it he hurts not the society, or any members of it, by taking from any member, or by hindering him from enjoying what he himself enjoys. The fruits of a man's honest industry are the just rewards of it, ascertained to him by natural and eternal equity, as is his title to use them in the manner which he thinks fit: and thus, with the above limitations, every man is sole lord and arbiter of his own private actions and property.

Lord Hugh Cecil

Conservative politician

What brought Conservatism into existence was the French Revolution.
> *Conservatism,* 1912

It is often assumed that Conservatism and Socialism are directly opposed. But this is not completely true. Modern

Conservatism inherits the traditions of Toryism which are favourable to the activity and authority of the State.
Ibid.

That authority should relieve suffering, that it should control and regulate trade; that it should restrain luxury; that it should suppress vice; that it should maintain religious truth—these were the principles which appealed to our forefathers as reasonable and especially to those among them who were Tories.
Ibid.

The socialist believes that it is better to be rich than poor, the Christian that it is better to be poor than rich.
Ibid.

Voting is not a right; voting is a public function. No one has any more right to be a voter than he has to be … a policeman, or a judge, or Prime Minister.
1931

Joseph Chamberlain

1836–1914; Civic leader and Liberal Imperialist

In almost every instance in which the rule of the Queen has been established and the great Pax Brittanica has been enforced, there has come with it greater security to life and property, and a material improvement in the condition of the bulk of the population.
Speech at Royal Colonial Institute, 1897

The day of small nations has long passed away. The day of Empire has come.
Former Colonial Secretary, 1904

It is said that the City is the centre of the world's finance, that the fate of our manufactures therefore is a secondary consideration … Now, I ask you, gentlemen, whether … that is not a very short-sighted view.
To City Financiers, 1904

Neville Chamberlain

1869–1940; Prime Minister 1937–40

In war, whichever side may call itself the victor, there are no winners, but all are losers.
Speech in Kettering, 4 July 1938

It is no part of a Prime Minister's duty to take a country into a war which he thinks you can't win.

However much we may sympathise with a small nation confronted by a big and powerful neighbour, we cannot in all circumstances undertake to involve the whole British Empire in a war simply on her account.
After Bad Godesberg, September 1938

How horrible, fantastic, incredible it is that we should be digging trenches and trying on gas masks here because of a quarrel in a faraway country between people of whom we know nothing.
Radio Broadcast on the Sudetenland crisis, 27 September 1938

In spite of the hardness and ruthlessness I thought I saw in his face, I got the impression that here was a man who could be relied upon when he had given his word.

This morning, I had another talk with the German Chancellor, Herr Hitler,

and here is the paper which bears his name upon it as well as mine...
> Speech at Heston, 30 September 1938

This is the second time in our history that there has come back from Germany to Downing Street peace with honour. I believe it is peace for our time.
> Speech in Downing Street, 1 October 1938

Our past experience has shown us only too clearly that weakness in armed strength means weakness in diplomacy, and if we want to secure a lasting peace … diplomacy cannot be effective unless the consciousness exists … that behind the diplomacy is the strength to give effect to it.
> After Munich, 1939

I have to tell you now that no such undertaking has been received, and that consequently, this country is at war with Germany.
> Radio speech, 3 September 1939

Whatever may be the reason—whether it was that Hitler thought he might get away with what he had got without fighting for it, or whether it was that after all the preparations were not sufficiently complete—however, one thing is certain—he missed the bus.
> Speech at Central Hall, Westminster, 5 April 1940

G. K. Chesterton

1874–1936; Novelist

All conservatism is based upon the idea that if you leave things alone you leave them as they are. But you do not. If you leave a thing alone you leave it to a torrent of change.
> Orthodoxy, 1908

A progressive is always a conservative; he conserves the direction of progress. A reactionary is always a rebel.
> Introduction to Carlyle's Past and Present.

The man who sees consistency in things is a wit, the man who sees the inconsistency in things is a humorist.

A nation without the means of reform is without the means of survival.

The prophet and the quack are alike admired for a generation and admired for the wrong reasons.

Tolerance is the virtue of a man without convictions.

Why shouldn't we quarrel about a word? What is the good of words if they aren't important enough to quarrel over? Why do we choose one word more than another if there isn't any difference between them.

Smile at us, pay us, pass us; but do not quite forget. For we are the people of England, that never have spoken yet.
> The Secret People

Lady Randolph Churchill

I shall never get used to not being the most beautiful woman in the room. It was an intoxication to sweep in and know every man had turned his head. It kept me in form.

Lord Randolph Churchill

1849–95; Conservative Politician, Chancellor of the Exchequer, 1886

If you want to gain the confidence of the working-classes, let them have a share, and a large, a real share, not a sham share, in your party councils and your party government.
Conservative Conference, 1883

We do not defend the Constitution from mere sentiment for the past, or from any infatuated superstition about divine right or hereditary excellence. We defend the Constitution solely on the ground of its utility to the people. It is on the grounds of utility alone that we go forth to meet our foes, and if we fail to make good our ground with utilitarian arguments and for utilitarian ends, then let the present combination of Throne, Lords and Commons be forever swept away …
'Trust the People' (Birmingham, 16 April 1884)

To tell the truth I don't know myself what Tory democracy is. But I believe it is principally opportunism.
1885

An old man in a hurry.
On Gladstone, 1886

Ulster will fight. Ulster will be right.
1886

Randolph Churchill

Conservative Politician

He never believed in doing something that he could get someone else to do for him.
On Stanley Baldwin

Winston Churchill

1874–1965; Prime Minister 1940–5, 1951–5

The maxim of the British people is 'Business as usual'
1914

Don't talk to me about naval tradition. It's nothing but rum, sodomy and the lash.

… A party of great vested interests … corruption at home, aggression to cover up abroad … sentiment by the bucket-load, patriotism by the imperial pint.
On the Tory Party while a Liberal MP

They told me how Mr Gladstone read Homer for fun, which I thought served him right.
My Early Life, 1930

India is no more a political personality than Europe. India is a geographical term. It is no more a united nation than the equator.
1931

We know that he has, more than any other man, the gift of compressing the largest amount of words into the smallest amount of thought.
On Ramsay MacDonald, 1933

I have waited fifty years to see the Boneless Wonder sitting on the Treasury bench.
On Ramsay MacDonald, 1933

Criticism may not be agreeable, but it is necessary. It fulfils the same function as pain in the body. It calls attention to an unhealthy state of things.

A fanatic is one who can't change his mind and won't change the subject.

The inherent vice of capitalism is the unequal sharing of blessings; the inherent virtue of socialism is the equal sharing of miseries.

The power of man has grown in every sphere, except over himself.

Mr [Joe] Chamberlain loves the working man. He loves to see him work

He looked at foreign affairs through the wrong end of a municipal drainpipe.

The price of greatness is responsibility.

The empires of the future are the empires of the mind.

It is no use saying, 'We are doing our best.' You have got to succeed in doing what is necessary.

He occasionally stumbled over the truth, but hastily picked himself up and hurried on as if nothing had happened.
> On Stanley Baldwin (attrib.)

I am certainly not one of those who need to be prodded. In fact, if anything, I am the prod.

Some regard private enterprise as if it were a predatory tiger to be shot. Others look upon it as a cow that they can milk. Only a handful see it for what it really is—the strong horse that pulls the whole cart.

I would say to the House, as I said to those who have joined this government: I have nothing to offer but blood, toil, tears and sweat.
> Speech made to House of Commons on May 13, 1940, three days after becoming Prime Minister.

The crafty, cold-blooded, black-hearted Italian.
> On Mussolini, 1944

Every day you may make progress. Every step may be fruitful. Yet there will stretch out before you an ever-lengthening, ever-ascending, ever-improving path. You know you will never get to the end of the journey. But this, so far from discouraging, only adds to the joy and glory of the climb.

Men stumble over the truth from time to time, but most pick themselves up and hurry off as if nothing happened.
A love of tradition has never weakened a nation, indeed it has strengthened nations in their hour of peril; but the new view must come, the world must roll forward.
> Speech in the House of Commons, November 29, 1944

Success is the ability to go from one failure to another with no loss of enthusiasm.

In the depths of that dusty soul is nothing but abject surrender.
> On Neville Chamberlain

When the eagles are silent, the parrots begin to jabber.

We shall show mercy, but we shall not ask for it.
> Speech in the House of Commons, July 14, 1940

Let us therefore brace ourselves to our duties, and so bear ourselves that if the British Empire and Commonwealth last for a thousand years, men will still say, 'This was their finest hour'.
> Speech delivered to the House of Commons on June 18, 1940 following the collapse of France

A pessimist sees the difficulty in every opportunity; an optimist sees the opportunity in every difficulty.

This is not the end. It is not even the beginning of the end. But it is, perhaps, the end of the beginning.
> Speech given at the Lord Mayor's Luncheon, Mansion House, London, November 10, 1942.

The greatest lesson in life is to know that even fools are right sometimes.

To build may have to be the slow and laborious task of years. To destroy can be the thoughtless act of a single day.

We shall not fail or falter; we shall not weaken or tire … Give us the tools and we will finish the job.
> BBC radio broadcast, Feb 9, 1941

Broadly speaking, the short words are the best, and the old words best of all.

It is no use saying, 'We are doing our best.' You have got to succeed in doing what is necessary.

There is nothing more exhilarating than to be shot at without result.

Although prepared for martyrdom, I preferred that it be postponed.

History will be kind to me for I intend to write it.

For myself I am an optimist—it does not seem to be much use being anything else.
> Speech at the Lord Mayor's banquet, London, November 9, 1954

The price of greatness is responsibility.

It is a good thing for an uneducated man to read books of quotations.
> *My Early Life,* 1930

Upon this battle [of Britain] depends the survival of Christian civilisation … Hitler knows that we will have to break us in this Island or lose the way. If we can stand up to him, all Europe may be free and the life of the world may move forward into broad sunlit, uplands …
> Speech to the House of Commons, 1940

Arm yourselves, and be ye men of valour, and be in readiness for the conflict; for it is better for us to perish in battle than to look upon the outrage of our nation and our altar.
> Broadcast on the BBC, May 19, 1940

Today we may say aloud before an awe-struck world: We are still masters of our fate. We are still captain of our souls.
> On the War Situation, House of Commons, September 9, 1941

I am a child of the House of Commons. I was brought up in my father's house to believe in democracy. Trust the people—that was his message … I cannot help reflecting that if my father had been American and my mother British, instead of the other way around, I might have got here on my own … I owe my advancement entirely to the House of Commons, whose servant I am. In my country, as in yours, public men are proud to be the servants of the State and would be ashamed to be its masters.

> Speech made to a Joint Session of the American Congress, December 26, 1941.

The Honourable Gentleman should not generate more indignation than he can conveniently contain.

> On William Wedgwood Benn

Television is a penny Punch and Judy show.

He will be as great a curse to this country in peace as he was a squalid nuisance in time of war.

Indeed I do not think we should be justified in using any but the more sombre tones and colours while our people, our Empire, and indeed the whole English-speaking world are passing through a dark and deadly valley.

> In the House of Commons, January 22, 1941

Canada is the linchpin of the English-speaking world. Canada, with those relations of friendly, affectionate intimacy with the United States on the one hand and with her unswerving fidelity to the British Commonwealth and the Motherland on the other, is the link which joins together these great branches of the human family, a link which, spanning the oceans, brings the continents into their true relation and will prevent in future generations any growth of division between the proud and the happy nations of Europe and the great countries which have come into existence in the New World.

> At a luncheon in honour of Mackenzie King, Prime Minister of Canada, Mansion House, London, September 4, 1941

Never give in—never, never, never, never, in nothing great or small, large or petty, never give in except to convictions of honour and good sense. Never yield to force; never yield to the apparently overwhelming might of the enemy.

> Speech made on 29 October 1941 to the boys at Churchill's old public [private] school, Harrow—not Oxford or Cambridge

When I warned them that Britain would fight on alone, whatever they did, their Generals told their Prime Minister and his divided cabinet that in three weeks, England would have her neck wrung like a chicken—Some chicken! Some neck!

> Speech made to the Canadian Parliament on December 30, 1941

Never in the field of human conflict was so much owed by so many to so few.

> In the House of Commons as the Battle Britain peaked, August 20, 1940.

We shall defend our island, whatever the cost may be. We shall fight on the beaches. We shall fight on the landing grounds. We shall fight in the fields, and in the streets, we shall fight in the hills. We shall never surrender!

> On Dunkirk, given in House of Commons June 4, 1940

I have not become the King's First Minister in order to preside over the dissolution of the British Empire.
1942

Victory at all costs, victory in spite of all terror, victory however long and hard the road may be; for without victory there is no survival.

There are few virtues that the Poles do not possess and there are few mistakes they have ever avoided.

A sheep in sheep's clothing.
On Clement Attlee, 1945

A modest little man with much to be modest about.
On Clement Attlee

I do not believe that a successful export trade can be founded on a starved home market.
1947

Socialism is the philosophy of failure, the creed of ignorance and the gospel of envy.
1948

A Labour Government is a government of the duds, by the duds and for the duds.

Trying to maintain good relations with the Communists is like wooing a crocodile. You do not know whether to tickle it under the chin or beat it over the head. When it opens its mouth you cannot tell whether it is trying to smile or preparing to eat you up.
Speech to the House of Commons, 1949

The difference between our outlook and the Socialist outlook on life is the difference between the ladder and the queue. We are for the ladder. Let all try their best to climb. They are for the queue. Let each wait his place until his turn comes.

But we ask: 'What happens if anyone slips out of his place in the queue?' 'Ah,' say the Socialists, 'our officials— and we have plenty of them—come and put him back in it, or perhaps put him lower down to teach others.'

And when they come to us and say: we have told you what happens when anyone slips out of the queue, but what is your answer to what happens if anyone slips off the ladder? Our reply is 'we shall have a good NHS and the finest social ambulance service in the world.'
1951

An appeaser is one who feeds a crocodile—hoping that it will eat him last.
Reader's Digest, 1954

It may well be that we shall, by a process of sublime irony, have reached a state in this story where safety will be the sturdy child of terror and survival the twin brother of annihilation.
On the nuclear deterrent, Last speech to the House of Commons as Prime Minister, 1955

Winston Churchill

1940–; Conservative MP 1970–97

You can sum up what CND means in three words—trust the Kremlin.

Cicero

106–43 BC; Roman Statesman and Writer

So long as the Empire of the Republic was maintained not by injustice but by the benefits it conferred … our government might have been called not so much Empire as a Protectorate of the whole world.
De Officiis

An army at home is of little use unless there are prudent counsels at home.
Ibid.

Laws are dumb in the midst of arms.
Pro Milone

The good of the people is the chief law.
De Legibus

Alan Clark

1928–; Conservative MP 1974–92, 1997–

Yesterday I travelled by train, and a plump young lady came into my compartment at Waterloo. She was not wearing a bra, and her delightful globes bounced prominently, but happily under a rope-knitted jersey. After a bit I moved over and sat beside her … She works as a shop assistant in Maidstone.
Alan Clark Diaries

Everyone in politics ought to be arrested at least once. It's an education.
After being arrested in Piccadilly for allegedly trying to cross a police cordon.

Give a civil servant a good case and he'll wreck it with clichés, bad punc-tuation, double negatives and convo-luted apology.

Bongo Bongo land.
On the origins of an African delega-tion, 1985

Might as well have a corncob up his arse.
On Douglas Hurd

Like most Chief Whips, he knew who the shits were.
On Michael Jopling, *Diaries,* 17 June 1987

There's nothing so improves the mood of the Party as the imminent execution of a senior colleague.
Diary, 13 July 1990

There are no friends in politics. We are all sharks circling and waiting for traces of blood to appear in the water.
Diary, 20 November 1990

As far as I am concerned, dirty tricks are part and parcel of effective govern-ment.
1993

The radiation and vitality was such that you felt electrified by it. But you also felt uncertain, you didn't know what was going to happen next. I never felt that with any other minister or any other member of the Government; I couldn't give a damn what they wanted. But with her, I wished to please her, and nor for my own ad-vancement. I wished to please her because she was such a remarkable individual.
On Margaret Thatcher

Gillian Clarke

Wife of Kenneth Clarke

A Cabinet Minister's wife needs a good hobby. I don't think there is much for a cabinet Minister's wife to do in London.

What should decide Ken's reputation is how he does his job, not anything else. I prefer to keep in the background.
> 1993

The lady may never have been for turning but she certainly turned heads. Everybody flirted with the Prime Minister. I think she took it as her due that you should flirt with her.
> On Margaret Thatcher, 1993

Kenneth Clarke

1940–; Conservative MP, 1970–, Cabinet Minister, 1985–97

Not only Celtic nationalists feel the need for a significant shift of power away from the centre of British politics … One practical answer could be the creation of new regional parliaments. They could strengthen the working of democracy in their areas. With some devolution of powers, they could also take a lot of the workload off Parliament.
> Birmingham Bow Group Pamphlet, 1968

It is surprising that the present bitter controversy has arisen between the Government and, on the one hand, the Labour Party—and to some extent the centre parties as well—and on the other the British Medical Opposition—The British Medical Association.

That is certainly my most Freudian slip of the tongue so far.
> Debate on the NHS, 1989

All those people who say that there will never be a single European Currency are trying to forecast history.
> As Chancellor of the Exchequer, 1993

At Consett you have got one of the best steelworks in Europe. It doesn't employ as many people as it used to because it is so modern.
> BBC Radio Newcastle, March, 1995. (The works had closed in 1980)

Tell your kids to get their scooters off my lawn.
> To Tory Party Chairman Brian Mawhinney

I think [Consett] is also one of the major centres for disposable baby nappies; diapers as well.
> c. March 1995 (The nappy factory had closed in 1991)

They are eighteen year-olds in the saloon bar trying every bottle on the shelf.
> On the Labour Party's Treasury team, 24 May 1997

William Cobbett

1763–1835; Journalist

… in the whole body of the industrious and working people of England, there was scarcely a single man to be found that had ever entertained the slightest thought of envying his richer neighbour, or wishing to share his property, or wishing all men pulled down to a level—I could never gather from one single working man, during the whole course of my communication with them, that he wished for anything beyond—that he wished for change other than—that which would leave him the enjoyment of the fair fruit of his earnings.

Rural Rides, 1830

It is a good people and not a gabbling people that is wanted in the country, and this smattering of education will only raise the labourers of this country above the situations best suited to their own interests ... It will put into their heads that they were not born to labour but to get their living without it.

1834

Samuel Taylor Coleridge

1722–1834; Poet, critic and social philosopher

No man does anything from a single motive.

In politics, what begins in fear usually ends in folly.

1830

The true patriot will reverence not only whatever tends to make the component individuals more happy, and more worthy of happiness; but likewise whatever tends to bind them together more closely as a people.

The Friend

Religion, true or false, is and ever has been the centre of gravity in a society to which all other things must and will accommodate themselves.

The cosmopolitanism which does not spring out of the blossom upon the deep-rooted stem of nationality, is a spurious and rotten youth.

Talk, Talk, 1835

Confucius

If a man takes no thought about what is distant, he will find sorrow near at hand.

The strength of a nation is derived from the integrity of its homes. Whoever serves his country well has no need of ancestors.

Joseph Conrad

1857–1924; Writer

Efficiency of a practically flawless kind may be reached naturally in the struggle for bread. But there is something beyond, a higher point, a subtle and unmistakable touch of love and pride beyond mere skill; almost an inspiration which gives to all work that finish which is almost art—which is art.

The Old Man of the Sea

Conservative Party

Forewords from Party Leaders

I had hoped to preserve the Coalition Government, comprising all Parties in the State, until the end of the Japanese war, but owing to the unwillingness of the Socialist and ... Liberal Parties to agree to my proposal, a General Election became inevitable, and I have formed a new National Government, consisting of the best men in all Parties who were willing to serve and some who are members of no Party at all.

Winston Churchill, *Mr Churchill's Declaration of Policy to the Electors,* 1945

It is a strong Government, containing many of those who helped me to carry the burdens of State through the darkest days and on whose counsel and executive ability I have learned to rely.

Ibid.

We seek the good of the whole nation, not that of one section or one faction. We believe in the living unity of the British people, which transcends class or party differences. It was this living unity which enabled us to stand like a rock against Germany when she over-ran Europe.

Ibid.

Upon our power to retain unity, the future of this country and of the whole world largely depends.

Ibid.

Britain is still at war, and must not turn aside from the vast further efforts still needed to bring Japan to the same end as Germany. Even when all foreign enemies are utterly defeated, that will not be the end of our task. It will be the beginning of our further opportu-nity—the opportunity which we snatched out of the jaws of disaster in 1940—to save the world from tyranny and then to play our part in its wise, helpful guidance.

Ibid.

… holding nothing back, we must now take stock of our resources and plan how the energies of the British people can best be freed for the work that lies ahead.

Ibid.

This is the time for freeing energies, not stifling them. Britain's greatness has been built on character and daring, not on docility to a State machine.

Ibid.

At all costs we must preserve that spirit of independence and that right to live by no man's leave underneath the law.

Ibid.

All who cherish the cause of our country at this fateful moment must cast their vote after hard and long thought, and make sure they cast it effectively.

Winston Churchill, *This is the Road*, 1950

We are confronted with a critical Election which may well be the turning point in the fortunes and even the life of Britain. We cannot go on with this evenly balanced Party strife and hold our own in the world, or even earn our living. The prime need is for a stable government with several years before it, during which time national interests must be faithfully held far above party feuds or tactics. We need a new Government not biased by privilege or interest or cramped by doctrinal prejudices or inflamed by the passions of class warfare. Such a Gov-ernment only the Conservative and Unionist Party can to-day provide.

Winston Churchill, *The Conservative Manifesto*, 1951

There must be no illusions about our difficulties and dangers. It is better to face them squarely as we did in 1940. The Conservative Party, who since victory have had no responsibility for the events which have led us to where we are now, offers no bribes to the electors. We will do our best to serve them and to make things better all round, but we do not blind ourselves to the difficulties that have to be overcome, or the time that will be required to bring us back to our rightful position in the world, and to revive the vigour of our national life and impulse.

Ibid.

We all seek and pray for peace. A mighty union of nations tread that path together, but we all know that peace can only come through their united strength and faithful brotherhood.

Ibid.

Contrast our position to-day with what it was six years ago. Then all our foes had yielded.

Ibid.

We all had a right to believe and hope that the fear of war would not afflict our generation nor our children. We were respected, honoured and admired throughout the world. We were a united people at home, and it was only by being united that we had survived the deadly perils through which we had come and had kept the flag of freedom flying through the fateful year when we were alone. There, at any rate, is a great foundation and inspiration. Everyone knows how the aftermath of war brings extraordinary difficulties. With national unity we could have

overcome them. But what has happened since those days?

Ibid.

In the year 1955—in this age of peril and promise—what needs to be done can be carried through only with the trust and goodwill of the people of this country.

Anthony Eden, *United For Peace and Progress* , 1955

As you know, much of my political life has been concerned with foreign affairs. Twice in a lifetime my generation has seen its world shaken, and almost destroyed, by a world war. Our civilisation could not hope to survive a third. It has been my work to do all I can to prevent such a catastrophe, and this will remain my firm resolve for the whole time I serve you.

Ibid.

But to secure peace we have to do more than just want it or just hope for it We must be firm and resolute.

Ibid.

I have no doubt that we are right to make the hydrogen bomb and it is a source of strength to the country that the Opposition should support us in that step. Mr Attlee, whose Government made the atomic bomb, has agreed that we must possess this newer and still more powerful deterrent In the face of its destructive power, any group of men would have to be not only bad, but mad, to unleash a war. This fact may be the greatest force for peace.

Ibid.

[At home] we must fight with vigour the war on the slums and the war against ill-health and disease. We must equip our rising generation with an education to fit them for the requirements of this new age and to enable them to make the best use of their talents. We must produce more and produce it more efficiently. We must capture new markets overseas. We must save to invest in the future—at home and in the Commonwealth and Empire.
Ibid.

Ownership can be expressed in the home, in savings or in forms of partnership in industry. It can take many shapes.
Ibid.

The essential theme is clear. We are against increased ownership of power and property by the State.
Ibid.

We seek ever wider ownership of power and property by the people. We aim at a community of free men and women working together for the common good.
Ibid.

This constructive programme—indeed its very title [*The Next Five Years*]—will show you that we do not intend to rest in the next five years upon the achievements of the past. We must both defend and develop the great gains that we have made. Our policy can be simply stated: Prosperity and Peace.
Harold Macmillan, *The Next Five Years*, 1959

I do not remember any period in my lifetime when the economy has been so sound and the prosperity of our people at home so widely spread ...
Ibid.

We must also remember what we can do to extend a generous helping hand to the Commonwealth family and others overseas.
Ibid.

As for peace, it is of course the supreme purpose of all policy. I have lived through two wars and all my efforts are directed to prevent a third. Events of the last few months give me hope that we may be moving into a more constructive period. Vital international negotiations lie ahead and I ask you to continue to entrust them to a Conservative Government.
Ibid.

Only by trusting the individual with freedom and responsibility shall we gain the vitality to keep our country great.
Alec Douglas-Home, *Prosperity with a Purpose*, 1964

... greatness is not measured in terms of prosperity alone. What counts is the purpose to which we put prosperity. The Conservative purpose is clear from our record and from our programme. It is to raise the quality of our society and its influence for good in the world. We are using the growth in wealth to expand opportunities for the young, to provide more generously for the old and the sick and the handicapped, to aid developing countries still battling against widespread poverty, and to maintain the strength on which na-

tional security and our work for peace depends.
Ibid.

In a world as dangerous as that in which we live it can make no sense whatever for Britain unilaterally to discard her strength.
Ibid.

We ... reject the idea of giving up our nuclear arm. We adopt instead a balanced policy of strength and reconciliation; strength to be used to stop wars before they start; conciliation to reach areas of agreement with the Soviet Union and the Communist world which will replace tension and potential conflict. The Nuclear Test Ban Treaty was one such achievement.
Ibid.

We mean to work for more until the danger of war is eliminated. The way will be rough but we will persevere. I ask you to conclude that we should retain British power and influence so they may be used for such high purpose.

I present to the people of Britain a manifesto which is also a blueprint.
Edward Heath, *Action Not Words: The New Conservative Programme,* 1966

... a blueprint not for a year but for a full Parliament. I am determined to promise nothing that we cannot achieve. I know that we shall inherit from the Labour Government a weak economic position, and I intend to give first priority to the management of our economy, to the strengthening of Britain's competitive position in

world markets and to the repayment of the heavy burden of debt which they have incurred.
Ibid.

I am determined to break away from the growing constraints of Socialism and the dreariness which stems from it: from the pattern of inflation and stagnant production which has been created.
Ibid.

I want to see our social services recognise the overriding claims of those in most need. I want to see choice becoming once more part of the pattern of life of the individual. I want to see our country with confidence in itself and in the future taking its place in the European Economic Community.
Ibid.

During the last six years we have suffered not only from bad policies, but from a cheap and trivial style of government.
Edward Heath, *A Better Tomorrow,* 1970

Decisions have been dictated simply by the desire to catch tomorrow's headlines. The short-term gain has counted for everything; the longer term objective has gone out of the window. Every device has been used to gain immediate publicity, and government by gimmick had become the order of the day.
Ibid.

Decisions lightly entered into have been as lightly abandoned.
Ibid.

It is not surprising that when I have travelled abroad in recent years friends of Britain have told be of their sadness at the way in which our reputation has shrunk. It is not surprising that young people in this country looking at politics for the first time should be suspicious and cynical.

Ibid.

I am determined therefore that a Conservative Government shall introduce a new style of government: that we shall re-establish our sound and honest British traditions in this field.

Ibid.

Once a decision is made, once a policy is established, the Prime Minister and his colleagues should have the courage to stick to it. Nothing has done Britain more harm in the world than the endless backing and filling which we have seen in recent years.

Ibid.

Whether it be our defence commitments, or our financial policies, or the reform of industrial relations, the story has been the same. At the first sign of difficulty the Labour Government has sounded the retreat, covering its withdrawal with a smokescreen of unlikely excuses.

Ibid.

Courage and intellectual honesty are essential qualities in politics, and in the interest of our country it is high time that we saw them again.

Ibid.

Today we face great dangers both from within our own country and from outside.

Edward Heath, *Firm Action for a Firm Britain,* 1974 (February)

The problems are formidable, but there is no reason why they should overwhelm us.

Ibid.

The world has changed dramatically since we last sought the support of the electorate.

Ibid.

In the last two years there has been a dramatic rise in the world price of almost all the essential raw materials and foods which we have to import from overseas.

Ibid.

On top of these increases comes the huge increase in oil prices, which in turn will effect the cost of almost everything that we produce or buy in this country.

Ibid.

Fortunately, as far as energy is concerned, Britain will in the long run be able to cope better than most. We have plentiful supplies of coal and natural gas. We are well advanced in the development of nuclear power ... within five years from now we should be able to satisfy the greater part of our needs with our own oil from the seas around our shores, provided that we make the determined effort that will be necessary.

Ibid.

[L]et no one suppose that as a nation we can deal with the immediate problem without hardship and sacrifice.
Ibid.

It will impose a greatly increased burden on our balance of payments and make us a poorer nation that we would otherwise have been.
Ibid.

Events from overseas have held us back. They will not destroy us.
Ibid.

What could destroy, not just our present standard of living but all our hopes for the future, would be inflation we brought upon ourselves.
Ibid.

[Prosperity] has now, for the time being, been blighted by the effects of the three-day week, forced upon us by the need to ration electricity so as to prevent our power stations from running out of coal altogether as a consequence of the industrial action taken by the National Union of Mineworkers.
Ibid.

A Britain united in moderation, not divided by extremism. A society in which there is change without revolution. A Government that is strong in order to protect the weak. A people who enjoy freedom with responsibility. A morality of fairness without regimentation. A nation with faith in itself, and a people with self-respect.
Ibid.

The dangers now facing Britain are greater than any we have seen since the last war. These dangers are both economic and political.
Edward Heath, *Putting People First,* 1974 October

Over recent months prices have been rising at an annual rate of over 20 per cent, and on present policies they will rise as much next year. This means that in two years the pound will be worth only 55p. Unemployment is rising rapidly, and the deficit in our balance of payments this year will be £4,000 million. By the end of the 1970s, on present forecasts, we are likely to owe £15,000 million for oil alone.
Ibid.

At the same time the rule of law is threatened, and there are conflicts within the nation.
Ibid.

If we do not solve our economic problems, our political difficulties will be made worse. And if we do not tackle our political problems, our economic difficulties will be insoluble.
Ibid.

Our main aim … is to safeguard the existence of our free society.
Ibid.

Inflation at its present pace threatens not only the standard of living of everybody in the country, but also the survival of our free and democratic institutions. No major democracy has ever survived such a catastrophic rise in the cost of living. We cannot be sure that we would be the exception.
Ibid.

[I]nflation and rising prices tear society apart. They destroy the confidence of people in one another and the future; they distort the existing relationships within our country; they poison the social environment; they wipe our people's savings; they imperil our economic system; they lead in the end to high unemployment and to widespread, if not national bankruptcy; and they bring particular hardship to the most vulnerable people in the land.
Ibid.

Trade unions are an important estate of the realm. We shall co-operate closely with them, and we hope that our proposals for industrial partnership will lead to close and effective co-operation both with employees and management. But we shall not be dominated by the trades unions.
Ibid.

They [trade unions] are not the government of the country.
Ibid.

Our nation still possess great moral reserves. Our patriotism, our knowledge that what unites us is far more significant than what divides us, our idealism, our wish to make our country better and to improve the lot of our fellow citizens—all these feelings and beliefs remain strong in Britain. But they can only by properly summoned to the service of our nation by a government that commands the confidence of the country because it puts the country first.
Ibid.

For me, the heart of politics is not political theory, it is people and how they want to live their lives.
Margaret Thatcher, *The Conservative Manifesto,* 1979

No one who has lived in this country during the last five years can fail to be aware of how the balance of our society has been increasingly tilted in favour of the State at the expense of individual freedom.
Ibid.

[The 1979] election may be the last chance we have to reverse that process, to restore the balance of power in favour of the people. It is therefore the most crucial election since the war.
Ibid.

There has been a feeling of helplessness, that we are a once great nation that has somehow fallen behind and that it is too late now to turn things round.
Ibid.

I don't accept [that it is too late to turn things round]. I believe we not only can, we must. This manifesto points the way. It contains no magic formula or lavish promises. It is not a recipe for an easy of a perfect life. But it sets out a broad framework for the recovery of our country, based not on dogma, but on reason, on common sense, above all on the liberty of the people under the law.
Ibid.

The things we have in common as a nation far outnumber those that set us apart.
Ibid.

In the last four years, Britain has recovered her confidence and self-respect. We have regained the regard and admiration of other nations. We are seen today as a people with integrity, resolve and the will to succeed.

Margaret Thatcher, *The Challenge of Our Times,* 1983

The choice before the nation is stark: either to continue our present steadfast progress towards recovery, or to follow policies more extreme and more damaging than those ever put forward by any previous opposition.

Ibid.

How to defend Britain's traditional liberties and distinctive way of life is the most vital decision that faces the people at this election.

Ibid.

Every thinking man and woman wants to get rid of nuclear weapons. To do this we must negotiate patiently from a position of strength, not abandon ours in advance.

Ibid.

The universal problem of our time, and the most intractable, is unemployment.

Ibid.

The answer [to unemployment] is not bogus social contracts and government overspending. Both, in the end, destroy jobs. The only way to a lasting reduction in unemployment is to make the right products at the right prices, supported by good services. The Government's role is to keep inflation down and offer real incentives for

enterprise. As we win back customers, so we win back jobs.

Ibid.

We are proud of the way we have shielded the pensioner and the National Health Service from the recession.

Ibid.

Only if we create wealth can we continue to do justice to the old and the sick and the disabled. It is economic success which will provide the surest guarantee of help for those that need it most.

Ibid.

Our history is the history of a free people—a great chain of people stretching back into the past and forward into the future.

Ibid.

All [British people] are linked by a belief in Britain's greatness. All are aware of their responsibility to contribute to both.

We have discovered a new strength and a new pride. We have fostered a new spirit of enterprise. We have risen to fresh challenges at home and abroad. Once again our economy is strong. Our industries are flourishing. Unemployment is falling.

Margaret Thatcher, *The Next Moves Forward,* 1987

Founded on this new prosperity, we are building a better Health Service and providing more care for those in need. Living standards are higher than ever before. Our people have the protection of a stronger defence and more police.

Ibid.

Britain has come right by her own efforts. We trusted in the character and talents of our people. The British instinct is for choice and independence. Given the opportunities provided by Conservative policies, many more families now enjoy the pride of ownership—of homes, of shares, of pensions.
Ibid.

Together we are building One Nation of free, prosperous and responsible families and people. A Conservative dream is at last becoming a reality.
Ibid.

At the end of this Parliament a new Millennium will be in view. We must raise our sights high. This Manifesto is about making our country respected and secure, and helping you to achieve a better, safer and more prosperous future. For I believe—strongly—that you, not the Government, should be in charge of your life. That's what Conservatism stands for. That principle underlies all the policies in this Manifesto.
John Major, *Conservative Party Manifesto,* 1992

The Conservative administrations elected since 1979 are among the most successful in British peacetime history. A country once the sick man of Europe has become its most successful economy. A country once brought to its knees by over-mighty trade unions now has industrial peace. Abroad, the cold war has been won; at home the rule of law restored. The enterprising virtues of the British people have been liberated from the dead hand of the

state. There can be no doubt that we have created a better Britain.
John Major, *You Can Only be Sure with the Conservatives,* 1997

Why … do we still need a Conservative Government? Because resting on what we have achieved is not enough. To stand still is to fall back. *Our goal must be for Britain to be the best place in the world to live.*
Ibid.

We live in a tougher, more uncertain world. A fast moving global free market is emerging. New economic powers are rising in the East. Family life and social attitudes are changing. Europe is adjusting to the end of Communism. The European social model is failing. The nation state is under threat. We must respond to these challenges.
Ibid.

We have turned around our economic fortunes. We have fewer people out of work and more in work than any other major European economy. British people now have the opportunity of a prosperous future. But that prosperity cannot be taken for granted. We have to compete to win. That means a constant fight to keep tight control of public spending and enable Britain to remain the lowest taxed economy in Europe. It means a continuing fight to keep burden off business, maintaining our opt-out of the European Social Chapter.
Ibid.

 If we relax for one moment, our hard won success will slip away again.
Ibid.

Conservative Party

On Socialism and the Labour Party

All that we long to achieve in making good the wartime shortage depends on attaining the highest possible levels of peacetime production as fast as we can. We shall fail in that if the British people, instead of fixing their eyes on production, are led off at this moment into academic and spiteful controversies about Socialism.

Conservative Party Manifesto, 1945

The duty of the [Labour] Government from their first day in office was to husband the national resources, to evoke the greatest efforts from all, to give every chance to enterprise and inventiveness and above all, not needlessly to divide the nation.

Conservative Party Manifesto, 1950

The Socialists have failed in their duty. National resources have been squandered. Individual effort has been discouraged or suppressed. National unity has been deeply injured. The Government have shrunk from the realities of the situation and have not told the people the truth.

Ibid.

[The Labour Government] tried to make out that before they got a majority the whole history of Great Britain, so long admired and envied throughout the world, was dark and dismal. They spread the tale that social welfare is something to be had from the State free, gratis and for nothing

Ibid.

There is no foundation for the Socialist claim to have brought us prosperity and security. Ministers themselves have declared that but for American Aid there would have been two million people unemployed.

Ibid.

During these bleak years [1945–50] Britain has lurched from crisis to crisis and from makeshift to makeshift.

Ibid.

In 1945, the Socialists promised that their methods of planning and nationalisation would make the people of Britain masters of their economic destiny. Nothing could be more untrue.

Ibid.

Socialism has imposed a crushing burden of taxation amounting to eight shillings of every pound earned in this country. Enterprise and extra effort have been stifled. Success has been penalised. Thrift and savings have been discouraged. A vote for Socialism is a vote to continue the policy which has endangered our economic and present independence both as a nation and as men and women.

Ibid.

Until the Socialist Government is removed neither Scotland nor Wales will be able to strike away the fetters of centralisation and be free to develop their own way of life.

Ibid.

Contrast our position to-day with what it was six years ago. Then all our foes had yielded

Ibid.

The attempt to impose a doctrinaire Socialism upon an Island which has grown great and famous by free enterprise has inflicted serious injury upon our strength and prosperity.

Ibid.

However well-meaning many of the present Socialist leaders may be, there is no doubt that in its complete development a Socialist State, monopolising production, distribution and exchange, would be fatal to individual freedom.

Ibid.

A vote for Socialism is a vote for the policy which was tried and which failed.

Conservative Party Manifesto, 1955

Under Conservative administration a working population of record peacetime size has been kept fully employed, without Socialist controls and without continual inflation.

Ibid.

Socialists, the makers of new monopolies, are posing now as the champions of the consumer. Multiply the Ministries and clamp on the controls is what, in effect, they say. But that was precisely their policy after the war. It led, despite heavy food subsidies, paid for out of taxation, to a 40 per cent rise in the cost of living in six years and to the perpetuation of shortages and queues, ration-books and black markets, snoopers and spivs.

Ibid.

Socialism would merely hinder this task [of facing the modern world]. Instead of thinking how to expand wealth in which all can share, the Socialists continue to 'plan' the equal division of scarcity.

Ibid.

[The Socialists] still cling to the broken reed of nationalisation; we work for a property-owning democracy.

Ibid.

The Socialists have learnt nothing in their period of Opposition save new ways to gloss over their true intentions. Their policies are old-fashioned and have no relevance to the problems of the modern world.

Conservative Party Manifesto, 1959

On examination, what the Labour Party have to offer is not a 'New Britain', but a camouflaged return to the dreary doctrines which had already proved a failure when they were last dismissed from office.

Conservative Party Manifesto, 1964

Labour's policies for the future are their policies of the past.

Conservative Party Manifesto, 1970

[The Labour Party] have little to boast of in their record. Even less to put forward for the future. So they talk, instead, of their ideals.

Ibid.

The Labour Party today faces the nation committed to a left-wing programme more dangerous and more extreme than ever before in its history.

Conservative Party Manifesto, October 1974

By practising the politics of envy and by actively discouraging the creation of wealth, [the Labour Party] have set one

group against another in an often bitter struggle to gain a larger share of a weak economy.
Conservative Party Manifesto, 1979

Labour's policy would mean not a secure Britain, but a neutralist Britain. And eventually for there can be no trifling with Soviet power a frightened and fellow-travelling Britain.
Conservative Party Manifesto, 1987

When the Exchange Rate Mechanism was being created, during the final days of the last Labour Government, the then Prime Minister decided Britain could not take part.
Conservative Party Manifesto, 1992

[The ERM] would not protect Labour; it would merely expose the folly of Labour policies.
Ibid.

With Socialism everywhere in rout or retreat, it is unclear what the Labour Party stands for. For public consumption, Labour leaders purport to have jettisoned the principles of a lifetime. But how much can they be trusted? How genuine is the conversion and what do they actually believe?
Ibid.

The free market is winning the battle of ideas the world over. From Russia to Vietnam, from China to Romania, people are realising that the socialist model has failed. This is not just an economic triumph. It is a triumph for human freedom. Britain helped to secure it. We should take pride in it.
Conservative Manifesto, 1997

Conservative Party
Britain in the World

Movement of men and women within the Empire must be made easier. A two-way traffic should grow. Those who wish to change their homes should be enabled to carry their national insurance rights with them wherever they go. Imperial ties should be knit together by closer personal contact and understanding
Conservative Party Manifesto, 1945

Our record in colonial government is unsurpassed. Our responsibility to the Colonies is to lead them forward to self-governing institutions; to help them to raise their standards of life by agricultural advance, the application of science and the building up of local industries; to improve conditions of labour and of housing, to spread education, to stamp out disease and to sustain health, vigour and happiness. The policy laid down in the Colonial Development and Welfare Acts must be keenly pressed forward. The resources of the Empire need to be developed for the benefit of all its many peoples.
Ibid.

Unless Britain can hold her place in the world, she cannot make her full contribution to the preservation of peace, and peace is our supreme purpose. Britain, wisely led, can bring together the Commonwealth and Empire, Western Europe and the Atlantic Powers into a partnership dedicated to the cause of saving world peace and of preserving democratic freedom and the rule of law.

Conservative Party Manifesto, 1950

Socialism abroad has been proved to be the weakest obstacle to Communism and in many countries of Eastern Europe has gone down before it. We are not prepared to regard those ancient states and nations which have already fallen beneath the Soviet yoke as lost for ever.

Ibid.

A Conservative Government will go forward resolutely to build, within the framework of the United Nations, a system of freedom based upon the rule of law.

Ibid.

We offer Empire producers a place in the United Kingdom market second only to the home producer. We claim the right to maintain whatever preferences or other special arrangements may be necessary. We shall be prepared to offer a guaranteed market at a remunerative price for some colonial products, and to concert plans with Commonwealth countries for the long-term expansion of production of food and raw materials.

Ibid.

Above all we seek to work in fraternal association with the United States to help by all means all countries, in Europe, Asia or elsewhere, to resist the aggression of Communism by open attack or secret penetration.

Ibid.

… banning the bomb alone would make the risks of war not smaller but greater, as long as the Communists retained their superiority in all other arms and in manpower.

Conservative Party Manifesto, 1955

National Service is … an instrument of our foreign and Imperial policy.

Ibid.

We should be wrong to minimise the fundamental issues of principle that divide us from the Communist world. We cannot ignore the post-war record of Communist subversion and attack, or their world-wide conspiracy to undermine free institutions and to divide and confuse the free peoples. We cannot excuse their denial of the rights of free worship and free expression. Whatever the origins of Communist theory, its practice has led to the extinction of freedom and the enthronement of tyranny wherever it has spread. Only if we are firm in faith and spirit, and united in common purpose with our allies, can we hope to achieve in time something better than a state of cold war.

Ibid.

The British Commonwealth and Empire is the greatest force for peace and progress in the world today. It comprises a quarter of the world's population. It contains peoples of every race, of every religion, of every colour, and at every stage of political and economic advance. It represents the most fascinating and successful experi-

ment in government and in international relations ever known.
Ibid.

We shall work to raise living standards and to guide Colonial peoples along the road to self-government within the framework of the Commonwealth and Empire.
Ibid.

Like all countries of advanced development and democratic tradition, we have responsibilities towards the less fortunate peoples of the world.
Ibid.

It is our responsibility to see that the rights of minorities are fully safeguarded, and self-government can be granted only when we are certain of this.
Ibid.

Whilst one hundred million people in Europe alone have, since the war, been forcibly absorbed into the Communist bloc and system, six times that number have been helped to nationhood within the British Commonwealth. It is our duty to ourselves and to the cause of freedom everywhere to see that the facts are known, and that misrepresentation about British 'colonialism' does not go unchallenged. Progressive expansion of overseas information services will remain our policy.
Conservative Party Manifesto, 1959

Further British capital will be made available through loans and grants for sound Commonwealth development.
Ibid.

… it remains vitally important to maintain our defensive alliances throughout the world. In Europe while we will work for the inspection and reduction of armaments in areas to be agreed, we are opposed to plans that would alter the military balance and weaken NATO.
Ibid.

This historic evolution [of colonies to nationhood] is now reaching its final stages. Of our remaining dependencies many are well on the road to sovereignty. A number have multi-racial populations presenting special problems. Others are too small to bear the burdens of separate statehood. In each case we shall work for a fair and practical solution which will protect the interests of the peoples concerned.
Conservative Party Manifesto, 1964

We propose next year to merge the Colonial Office with the Commonwealth Relations Office, and it and the Foreign Office will be staffed from a single Diplomatic Service.
Ibid.

More than 50,000 students from developing countries were in full-time courses in Britain last year, while some 19,000 British men and women were serving in the developing countries under our Government's auspices. An important feature has been the growing opportunity for young people to find scope for their energy and idealism in voluntary overseas service. Through the initiative of voluntary organisations, and with increasing Government support, the numbers are rising fast.

Ibid.

Help immigrants already here to rejoin their families in their countries of origin, or to return with their families to these countries, if they so wish.

Conservative Party Manifesto, 1966

Strengthen and expand existing Commonwealth links by making full use of the Commonwealth Foundation, by encouraging the professional, legal, medical and educational Commonwealth Conferences and by acting on their recommendations where appropriate.

Ibid.

We believe it right to allow an existing Commonwealth immigrant who is already here to bring his wife and young children to join him in this country. But for the future, work permits will not carry the right of permanent settlement for the holder or his dependents.

Conservative Party Manifesto, 1970

We will vigorously pursue international agreements for the safeguarding and improvement of the environment. We will set clearly defined aims and target-dates for the achievement of cleaner air and rivers, and for the clearance of derelict land.

Ibid.

Britain must play a proper part in dealing with world poverty.

Ibid.

W e have acted so that people might live in freedom and justice. The bravery,

skill and determination with which Britain's task force recaptured the Falklands reverberated around the world. Many small nations gave thanks for that stand; and our allies in the North Atlantic are heartened by what Britain achieved in the South Atlantic.

Conservative Party Manifesto, 1983

Labour's support for gestures of one-sided disarmament is reckless and naive. There is no shred of evidence to suggest that the Soviet bloc would follow such an example.

Ibid.

Labour would give up Britain's nuclear deterrent and prevent the United States from using its bases in Britain which are part of its nuclear shield over Europe. That would shatter the NATO Alliance, and put our safety in the greatest jeopardy.

Ibid.

Britain is once again giving a lead in world affairs.

Conservative Party Manifesto, 1987

The world has been transformed in recent years. Communism has collapsed in Eastern Europe, and the Soviet Union has fallen apart. Everywhere Socialism is in retreat and democracy, human rights and market economics are advancing.

Conservative Party Manifesto, 1992

Britain has led the world in helping the reforms in the former Soviet Union.

Ibid.

Britain is a world leader as well as a European nation. Our economic strength, our history and our language make us a global trading nation with links right around the world. Only the United Kingdom is a member of the European Union, the United Nations Security Council, the Commonwealth, NATO and the Group of Seven leading industrial nations.

Conservative Party Manifesto, 1997

Conservative Party

Britain and European Integration

Entry into the European Economic Community is not open to us in existing circumstances, and no question of fresh negotiations can arise at present. We shall work, with our EFTA partners, through the Council of Europe, and through Western European Union, for the closest possible relations with the Six consistent with our Commonwealth ties.

Conservative Party Manifesto, 1964

We are about to join an economic association of Seven European countries; our aim remains an industrial free market embracing all Western Europe.

Conservative Party Manifesto, 1966

We are determined to give Britain a respected place in the world again and lead her into the European Community.

Ibid.

TO GET INTO EUROPE :
Work energetically for entry into the European Common Market at the first favourable opportunity.
Prepare for entry by relating the development of our own policies to those of the Common Market, wherever appropriate.

Encourage co-operation with other European countries in joint projects which need not await our membership of the Common Market: particularly where large-scale scientific and technological resources are called for.

Ibid.

If we can negotiate the right terms, we believe that it would be in the long-term interest of the British people for Britain to join the European Economic Community, and that it would make a major contribution to both the prosperity and the security of our country.

Conservative Party Manifesto, 1970

The opportunities are immense. Economic growth and a higher standard of living would result from having a larger market.

Ibid.

Every aspect of world affairs underlines the need for a Europe which is united and can carry the maximum weight in the councils of the world.

Conservative Party Manifesto, February 1974

By far the most historic achievement of the last Conservative government was to bring about British entry into the European Community. Membership of the EEC brings us great economic advantages, but the European Community is not a matter of accountancy. There are two basic ideas behind the formation of the Common Market; first, that having nearly destroyed themselves by two great European civil wars, the European nations should make a similar war impossible in future; and, secondly, that only through unity could the Western European nations recover control over their destiny—a control which they had lost after two wars, the division of Europe and the rise of the United States and the Soviet Union.

Conservative Party Manifesto, October 1974

British withdrawal [from the Common Market] would mean the abandonment of export opportunities, the decline of industrial development in this country and the loss of jobs. Withdrawal would give us less power and influence in the world not more. Withdrawal would confront us with the choice of almost total dependence on others or retreat into weak isolation. We reject such a bleak and impotent future for Britain.

Ibid.

Europe gives us the opportunity to reverse our political and economic decline. It may be our last.

Ibid.

We believe that radical changes in the operation of the Common Agricultural Policy (CAP) are necessary. We would, in particular, aim to devalue the Green Pound within the normal lifetime of a Parliament to a point which would enable our producers to compete on level terms with those in the rest of the Community.

Conservative Party Manifesto, 1979

If we wish to play our full part in shaping world events over the next few critical years, we must also work honestly and genuinely with our partners in the European Community. There is much that we can achieve together, much more than we can achieve alone

Ibid.

We shall work for a common-sense Community which resists excessive bureaucracy and unnecessary harmonisation proposals, holding to the principles of free enterprise which inspired its original founders.

Ibid.

We intend to remove lead from petrol, and are taking the initiative with our European partners to achieve this at the earliest possible date. We will press ahead with our plans to reduce lead in paints, food and drinking water

Conservative Party Manifesto, 1983

We have stood up for Britain's interests, and substantially reduced our net contribution to the Community Budget.

Ibid.

We shall continue both to oppose petty acts of Brussels bureaucracy.

Ibid.

The Labour Party wants Britain to withdraw from the Community, because it fears that Britain cannot compete inside and that it would be easier to build a Socialist siege economy if we withdrew.

Ibid.

The European Community is the world's largest trading group. It is by far our most important export market. Withdrawal would be a catastrophe for this country.

Ibid.

Being good Europeans does not prevent us from standing up for British interests.

Conservative Party Manifesto, 1987

The Maastricht Treaty was a success both for Britain and for the rest of Europe.

Conservative Party Manifesto, 1992

British proposals helped to shape the key provisions of the Treaty including those strengthening the enforcement of Community law, defence, subsidiarity and law and order.

Ibid.

The Treaty negotiated at Maastricht laid down the process under which the Community can, if its members meet certain economic conditions, create a monetary union with a single currency for some or all of them.

Ibid.

We will play our full part in the design and discussion of monetary institutions for Europe.

Ibid.

When or if other members of the EC move to a monetary union with a single currency, we will take our own unfettered decision on whether to join. That decision will be taken by the United Kingdom Parliament.

Ibid.

The government has a positive vision for the European Union as a partnership of nations. We want to be in Europe, but not run by Europe.

Conservative Party Manifesto, 1997

Conservative Party

Liberating the Economy

Our war budget has been rendered possible only by the severest taxation pressing heavily on everybody, by borrowing on a vast scale to meet the passing crisis, by huge Lend-Lease supplies from the United States and by generous gifts from Canada and elsewhere. All this cannot go on.

Conservative Party Manifesto, 1945

The State has no resources of its own. It can only spend what it takes from the people in taxes or borrowing. Britain is now a nation of taxpayers. Its record of providing more than half of the national expenditure during the last years of the war from taxation is unsurpassed. The willingness of this generation to bear their fair share of sacrifices must, though we hope for relief, be continued. Our future needs for the war against Japan, for winding up the German war, and the plans for social progress which we are determined to carry out, cause and require a much higher rate of national expenditure than before the war.

Ibid.

Where all benefit, all will have to contribute. The revenue is not created by waving a magic wand. It is drawn from the fruits of the nation's industry, agriculture and commerce. It is won by work and paid in taxes. The present level of taxation drastically restricts the ability of the ordinary citizen to satisfy his personal desires. It is discouraging

to his enterprise and his efforts to better himself by doing the bit extra, for so large a part of anything he gains to be removed by the tax-collector.
Ibid.

As against the advocates of State ownership and control, we stand for the fullest opportunity for go and push in all ranks throughout the whole nation. This quality is part of the genius of the British people, who mean to be free to use their own judgement and never intend to be State serfs, nor always to wait for official orders before they can act.
Ibid.

We must guard against abuses to which monopolies may give rise.
Ibid.

Nationalisation involves a State monopoly, with no proper protection for anyone against monopoly power.
Ibid.

We intend to guard the people of this country against those who, under guise of war necessity, would like to impose upon Britain for their own purposes a permanent system of bureaucratic control, reeking of totalitarianism.
Ibid.

Opportunities to increase the nation's resources by harnessing water power also will be scientifically investigated and followed up.
Ibid.

Britain can resolve her economic difficulties not only by reviving her native strength but by fortifying every link with the nations of our Empire and Commonwealth.
Conservative Party Manifesto, 1950

Conservatives believe in enterprise. We believe that the quality of daring was never more needed than today.
Ibid.

The true value of money must be honestly maintained.
Ibid.

The time has come to restore the business of food purchase to the experienced traders in food and to end direct Government buying.
Ibid.

We regard present high taxation as a grave evil.
Ibid.

The foundation of industrial endeavour must be good human relationships, not impersonal control from aloft and afar.
Ibid.

Almost every incident of daily life is bound by controls which Parliament has had little chance to debate. These controls shelter the sluggish from failure while holding back the adventurous from success.
Ibid.

We shall bring Nationalisation to a full stop here and now.
Ibid.

'British Railways' should be re-organised into a number of regional railway systems each with its own pride of identity and each administered by its own Board of Direction whose mem-

bers must have varied practical experience of serving public needs.
Ibid.

Devaluation was the offspring of wild, profuse expenditure, and the evils which we suffer to-day are the inevitable progeny of that wanton way of living.
Conservative Party Manifesto, 1951

To foster commerce within the Empire we shall maintain Imperial Preference.
Ibid.

We shall stop all further nationalisation.
Ibid.

We have proved, by re-establishing confidence in our currency, by maintaining full employment, by restoring housewives' choice and by smashing housing records, that Conservative freedom works.
Conservative Party Manifesto, 1955

We believe that the British people have a real chance during the coming twenty-five years to double their standard of living. The future beckons to this generation with a golden finger.
Ibid.

We live by world trade: the more world trade there is, the better we shall live. We share in it, we ship it, we insure it and we help finance it. We have been selling, and we shall have to go on selling, against fierce competition in the markets of the world. The first object of our policy must be to enable British industry to do this in what is likely to remain a buyer's market.
Ibid.

We must re-establish sterling in a position so strong and respected that it can play its full part as a major international currency.
Ibid.

Where they are suitable and desired, co-partnership and profit-sharing schemes should be encouraged. They give employees a stake in the prosperity of their firm and so contribute to our concept of a property-owning democracy. We shall continue to assist better training within industry.
Ibid.

... those sections of our economy that remain nationalised must be brought to a higher peak of efficiency. Here again, investment is an important factor.
Ibid.

The new medium of television, which is becoming ever more important in our lives, must not be under monopoly control. Conservatives have ensured that alternative and competing television programmes will soon be available.
Ibid.

Conservative policy is to double the British standard of living in this generation and ensure that all sections of society share in the expansion of wealth.
Ibid.

Sterling is the currency in which nearly half the world's trade is done. Our paramount aim will be to maintain international confidence in it as a sound and stable medium of exchange.
Ibid.

The long-term problem of the balance of payments can only be solved by bringing our trading economy to the highest pitch of competitiveness and modern efficiency.

Conservative Party Manifesto, 1964

Our aim is an economy in which earnings rise in step with productivity and do not outpace it.

Ibid.

… the rapidly changing world of industrial technology is the last place for Socialism. It calls for a flexibility, and a response to new ideas and requirements, which a system of free competitive enterprise is best suited to provide

Ibid.

Britain now faces the worst inflation for twenty years. This is mainly the result of tax increases and devaluation. In implementing all our policies, the need to curb inflation will come first. For only then can our broader strategy succeed.

Conservative Party Manifesto, 1970

We will reduce taxation. We will simplify the tax system.

Ibid.

Other countries achieve a low-cost high-wage economy. So can we.

Ibid.

It is largely because of [poor industrial relations] that our economic progress since the war has consistently lagged behind that of most other industrial nations—and will continue to do so in the future, with grave consequences, unless a major improvement in industrial relations can be secured.

Conservative Party Manifesto, February 1974

There is no majority for a massive extension of nationalisation. There is no majority for the continued harrying of private enterprise. There is no majority for penalising those who save, own property or make profits.

Conservative Party Manifesto, October 1974

The first priority for any government must be to defend the value of the currency and to bring inflation down from the present ruinous rates. This cannot be done overnight; it cannot be done by using only one weapon; and it cannot be done without united effort. If it is not done, the effects on every family will be calamitous.

Ibid.

Every reasonable person knows that if we pay ourselves higher wages than we can afford, sooner or later we shall have to pay higher bills than we can afford.

Ibid.

What we do oppose are ill-considered and damaging additional burdens piled on top of existing penal and comprehensive taxes. Britain already has higher taxes on both capital and income than other countries—with a top rate for income tax of 98 per cent. Tax on tax on tax: this is a prescription, not for a fairer society, but for a poorer and more bitter one.

Ibid.

The centre-piece of our social pro-gramme will be the Tax-Credit scheme—the most advanced anti-poverty programme set in hand by any western country. This scheme will provide cash help, related to family circumstances, automatically and with-out special means test.
Ibid.

Inflation ... has come near to destroy-ing our political and social stability
Conservative Party Manifesto, 1979

Even in the depression of the 1930s the British economy progressed more than it has under this Labour government.
Ibid.

We shall cut income tax at all levels to reward hard work, responsibility and success; tackle the poverty trap; encourage saving and the wider ownership of property; simplify taxes—like VAT; and reduce tax bureaucracy.
Ibid.

Profits are the foundation of a free enterprise economy. In Britain profits are still dangerously low.
Ibid.

Too much emphasis has been placed on attempts to preserve existing jobs. We need to concentrate more on the creation of conditions in which new, more modern, more secure, better paid jobs come into existence.
Ibid.

We will offer to sell back to private ownership the recently nationalised aerospace and shipbuilding concerns,

giving their employees the opportunity to purchase shares.
Ibid.

Just as we reject nationalisation, so we are opposed to the other Socialist panacea—import controls. They would restrict consumer choice, raise prices and invite damaging retaliation against British goods overseas.
Ibid.

We did not disguise the fact that putting Britain right would be an extremely difficult task. The second sharp oil price increase and the deepest world recession since the 1930s have made those difficulties worse. At the same time, the Western world is passing through another transformation from the age of the smokestack to the era of the micro-chip. Traditional industries are being transformed by the new technologies. These changes have led to a rapid rise in unemployment in almost every Western country.
Conservative Party Manifesto, 1983

We have paid off nearly half the overseas debts the Labour Party left behind. Once the IMF's biggest bor-rower, we are now playing a leading part in strengthening international trade and finance—to the benefit of the poorest countries on earth.
Ibid.

In the next Parliament, we shall en-deavour to bring inflation lower still. Our ultimate goal should be a society with stable prices.
Ibid.

There has been a rapid shift of jobs from the old industries to the new, concentrated on services and the new technologies. Tragically, trade unions have often obstructed these changes. All too often this has delayed and reduced the new and better-paid jobs which could replace those that have been lost.
Ibid.

Most decisions worth taking are difficult.
Ibid.

Is it really only such a short time ago that inflation rose to an annual rate of 27 per cent? That the leader of the Transport and General Workers' Union was widely seen as the most powerful man in the land?
Conservative Party Manifesto, 1987

There is no better yardstick of a party's fitness to govern that its attitude to inflation. Nothing is so politically immoral as a party that ignores that yardstick.
Ibid.

We are the only Party that believes in lower taxation.
Ibid.

Self-employment is the seedcorn of the new enterprises of tomorrow.
Ibid.

Like other sections of British industry … the City was held back by restrictive practices until they were swept away in last year's 'big bang'. This has brought nearer the day when shares can be bought and sold over the counter in every high street.
Ibid.

In 1990, a Conservative Government joined the ERM.
Conservative Party Manifesto, 1992

Membership of the ERM is now central to our counter-inflation discipline. But the ERM is not a magic wand.
Ibid.

In due course, we will move to the narrow bands of the ERM.
Ibid.

Curbing the power of the trade unions, opening up markets and cutting red tape, has given us a low-strike, lost-cost economy: and as a result Britain is the number one location for foreign investment in Europe.
Conservative Party Manifesto, 1997

Conservative Party

Domestic Concerns

In local government we favour more devolution to the boroughs and district councils to avoid the swarms of full-time organisers and supervisors like those who have sprung up in the health services.
Ibid.

We shall make it our special care to foster Welsh culture and the Welsh language.
Conservative Party Manifesto, 1950

We shall restore the University constituencies.
Conservative Party Manifesto, 1951

The first great motorways to be built in this country will help traffic to flow between our cities. But we will not sacrifice safety to speed.
Ibid.

The peaceful uses of nuclear energy can make an incalculable contribution to the raising of living standards. A new industrial era may indeed be ushered in when the atom has been harnessed to bring everyday heat, light and power to factory, farm and home
Ibid.

The Conservative Party gives a pledge to the farming community that so long as we are responsible there will be fair prices for good farming, orderly marketing of the main farm products, and no nationalisation of the land.
Ibid.

We shall cherish local democracy.
Ibid.

We shall root out the slums at an increasing pace, and aim to re house at least 200,000 people a year from them.
Ibid.

More than a thousand new telephones a day are now being installed, and we intend to speed up this record progress
Ibid.

Conservatives will continue to guarantee the present freedom of the Universities from Government interference.
Ibid.

By raising living standards and by social reform we are succeeding in creating One Nation at home.
Conservative Party Manifesto, 1959

Reorganisation and re-equipment of the Lancashire cotton industry has got away to a good start. With the help of the Act we have passed it can have a prosperous future.
Ibid.

We shall go ahead with a 'round-the-world' telephone cable in co-operation with the Commonwealth, and maintain our lead in telecommunications by building a new large cable-laying ship.
Ibid.

Two out of three families in the country now own TV, one in three has a car or motor-cycle, twice as many are taking holidays away from home—these are welcome signs of the increasing enjoyment of leisure. They are the fruits of our policies.
Ibid.

… all this represents a challenge to make the growth of leisure more purposeful and creative, especially for young people.
Ibid.

Our policy of opportunity will … be extended. In particular, we propose to reorganise and expand the Youth Service. Measures will be taken to encourage Youth Leadership and the provision of attractive youth clubs, more playing fields and better facilities for sport. We shall do more to support the arts including the living theatre. Improvements will be made in museums and galleries and in the public library service. Particular attention will be given to the needs of provincial centres.
Ibid.

The restrictions on shop hours, which are particularly inconvenient for the growing number of women at work, are being reviewed.
Conservative Party Manifesto, 1964

We intend to press ahead with negotiations for the Channel Tunnel so that an early start can be made
Ibid.

There is an enormous growth in the variety and richness of leisure-time activity. Appreciation of the arts, hobbies and handicrafts of every kind, physical sports, home and foreign travel—these and other pursuits are increasing year by year. They are a cheerful measure of rising prosperity. For the 'affluence' at which Socialists sneer is enabling people, not only to satisfy material wants, but to develop their interests and their feel for the quality of life.
Ibid.

We shall also seek to promote higher standards of architecture and civic planning, and commission works by contemporary artists for public buildings.
Ibid.

[We shall] ensure that all immigrants living in Britain are treated in all respects as equal citizens and without discrimination.
Conservative Party Manifesto, 1966

Combine stricter control of entry with special help where necessary to those areas where immigrants are concentrated.
Ibid.

Farmers are frustrated and disgruntled.
Conservative Party Manifesto, 1970

We will bring forward a sensible measure of local government reform which will involve a genuine devolution of power from the central government and will provide for the existence of a two-tier structure.
Ibid.

We will ensure that the natural beauty of our British countryside and seashore is conserved and wildlife is allowed to flourish.
Ibid.

Food has been relieved of tax altogether.
Ibid.

And we have replaced both Purchase Tax and SET by a 10 per cent Value Added Tax—the lowest standard VAT rate in Europe.
Ibid.

We will continue with our slum clearance programme designed to clear the slums by 1982.
Ibid.

We shall further extend and protect the Green Belt.
Ibid.

We do not accept that, by becoming more prosperous, we will destroy the quality of our environment.
Conservative Party Manifesto, October 1974

In the interests of good race relations, and for the benefit of immigrants already in Britain, as well as for the wider community, a Conservative government will follow a policy of strictly limited immigration.
Ibid.

The new Conservative government will strengthen the police force, our principal defenders against internal attack.
Ibid.

We are utterly opposed to racial discrimination wherever it occurs, and we are determined to see that there is real equality of opportunity.
Conservative Party Manifesto, 1983

To have good community relations, we have to maintain effective immigration control.
Ibid.

We shall legislate to curb excessive and irresponsible rate increases by high-spending councils, and to provide a general scheme for limitation of rate increases for all local authorities to be used if necessary.
Ibid.

The Metropolitan Councils and the Greater London Council have been shown to be a wasteful and unnecessary tier of government.
Ibid.

We have to cure the disastrous mistakes of decades of town-hall Socialism by striking a better balance between public and private effort.
Ibid.

We shall transfer more state-owned businesses to independent ownership.
Ibid.

Britain has come from nowhere to be the world's fifth largest oil producer.
Ibid.

The peaceful application of nuclear energy, if properly controlled (as it always has been in this country), will be beneficial to the environment as well as to the economy.
Ibid.

Conservatives are by instinct conservationists—committed to preserve all that is best of our country's past.
Conservative Party Manifesto, 1987

We will reform local government finance to strengthen local democracy and accountability.
Ibid.

A more prosperous Britain can afford to be ambitious. We can aspire to excellence in the arts, broadcasting and sport. We can use our increased leisure time, energy and money, to improve life for ourselves and our families. The National Lottery we propose to introduce can be used to restore our heritage and promote projects which will become a source of national pride.
Conservative Party Manifesto, 1992

Britain is blessed with some of the most beautiful countryside in Europe. We have to strike a balance: our rural communities must not become rural museums, but remain vibrant places to live and work.
Conservative Party Manifesto, 1997

Conservative Party
The Welfare State

One of our most important tasks will be to pass into law and bring into action as soon as we can a nation-wide and compulsory scheme of National Insurance based on the plan announced by the Government of all Parties in 1944.
Conservative Party Manifesto, 1945

The health services of the country will be made available to all citizens. Everyone will contribute to the cost, and no one will be denied the attention, the treatment or the appliances he requires because he cannot afford them.
Ibid.

We propose to create a comprehensive health service covering the whole range of medical treatment from the general practitioner to the specialist, and from the hospital to convalescence and rehabilitation; and to introduce legislation for this purpose in the new Parliament
Ibid.

Motherhood must be our special care.
Ibid.

On the birth, the proper feeding and the healthy upbringing of a substantially increased number of children, depends the life of Britain and her enduring glory.
Ibid.

Our object is to provide education which will not produce a standardised or utility child, useful only as a cog in a nationalised and bureaucratic machine, but will enable the child to develop his or her responsible place, first in the world of school, and then as a citizen. Many parents will be able to choose the school they like and to play their part with the educational authorities in the physical and spiritual well-being of their children.
Ibid.

No system of education can be complete unless it heightens what is splendid and glorious in life and art. Art, science and learning are the means by which the life of the whole people can be beautified and enriched.
Ibid.

The Social Services were born of Parliaments with Conservative and Liberal majorities. They rest upon the productive effort of British industry and agriculture. The Socialists have by inflation reduced their value and compromised their future.
Conservative Party Manifesto, 1950

We regard social security, not as a substitute for family thrift, but as a necessary basis or supplement to it. We think of the National Health Service as a means, not of preventing anyone from paying anything for any service, but of ensuring that proper attention and treatment are denied to no-one.
Conservative Party Manifesto, 1955

We are anxious that the status and rewards of the teaching profession should continue to attract men and women of high attainment and character.
Ibid.

More and more [school children] who have the ability to benefit will stay on to 17 and 18 and go forward to higher education. This will be made possible by our plans for the universities, colleges of advanced technology, higher technical institutions and teacher training colleges. There will be places for 100,000 extra students by 1968, and for a steadily growing number after that.
Conservative Party Manifesto, 1964

One family in every four is living in a new home built under the Conservatives.

Ibid.

In the towns and cities where most remaining slums are concentrated, clearance rates are being doubled. We aim to clear by 1973 virtually all the known slums.

Ibid.

A royal commission has been set up to report on sentencing policies and the most effective methods for the treatment of offenders. We have asked it to give urgent priority to the growing problem of crime among the young.

Ibid.

Much juvenile delinquency originates in broken or unhappy homes. We shall continue to support the work of marriage guidance.

Ibid.

New drive and impetus is urgently needed to reverse the biggest decline in the housing programme for a quarter of a century.

Conservative Party Manifesto, 1970

The fundamental problem of all Britain's social services—education, health, provision for the old and those in need—is the shortage of resources.

Ibid.

In forward planning for health, we will put more emphasis on community services.

Ibid.

Labour see 'danger' in the growth of private provision in health and welfare.

Ibid.

We wish to move the debate away from the kind of school which children attend and concentrate on the kind of education they receive.

Conservative Party Manifesto, February 1974

We must take speedy action to raise standards of teaching and education. This will involve a considerable strengthening of the system of schools inspection. More inspectors will need to be recruited. National standards of reading, writing and arithmetic will be set. And the training period for teachers should give more attention to teaching the three basic skills and how to maintain discipline.

Conservative Party Manifesto, October 1974

We will encourage schools to publish prospectuses about their record, existing character, specialities and objectives.

Ibid.

It must pay a man or woman significantly more to be in, rather than out of, work.

Conservative Party Manifesto, 1979

We need more compulsory attendance centres for hooligans at junior and senior levels. In certain detention centres we will experiment with a tougher regime as a short, sharp shock for young criminals.

Ibid.

For school leavers, we have provided the most imaginative and far-reaching scheme in our history. The Youth Training Scheme offers every 16–year old a year of serious training for work.

Conservative Party Manifesto, 1983

We recognise the importance of teachers and wish to enhance their professional status.

Conservative Party Manifesto, 1987

We will give greater emphasis to the prevention of avoidable illness and the promotion of good health to make the NHS more truly a health service and not merely a sickness service.

Ibid.

To fight AIDS, the Government has undertaken the biggest health education campaign ever seen in this country one much admired abroad and is fully supporting the Medical Research Council in a special programme of research towards treatments and vaccines.

Ibid.

Elderly, disabled, mentally ill and mentally handicapped people, should be cared for within the community whenever this is right for them.

Conservative Party Manifesto, 1987

The battle against drugs can and must be won. Already there are some signs that the heroin problem may have passed its peak. The cocaine explosion has never happened. It need never happen.

Ibid.

The origins of crime lie deep in society: in families where parents do not support or control their children; in schools where discipline is poor; and in the wider world where violence is glamorised and traditional values are under attack

Ibid.

By the year 2000, one in three young people will follow full-time higher education courses. Meanwhile, the number of mature entrants to higher education has risen by 65 per cent since 1979. And our universities are attracting increasing numbers of foreign students.

Conservative Party Manifesto, 1992

Despite this huge expansion, our students enjoy one of the most generous support systems in the world. The introduction of student loans has given students 30 per cent more money for their living costs than the former system of grants alone.

Ibid.

The public sector is being transformed the world over. Britain is in the vanguard. Everyone wants to learn from our vision of a smaller state doing fewer things and doing them better.

Conservative Party Manifesto, 1997

We are launching an ambitious programme with industry to spread 'IT for All', giving every adult the opportunity to try our and learn about the new IT services. We will work with industry to ensure that all schools are connected to the information superhighway.

Ibid.

Conservative Party

Industrial Relations

Conservatives should not hesitate to join Trade Unions as so many of our Party have already done, and to play their full part in their union affairs.

Conservative Party Manifesto, 1950

The foundation of industrial endeavour must be good human relationships, not impersonal control from aloft and afar.
Ibid.

We must free ourselves from our impediments. Of all impediments the class war is the worst.
Conservative Party Manifesto, 1951

We intend to reform both British management and British trade unions.
Conservative Party Manifesto, 1959

Everyone is fed up with pointless strikes and outdated management.
Ibid.

Pass a new Industrial Relations Act and establish a new Code of Good Industrial Relations Practice.
Ibid.

It is manifestly unfair that those who do not go on strike are, in effect, obliged to subsidise those who do. It is no part of our policy to see the wives and children of men on strike suffering. But it is only right that the unions themselves, and not the taxpayer, should accept their primary responsibility for the welfare of the families of men who choose to go on strike; and after discussions with trade unions and employers, we will amend the social security system accordingly.
Conservative Party Manifesto, February 1974

[T]he Achilles heel of the British economy has long been, and continues to be, industrial relations.
Ibid.

The need for action on this front was recognised by our predecessors, who first set up a Royal Commission to inquire into the subject and then prepared a major Bill to reform trade union law—only to withdraw it in an abject and humiliating surrender to trade union pressure.
Ibid.

We believe that the great majority of the trade union movement will be prepared to work with the democratically elected government of the country for the public good.
Conservative Party Manifesto, October 1974

Much of the friction in our industrial relations is a symptom of the frustration and boredom found in many jobs in modern industry.
Ibid.

During the industrial strife of last winter, confidence, self-respect, common sense, and even our sense of common humanity were shaken. At times this society seemed on the brink of disintegration.
Ibid.

The trade union movement, which sprang from a deep and genuine fellow-feeling for the brotherhood of man, is today more distrusted and feared than ever before.
Ibid.

Between 1974 and 1976, Labour enacted a 'militants' charter' of trade union legislation.
Conservative Party Manifesto, 1979

Does anyone suppose that the Labour Party would have resisted, let alone defeated, the violence and intimidation in the coal strike? Or that the Liberals or the Social Democrats would have fought so hard for our rebate from the European Community? Or that any of the Opposition parties would have persevered through all these difficulties to break the back of inflation and restore honest money?
Conservative Party Manifesto, 1987

Conservative Party

The Individual

It will be our aim and purpose to make an early reduction in taxation in a way that will stimulate energy and permit free individual choice.
Conservative Party Manifesto, 1945

All possible encouragement will be given to the enterprise of individuals and firms to take advantage of export opportunities of all kinds, and nothing must be done to paralyse the spirit of adventure.
Ibid.

The small man in trade or industry, who adventures all he has in the effort to make a success of the business he undertakes, must be given every chance to make good. His independence of spirit is one of the essential elements that made up the life of a free society. Many thousands of such men have been hit bitterly hard by war. Other men may have jobs to go back to, but the businesses of some of these men are gone, or hanging by a thread.
Ibid.

We intend to help all those who wish to own a house of their own or a smallholding. A true property-owning democracy must be based upon the wide distribution of private property, not upon its absorption in the State machine.
Conservative Party Manifesto, 1950

it is certainly no proper function of the State in normal times to go into trade itself, to interfere in the day-to-day running of business, or to tell housewives how to do their shopping.
Conservative Party Manifesto, 1955

[The Socialists] seem to think that the British housewife is incapable of deciding for herself; we are sure that it is the customer, and not 'the gentleman in Whitehall,' who knows best.
Ibid.

Our theme is that property, power and responsibility alike must not become absorbed into the State machine, but be widely spread throughout the whole of the community.
Ibid.

To this end, we shall encourage home ownership. We shall foster thrift. We shall stimulate a spirit of partnership in industry. We shall maintain the independence of the small trader and landowner and of the professional man.
Ibid.

Owner-occupation has spread to 44 per cent of families. Conservatives will encourage its continued increase.
Conservative Party Manifesto, 1964

Small businesses have had a raw deal from Labour. They have had to suffer

higher and more complicated taxes, and waste more time filling up forms.
Conservative Party Manifesto, 1970

Protection of the individual citizen is a prime duty of government. Urgent action is needed to check the serious rise in crime and violence.
Ibid.

People feel increasingly frustrated and even oppressed by the impact on their lives of remote bureaucracy, and of events which seem to be entirely beyond their control or that of our democratic institutions.
Conservative Party Manifesto, October 1974

People want to be helped to achieve, not encouraged to envy.
Ibid.

We want also to help the small, often family-owned businesses which form the backbone of British enterprise.
Ibid.

An important part of the distinct Conservative policy on education is to recognise parental rights. A say in how their children are to be brought up is an essential ingredient in the parental role.
Ibid.

Through the centuries, the law in Britain has acted as the defence of the small man against the great, of the weak against the strong.
Ibid.

By enlarging the role of the State and diminishing the role of the individual, [the Labour Party] have crippled the enterprise and effort on which a prosperous country with improving social services depends.
Conservative Party Manifesto, 1979

We want to work with the grain of human nature, helping people to help themselves—and others. This is the way to restore that self-reliance and self-confidence which are the basis of personal responsibility and national success.
Ibid.

For the first time, the new Enterprise Allowance Scheme offers many thousands of unemployed people the support they need, but previously could not get, while they start their own businesses
Conservative Party Manifesto, 1983

Freedom and responsibility go together. The Conservative Party believes in encouraging people to take responsibility for their own decisions.
Ibid.

Of course, it is not possible to give people independence. That is something we must all achieve by our own efforts.
Conservative Party Manifesto, 1987

In this way One Nation is finally reached not by a single people being conscripted into an organised socialist programme but by millions of people building their own lives on their own .
Ibid.

We were determined to make share-ownership available to the whole nation. Just as with cars, television sets, washing machines and foreign holidays, it would no longer be a privilege of

the few; it would become the expectation of the many.
Ibid.

Small businesses are the seedcorn of the economy
Conservative Party Manifesto, 1992

The Citizen's Charter is the most far-reaching programme ever devised to improve quality in public services.
Ibid.

The [Citizen's] Charter will be at the centre of government's decision-making throughout the 1990s.
Ibid.

Conservative Party

The Constitution

With out mandate and without good reason [the socialists] have reduced the powers of the House of Lords and taken the country a long way towards single-chamber government. By over-centralisation of power they have gravely weakened our system of democratic local government.
Conservative Party Manifesto, 1950

... we must guard the British way of life, hallowed by centuries of tradition. We have fought tyrants at home and abroad to win and preserve the institutions of constitutional Monarchy and Parliamentary government.
Conservative Party Manifesto, 1951

We have cut back war-time powers and regulations which trespassed upon British liberties.
Conservative Party Manifesto, 1955

The functions and powers of government have expanded so much in recent years that the traditional safeguards for the citizen no longer suffice. Although we will reduce government activity and interference, a better system of control and examination of decisions by civil servants, public bodies and local authorities which affect individual citizens is also needed. Parliament during recent years has often passed government legislation which has infringed individual rights and given wide discretionary powers to Ministers and their civil servants. We will closely examine ways of safeguarding more effectively and equitably the rights and freedom of the individual citizen.
Conservative Party Manifesto, 1970

We do not believe that the great majority of people want revolutionary change in society, or for that matter that the future happiness of our society depends on completely altering it.
Conservative Party Manifesto, October 1974

At a time when there are too many people prepared to take the law into their own hands, a Conservative government, backed by public opinion, will uphold the rule of law. Without law, there can be no freedom.
Ibid.

By heaping privilege without responsibility on the trade unions, Labour have given a minority of extremists the power to abuse individual liberties and to thwart Britain's chances of success.
Conservative Party Manifesto, 1979

We will see that Parliament and no other body stands at the centre of the nation's life and decisions, and we will seek to make it effective in its job of controlling the Executive.

Ibid.

Labour want not merely to abolish the House of Lords but to put nothing in its place. This would be a most dangerous step. A strong Second Chamber is necessary not only to revise legislation but also to guarantee our constitution and liberties.

Ibid.

The rule of law matters deeply to every one of us. Any concession to the thief, the thug or the terrorist undermines that principle which is the foundation of all our liberties. That is why we have remained firm in the face of the threats of hijackers and hunger strikers alike. The defeat of the occupation of the Iranian Embassy is only one example of our determination to be patient but still unyielding.

Conservative Party Manifesto, 1983

The British Constitution has outlasted most of the alternatives which have been offered as replacements. It is because we stand firm for the supremacy of Parliament that we are determined to keep its rules and procedures in good repair.

Ibid.

Labour want to abolish the House of Lords. We will ensure that it has a secure and effective future. A strong Second Chamber is a vital safeguard for democracy and contributes to good government.

Ibid.

Cutting a clear path through the jungle of a modern bureaucracy is hard going.

Ibid.

Radical changes that alter the whole character of our constitutional balance could unravel what generations of our predecessors have created. To preserve that stability in future—and the freedom and rights of our citizens—we need to continue a process of evolution, not revolution.

Conservative Party Manifesto, 1997

Conservative Party

A Conservative Britain

Ours is a great nation and never in its history has it stood in higher repute in the world than today. Its greatness rests not on its material wealth, for that has been poured out in full measure, nor upon its armed might, which other nations surpass. It has its roots in the character, the ability, and the independence of our people and the magic of this wonderful island. British virtues have been developed under the free institutions which our fathers and forefathers struggled through the centuries to win and to keep. We of this generation are trustees for posterity, and the duty lies upon us to hand down to our children unimpaired the unique heritage that was bequeathed to us.

Conservative Party Manifesto, 1945

This is a country built on family life. War and separation have strengthened, not impaired, the love of home. The children must always come first. The Education Act, school meals, family allowances, all show that Parliament is realising that. Family life is a precious asset to be defended at all costs.

Ibid.

We are dedicated to the purpose of helping to rebuild Britain on the sure foundations on which her greatness rests. In recent generations, enormous material progress has been made. That progress must be extended and accelerated not by subordinating the individual to the authority of the State, but by providing the conditions in which no one shall be precluded by poverty, ignorance, insecurity, or the selfishness of others from making the best of the gifts with which Providence has endowed him.

> Ibid.

Our programme is not based upon unproved theories or fine phrases, but upon principles that have been tested anew in the fires of war and not found wanting. We commend it to the country not as offering an easy road to the nation's goal but because, while safeguarding our ancient liberties, it tackles practical problems in a practical way.

> Ibid.

We shall make Britain once again a place in which hard work, thrift, honesty and neighbourliness are honoured and win their true reward in wide freedom underneath the law. Reverence for Christian ethics, self-respect, pride in skill and responsibility, love of home and family, devotion to our country and the British Empire and Commonwealth, are the pillars upon which we base our faith.

> Conservative Party Manifesto, 1950

This is an age of challenge and opportunity. In the first half of the century we had to sacrifice our wealth and our overseas investments in two world wars: in the struggle for life and freedom we diminished our commercial strength. Now in this second half of the century, more dependent than ever on our foreign trade in an increasingly competitive world, we must venture for livelihood and prosperity.

> Conservative Party Manifesto, 1955

We Conservatives place our political faith in the unity of our country, in the neighbourliness of its spirit, in the vigour of its character, and in the liberties of its subjects.

> Ibid.

Conservatism is more than successful administration. It is a way of life. It stands for integrity as well as for efficiency, for moral values as well as for material advancement, for service and not merely self-seeking.

> Conservative Party Manifesto, 1959

In thirteen years of Conservative government the living standards of the British people have improved more than in the whole of the previous half-century.

> Conservative Party Manifesto, 1964

As a nation, we have been starved of achievement. We have become conditioned to failure.

> Conservative Party Manifesto, 1970

Conservatives are proud of yesterday's achievements. Angered by today's failures. Determined that tomorrow shall be better again.

> Ibid.

Under a Conservative Government, the gap between the politician's prom-

ise and government performance will be closed, so that people and government can be brought together again in one nation united in a common purpose—a better tomorrow.
Ibid.

What has happened to our country, to the values we used to share, to the success and prosperity we once took for granted?
Conservative Party Manifesto, 1979

Our country's relative decline is not inevitable.
Ibid.

The Conservative government's first job will be to rebuild our economy and reunite a divided and disillusioned people.
Ibid.

Our five tasks are:
1 To restore the health of our economic and social life, by controlling inflation and striking a fair balance between the rights and duties of the trade union movement.
2 To restore incentives so that hard work pays, success is rewarded and genuine new jobs are created in an expanding economy.
3 To uphold Parliament and the rule of law.
4 To support family life, by helping people to become home-owners, raising the standards of their children's education, and concentrating welfare services on the effective support of the old, the sick, the disabled and those who are in real need.

5 To strengthen Britain's defences and work with our allies to protect our interests in an increasingly threatening world.
Ibid.

The years of make-believe and false optimism are over. It is time for a new beginning.
Ibid.

We shall never lose sight of the British traditions of fairness and tolerance. We are also determined to revive those other British qualities—a genius for invention and a spirit of enterprise.
Ibid.

Under Conservative government, confidence is brushing aside pessimism at home. Abroad, Britain is regarded for the first time in years as a country with a great future as well as a great past.
Ibid.

Remember the conventional wisdom of the day. The British people were 'ungovernable'. We were in the grip of an incurable 'British disease'. Britain was heading for 'irreversible decline'.
Conservative Party Manifesto, 1987

Well, the people were not ungovernable, the disease was not incurable, the decline has been reversed.
Ibid.

In this election, only the Conservative Party is offering strong, decisive and united government. We intend to press on with the radical Conservative reform which we embarked upon in 1979, and which has already revived the spirit of our people and restored the reputation of our country.
Ibid.

In twenty years, privatisation has gone from the dream of a few Conservative visionaries to the big idea which is transforming decaying public sector industries in almost every country in the world. Britain has led the world with this new industrial revolution: we can be proud of what we have achieved.

Conservative Party Manifesto, 1997

Calvin Coolidge

1872–1933; American President 1923–8

The business of America is business.
1925

Don't expect to build up the weak by pulling down the strong.

Ultimately property rights and personal rights are the same thing.

Julian Critchley

1930– ; Conservative MP 1959–64, 1970–97

Humming, hawing and hesitation are the three Graces of contemporary Parliamentary oratory.

The *Times,* 1982

Like Marxism, Thatcherism is, in fact, riddled with contradictions. Mrs Thatcher, on the other hand, is free of doubt. She is the label on the can of worms.

Palace of Varieties, 1989

Disloyalty is the secret weapon of the Conservative Party.

The *Observer,* November 1990

She cannot see an institution without hitting it with her handbag.

On Margaret Thatcher, 1982

If she has a weakness it is for shop-keepers, which probably accounts for the fact that she cannot pass a branch of Marks & Spencers without inviting the manager to join her private office.

On Margaret Thatcher

Mrs Thatcher is a woman of common views but uncommon abilities.

As Margaret Thatcher came up in the world, so the Conservative Party came down.

Julian Critchley, BBC TV, 1991

The only safe pleasure for a parliamentarian is a bag of boiled sweets.
1982

He could not see a parapet without ducking beneath it.

On Michael Heseltine

Edwina Currie

1946–; Conservative MP, 1983–97

I'm quite deliberate sometimes about getting into the tabloid press and on TV because I think that if responsible politicians don't do it, then irresponsible ones will.
1983

There's no smoke without mud being flung around.
1989

Most of the egg production in this country sadly is now infected with salmonella.

As junior health minister, 1988 (she resigned two weeks later)

People in the north die of ignorance and crisps.

As junior health minister, 1986

Cervical cancer is the result of being far too sexually active—nuns don't get it.
> As junior health minister

Good Christian people … will not catch AIDS.
> As junior health minister

Take the wife.
> As junior health minister on how businessmen travelling abroad should avoid AIDS.

Buy long johns, check your hot water bottles, knit gloves and scarves and get your grandchildren to give you a woolly night-cap.
> As junior health minister, advice to pensioners for keeping warm in winter

The strongest possible piece of advice I would give to any young woman is: Don't screw around, and don't smoke.
> 1988

I have nothing to do with any aspects of advertising. I can't even tell a Cinzano from a Martini. But I do trust the public to tell the difference between real life and advertisements which is more than better educated worthies seem willing to do.
> Denying that advertising on the BBC would be bad for the public, 1989

Lord Curzon

1859–1925; Conservative MP 1886–98, Cabinet Minister 1916–24

That strange, powerful, inscrutable and brilliant obstructive deadweight at the top.
> On Robert Cecil, Lord Salisbury

Not even a public figure. A man of no experience. And of the utmost inexperience.
> On Stanley Baldwin

When a group of Cabinet Ministers begins to meet separately and to discuss independent action, the death tick is audible in the rafters.
> November 1922

I think and hope that we have conveyed not merely the impression, but the conviction that, whatever other countries or governments may do, the British government is never untrue to its word, and is never disloyal to its colleagues or its allies, never does anything underhand or mean; and if this conviction be widespread—as I believe it to be—that is the real basis of the moral authority which the British Empire has long exerted and I believe will long continue to exert in the affairs of mankind.
> As Foreign Secretary, 1923

Dante

Poet

The hottest places in Hell are reserved for those who in time of great moral crisis maintain their neutrality.

Lord Darlington

With the feelings of an Englishman, I protest against this secret and unmanly mode of voting … I do not think that any public benefit can arise from this change … Is it desirable that men should make a promise with one hand and break it with the other?
> Opposing secret voting, 1833

Charles de Gaulle

1890–1970; President of France, 1945–6, 1958–69

How can you govern a nation which has 246 varieties of cheese?
>   1962

Politics are too serious a matter to be left to the politicians.

Since a politician never believes what he says, he is quite surprised to be taken at his word.

Anthony De Jasay

People who live in states have as a rule never experienced the state of nature and vice-versa, and have no practical possibility of moving from the one to the other ... On what grounds, then, do people form hypotheses about the relative merits of state and state of nature? ... My contention here is that preferences for political arrangements of society are to a large extent produced by these very arrangements, so that political institutions are either addictive like some drugs, or allergy-inducing like some others, or both, for they may be one thing for some people and the other for others.
>   *The State*

Bertrand De Jouvenel

The more one considers the matter, the clearer it becomes that redistribution is in effect far less a redistribution of free income from the richer to the poorer, as we imagined, than a redistribution of power from the individual to the State.
>   *The Ethics of Redistribution*

Lord Denning

1899–1998; High Court Judge

The Treaty of Rome is like an incoming tide. It flows into the estuaries and up the rivers. It cannot be held back.
>   1975

Earl of Derby

1799–1869; Prime Minister 1852, 1858–9, 1866–8

I am an advocate in a cause which I believe to be that of policy, of justice and humanity. I am an advocate for weakness against power, for perplexed and bewildered barbarism against the arrogant demands of overweening, self-styled civilisation. I am an advocate for the feeble defencelessness of China against the overpowering might of Great Britain.
>   Speech in the House of Lords attacking Palmerston's policy on China, 24 February 1857

No doubt we are making a great experiment and taking a leap in the dark but I have the greatest confidence in the sound sense of my fellow countrymen, and I entertain a string hope that the extended franchise which we are now conferring upon them will be the means of placing the institutions of this country on a firmer basis, and that the passing of this measure will tend to increase the loyalty and contentment of a great portion of Her Majesty's subjects.
>   After the Third Reading of the Reform Bill, 6 August 1867

The foreign policy of the Noble Earl may be summed up in two expressive words—meddle and muddle.

> On Lord John Russell, speech in the House of Lords, February 1864

Geoffrey Dickens

1931–96; Conservative MP, 1979–96

I believe that people like myself should stand shoulder to shoulder with the homosexual fraternity … but you're only going to get that support if you don't continue to flaunt your homosexuality and stuff it down other people's throats.

> 1988

Denis Diderot

1713–84; French philosopher

From fanaticism to barbarism is only one step.

Benjamin Disraeli

1804–1881; Prime Minister 1868, 1874–80

There are three kinds of lies; lies, damned lies and statistics.

The wisdom of the wise and the experience of the ages are perpetuated by quotations.

Mr Speaker, I withdraw. Half the Cabinet are not asses.

> On being reprimanded by the Speaker for saying that 'half the Cabinet are asses'.

I repeat that all power is a trust—that we are accountable for its exercise—that, from the people, and for the people, all springs, and all must exist.

> *Vivian Grey*, 1826

There is no act of treachery or meanness of which a political party is not capable; for in politics there is no honour.

> *Vivian Grey*, 1826

A nation is a work of art and a work of time. A nation is gradually created by a variety of influences—the influence of original organisation, of climate, soil, religion, customs, manners, extraordinary accidents and incidents in their history, and the individual character of their illustrious citizens. These influences create the nation—these form the national mind …

> *The Runnymede Letters*, 1836

An arch-mediocrity presiding over a Cabinet of mediocrities.

> On Lord Liverpool

Every man has a right to be conceited until he is successful.

Though I sit down now, the time will come when you will hear me.

> Maiden Speech in the House of Commons, 7 December 1837

The Continent will [not] suffer England to be the workshop of the world.

> House of Commons, 15 March 1838

The House of Commons is absolute. It is the State. L'Etat c'est moi.

> *Coningsby*, 1844

No government can long be secure without a formidable opposition.

> 1844

I have not been ever of the opinion that revolutions are not to be evaded.

This respect for precedent, this clinging to prescription, this reverence for antiquity which all too often ridiculed by conceited and superficial minds, and more the special contempt of the gentleman who admire abstract principles, appear to me to have their origin in a profound knowledge of human nature and in a fine observation of public affairs, and satisfactorily account for the permanent character of our liberties. Our constitution is a prescriptive constitution, it is a constitution whose sole authority is that it has existed time out of mind ... it is a constitution made by what is ten thousand times better than choice. It is made by the peculiar circumstances, occasions, tempers, dispositions and moral, social and civil habitudes of the people, which disclose themselves only in a long space of time.

Vindication of the English Constitution

A Conservative government is an organised hypocrisy.

Debate in the House of Commons on the Corn Laws, 17 March 1845

He never wrote an invitation to dinner without an eye on posterity.

On writer and politician, Edward Bulwer

The European talks of progress because, by the aid of a few scientific discoveries, he has established a society which has mistaken comfort for civilisation.

Conservatism discards prescription, shrinks from Principle, disavows progress; having rejected all respect for antiquity, it offers no redress for the present, and makes no preparation for the future.

Coningsby, 1844

A sound Conservative Government? I understand: Tory men and Whig measures.

Coningsby, 1844

Thus you have a starving population, an absentee aristocracy, and an alien church, and in addition the weakest executive in the world. That is the Irish question.

16 February 1844

His temper naturally morose, has become licentiously peevish. Crossed in his Cabinet, he insults the House of Lords, and plagues the most eminent of his colleagues with the crabbed malice of a maundering witch.

On the Earl of Aberdeen

Gladstone, like Richelieu, can't write. Nothing can be more unmusical, more involved or more uncouth than all his scribblement.

That fatal drollery called a representative government.

Tancred, 1847

Justice is truth in action.

11 February 1851

England does not love coalitions.

House of Commons, 16 December 1852

If a traveller were informed that such a man was the Leader of the House of Commons, he might begin to comprehend how the Egyptians worshipped an insect.

On Lord John Russell

I doubt very much whether a democracy is a government that would suit this country.

1865

Individuals may form communities, but it is institutions alone that can create a nation.

> Speech in Manchester, 1866

I have climbed to the top of the greasy pole.

> On becoming Prime Minister, 1868

... honest in the most odious sense of the word.

> On Gladstone (attrib.)

[The result of widening the franchise would be] a Parliament of no statesmanship, no eloquence, no learning, no genius. Instead of these ,you will have a horde of selfish and obscure mediocrities incapable of anything but mischief ... devised and regulated by the raging demagogue of the hour.

> Opposing reform, 1866

For my part I do not believe that the country is in danger, I think England is safe in the care of men who inhabit her; that she is safe in something much more precious than her accumulated capital—her accumulated experience; she is safe in her national character, in her fame, in the traditions of a thousand years, and in that glorious future which I believe awaits her.

> Speech to the House of Commons,
> third reading of the Reform Bill, 1867

You know who critics are? The men who have failed in literature and art.

> Lothair, 1870

I look upon Parliamentary government as the noblest government in the world.

> 3 April 1872

I believe that without *party* Parliamentary government is impossible.

> 3 April 1872

In my opinion no minister in this country will do his duty who neglects any opportunity of reconstructing as much as possible our colonial empire, and of responding to those distant sympathies which may become the source of incalculable strength and happiness to this land.

> 1872

The principles of liberty, of order, of law and of religion ought not to be entrusted to individual opinion or to the caprice and passion of multitudes, but should be embodied in a form of permanence and power. We associate with the monarchy the ideas which it represents—the majesty of the law, the administration of justice, the fountain of mercy and of honour.

> 1872

The issue is no mean one. It is whether you will be content to be a comfortable England, modelled and moulded upon continental principles, and meeting in due course an inevitable fate, or whether you will be a great country, an imperial country, a country where your sons when they rise, rise to paramount positions, and obtain not merely the esteem of their countrymen, but command respect in the rest of the world.

> Speech at Crystal Palace, 1872

If Gladstone fell into the Thames, that would be a misfortune, and if anybody pulled him out that, I suppose, would be a calamity.

The world is weary of statesmen whom democracy has degraded into politicians.

I am dead: dead, but in the Elysian fields.

> On his elevation to the House of Lords, 1876

Lord Salisbury and myself have brought you back peace—but a peace I hope with honour.

> On returning from the Congress of Berlin

A sophistical rhetorician, inebriated with the exuberance of his own verbosity, and gifted with an egotistical imagination, that can at all times command an interminable and incon-sistent series of arguments, malign an opponent and glorify itself.

> On Gladstone, speech at Knightsbridge, 1878

As I sat opposite the Treasury Bench, the ministers reminded me of one of those marine landscapes not very unusual on the coasts of South America. You behold a range of ex-hausted volcanoes, not a flame flickers on a single pallid crest, but the situation is still dangerous. There are occasional earthquakes, and ever and anon the dark rumbling of the sea.

Posterity will do justice to that unprin-cipled maniac Gladstone, an extraordi-nary mixture of envy, vindictiveness, hypocrisy and superstition; and with one commanding characteristic whether Prime Minister, or Leader of the Opposition, whether preaching, praying, speechifying or scribbling, never a gentleman.

> Letter to Lord Derby, 1878

What you say about Gladstone is most just. What restlessness! What vanity!

And what unhappiness must be his! Easy to say he is mad. It looks it. My theory about him is unchanged; a ceaseless Tartuffe from the beginning. That sort of man does not get mad at seventy.

> Letter to Lord Bradford, 1879

One of the greatest of Romans, when asked what were his policies, replied, *Imperium et Libertas*. That would not make a bad programme for a British Ministry.

> Mansion House Speech, 1879

The greatest opportunity that can be offered to an Englishman—a seat in the House of Commons.

> *Endymion*, 1880

Action may not always bring happiness; but there is no happiness without action.

Nurture your mind with great thoughts.

When I want to read a novel, I write one.

In a progressive country change is constant, and the great question is, not whether you should resist change which is inevitable, but whether that change should be carried out in deference to the manners, the customs, the laws, and the traditions of the people, or in deference to abstract principles and arbitrary and general doctrines.

I never offered an opinion until I was sixty, and then it was one which had been in our family for generations.

Robert Dole

1923–; US Senator

Good news is, a bus full of supply-siders went over the cliff. Bad news is, there were three empty seats.

A little gridlock might be food from time to time.

Stephen Dorrell

1952–; Conservative MP, 1979–, Cabinet Minister

Even if science was wrong on that subject, we've removed from the human food chain the organs that could conceivably be linked to a transmission.
1995

Dostoevsky

1821–1881; Russian novelist

What man want is simply independent choice, whatever that independence may cost and wherever it may lead.
Notes from the Underground, 1864

The Socialist who is a Christian is more to be dreaded than the Socialist who is an atheist.
The Brothers Karamazov, 1880

Alan Duncan

1957–; Conservative MP, 1992–

At least if I'd been f★★cking somebody I would have been having some fun.
after being criticised for a property deal, 1994

'Communities' do not exist. The new communitarianism shares the contradiction that which bedevils all collectivist philosophies. It is that collective activities are not practicable much above the level of the family or the team-sport.
Saturn's Children, 1990

The idea of a 'community' is either a meaningless metaphysical abstraction, a banal shorthand description of existing social realities, or a euphemism for State power. No coherent policy can be derived from it.
Ibid.

... it is pointless to persist with the conventional responses to the increase in crime. More police, more prisons and more effective judicial procedures are clearly not working, except in so far as they satisfy a patent public thirst for retribution.
Ibid.

The analysis of the economics of the drugs trade is too compelling to ignore. Logic suggests that the only completely effective way to ameliorate the problem, and especially the crime which results from it, is to bring the industry into the open by legalising the distribution and consumption of all dangerous drugs, or at the very least decriminalising their consumption.
Ibid.

There is no reason to suppose that the number of consumers would increase if dangerous drugs were legalised. A sensible legislation would retain strict official control over the distribution and quality of drugs, and perhaps include the establishment of a register of users of hard drugs. Evidence from Holland and the United States, where

experiments in the decriminalisation of soft drugs are taking place, suggests consumption tends not to rise, but drug-related crime does tend to fall.
Ibid.

Although the democratic State has a constant urge, as de Tocqueville forecast, to act as an 'immense, protective power which is alone responsible for securing their enjoyment and watching over their fate', it is perfectly respectable to believe that people are a judge of their own best interests, even if they choose to consume harmful drugs.
Ibid.

William Durant and Ariel Durant

1885–1981 and 1888–1981; American Political Philosophers

The experience of the past leaves very little doubt that every economic system must sooner or later rely upon some form of the profit motive to stir individuals and groups to productivity. Substitutes like slavery, police supervision, or ideological enthusiasm prove too unproductive, too expensive or too transient.
The Lessons of History, 1968

Nothing is clearer in history than the adoption by successful rebels of the methods they were accustomed to condemn in the forces they deposed.
Ibid.

Utopias of equality are biologically doomed, and the best that the amiable philosopher can hope for is an approximate equality of legal opportunity. A

society in which all potential abilities are allowed to develop and function will have a survival advantage in the competition of groups,
Ibid.

A great civilisation is not conquered from without until it has destroyed itself within. The essential cause of Rome's decline lay in her people, her morals, her class struggle, her failing trade, her bureaucratic despotism, her stifling taxes, her consuming wars.
Caesar and Christ, 1944

Max Eastman

1883–1969; American Intellectual and Poet

I never dreamed that, however that they, [the American intelligentsia] could sink to the depth of maudlin self-deception and perfectly abject treason to truth, freedom, justice, and mercy that many of them have reached in regard to the Russian debacle.
On the failure of liberals to confront the failure of the Russian socialist revolution. *Reflections on the Failure of Socialism,* 1955

Anthony Eden

1897–1977; Prime Minister 1955–57

That is a good question for you to ask, not a wise question for me to answer.
On being asked what effect the death of Stalin would have on international affairs, 1953

[Nasser] is the best sort of Egyptian and a great improvement on the Pashas of the past.
After meeting Nasser in Cairo, February 1955

We are in armed conflict; that is the phrase I have used. There has been no declaration of war.

On the Suez Crisis, 1 November 1956

Dwight D. Eisenhower

1890–1969; American President 1952–60

You do not lead by hitting people over the head—that's assault, not leadership. Humility must always be the portion of any man who receives acclaim earned in blood of his followers and sacrifices of his friends.

Guildhall Address, London, June 12, 1945

I hate war as only a soldier who has lived it can, only as one who has seen its brutality, its stupidity.

Canadian Club, Ottawa, January 10, 1946

A people that values its privileges above its principles soon loses both.

First Inaugural Address, January 20, 1953

There is in world affairs a steady course to be followed between an assertion of strength that is truculent and a confession of helplessness that is cowardly.

State of the Union Address, February 2, 1953

Every gun that is made, every warship launched, every rocket fired signifies, in the final sense, a theft from those who hunger and are not fed, those who are cold and are not clothed.

The Chance for Peace Address, April 16, 1953

The world moves, and ideas that were good once are not always good.

Press Conference, Washington D.C. August 31,1955

The only way to win World War III is to prevent it.

Radio and TV Address, September 19, 1956

The final battle against intolerance is to be fought—not in the chambers of any legislature—but in the hearts of men.

Campaign Speech, Los Angeles, October 19, 1956

I like to believe that people in the long run are going to do more to promote peace than our governments. Indeed, I think that people want peace so much that one of these days governments had better get out of their way and let them have it.

TV Talk with Harold Macmillan August 31, 1959

In the councils of government, we must guard against the acquisition of unwarranted influence, whether sought or unsought, by the military–industrial complex.

Farewell Address, Radio and TV January 17, 1961

T. S. Eliot

1888–1965; Poet and Critic

Envy is everywhere.
Who is without envy? And most people
Are unaware or unashamed of being envious.

The Elder Statesman, 1958

The difference between being an elder
statesman
And posing successfully as an elder
statesman
Is practically negligible.
> Ibid.

The historical sense involves a percep-
tion, not only of the pastness of the
past, but of its presence.
> *Tradition and the Individual Talent,*
> 1920

It is not enough to understand what we
ought to be, unless we know what
we are;
And we do not understand what we are,
Unless we know what we ought to be.
> *Religion and Literature,* 1935

We know too much, are convinced of
too little. Our literature is a substitute
for religion, and so is our religion.

Ebeneezer Elliott

1781–1849; Poet

What is a communist? One who has
yearnings
For equal division of unequal earnings
Idler or bungler, or both, he is willing,
To fork out his copper and pocket
your shilling.
> *Corn-Law Rhymes,* 1831

Ralph Waldo Emerson

1803–82

The punishment which the wise suffer,
who refuse to take part in the government—is to live under the government
of worse men.
> *Epigrams*

There is always a certain meanness in
the argument of conservatism, joined
with a certain superiority in its fact.

The democrat is a young conservative,
the conservative is an old democrat.
The aristocrat is the democrat ripe and
gone to seed.

Democracy becomes a government of
bullies tempered by editors.

The two parties which divide the state,
the party of Conservatism and that of
Innovation, are very old, and have
disputed the possession of the world
ever since it was made.

Euripides

480–405 BC; Greek Dramatist

Moderation, the noblest gift of heaven.
> *Medea*

Nigel Evans

1957–; Conservative MP 1991–

I am proud to be Welsh and I am also
an unashamed, Union-Jack waving
Brit.

I'm used to being unpopular. I am a
Conservative and I'm from Wales.

Michael Fabricant

1950–; Conservative MP, 1992–

Much as I would like the whole world
to disarm and allow a free market to
operate, as long as other countries
support their industries, we must
intervene to do the same.
> May 1993

Nicholas Fairbairn

1933–94; Conservative MP, 1974–92

A little boy sucking his misogynist thumb and blubbing and carping in the corner of the front bench below the gangway is a mascot which Parliament can do without.
>On Edward Heath

He has no place in the Party. He has no future in Parliament. He has no place, for Parliament is a generous place; democracy a generous thing. May I suggest he pursues his alternative career and conducts orchestras, since he does not know how to conduct himself.
>On Edward Heath

What's a skirt but an open gateway?

You are a silly, crude bitch and since you are a potential breeder, God help the next generation.
>To a young woman heckler

The Hon. Lady was once an egg and people on both sides of this House greatly regret its fertilisation.
>To Edwina Currie referring to the 'Salmonella in eggs affair', 1988

She is a lady short on looks, absolutely deprived of any dress sense, has a figure like a Jurassic Park monster, is very greedy when it comes to loot, no tact and wants to upstage everybody else. I cannot think of anybody else I would sooner not appoint to this post than the Duchess of York.
>On the suggestion that the Duchess of York should become UN ambassador.

Lord Falkland

When it is not necessary to change, it is necessary not to change.

Herbert Fisher

Purity of race does not exist. Europe is a continent of energetic mongrels.
>*A History of Europe,* 1934

Howard Flight

1948–; Conservative MP 1997–

I've always been a passionate believer in capitalism; to me it is like a Bach fugue—a wonderfully complicated thing which has come about naturally and works.

Malcolm Forbes jr

Capitalism works better than any of us can conceive. It is also the only truly moral system of exchange.
>May 1993

Capitalism is the real enemy of tyranny.
>Ibid.

Gerald Ford

1909–; US President, 1974–76

Get those nigger babies off my TV set.
>To White House Staff after watching pictures of the war in Biafra, Nigeria

If the Government is big enough to give you everything you want, it is big enough to take away everything you have.
>1960

Our long national nightmare is over. Our Constitution works. Our great Republic is a Government of laws and not of men.

Following Watergate, 1974

Truth is the glue that holds governments together.

1974

There is no Soviet domination of Eastern Europe and there never will be under a Ford administration.

1976

Earl Fortescue

It has been said that children should be kept at school until fourteen years of age; but the amount and importance of the labour which lads between ten and fourteen can perform should not be ignored. Since the present educational system has come into operation, the weeds have very much multiplied in Norfolk which was once regarded as quite the garden of England, weeding being particularly the work of children whose labour is cheap, whose sight is keen, bodies flexible and fingers nimble.

1880

Eric Forth

1944–; Conservative MP 1983–

Reading, 'riting, 'rithmetic, right and 'rong'.

On the 5 Rs

Liam Fox

1961–; Conservative MP, 1992–

Nothing could do more to harm the opponents of the Government than the shocking and sickening violence of the agitators outside the Wapping plant who feel they are justified in provoking scenes of carnage to make their point and who regard the police with malevolent contempt.

January 1987

I believe strongly in competition, the supremacy of the market, in the fact that capitalism and multi-party democracies are better than other systems and that people should be supported when they can't help themselves and not when they won't help themselves.

Felix Frankfurter

1882–1965; American judge

Freedom of the press is not an end in itself but a means ... to a free society. The history of liberty has largely been the history of the observance of procedural standards.

1943

It is a fair summary of history to say that the safeguards of liberty have been forged in controversies involving not very nice people.

1950

Benjamin Franklin

1706–90; American politician

... in this world nothing is certain but death and taxes.

Letter to M. Lewy, 1789

Necessity has no law; I know some attorneys of the same.

They that can give up essential liberty to obtain a little temporary safety deserve neither liberty nor safety.
1759

No nation was ever ruined by trade.

Roger Freeman

1942–; Conservative MP, 1983–97, Cabinet Minister, 1995–97

There's a lot that can be done in terms of encouraging more people to enjoy a cheap and cheerful service at one moment in the day for the typists and perhaps a more luxurious service for the civil servants and businessmen who might travel at a slightly different time.
As a public transport minister, 1994

David Friedman

Economist

Suppose one little old lady in ten carries a gun. Suppose that one in ten of those, if attacked by a mugger, succeeds in killing the mugger instead of being killed by him — or shooting herself in the foot. On average, the mugger is much more likely to win the encounter than the little old lady. But — also on average — every hundred muggings produces one dead mugger. At those odds, mugging is an unprofitable business — not many little old ladies carry enough money to justify one chance in a hundred of being killed getting it. The number of muggers declines drastically, not because they have all been killed but because they have, rationally, sought safer professions.
Hidden Order: The Economics of Everyday Life

Milton Friedman

1912– ; American economist

Thank heavens we do not get all of the government that we are made to pay for.

History suggests that Capitalism is a necessary condition for political freedom.
Capitalism & Freedom, 1962

Nothing is so permanent as a temporary government program.

Governments never learn. Only people learn.

Inflation is taxation without legislation.

Hell hath no fury like a bureaucrat scorned.

The government solution to a problem is usually as bad as the problem.

There is an invisible hand in politics that operates in the opposite direction to the invisible hand in the market. In politics, individuals who seek to promote only the public good are led by an invisible hand to promote special interests that it was no part of their intention to promote.
1983

Why would anyone be foolish to worry about money supply? The more money the merrier, right? Wrong ... If the amount of money overwhelms the capacity to produce goods, consumers, with more money to spend, bid up prices ... [People are] no wealthier than before; more bills do not bring a higher standard of living any more than if everyone added to zeroes to his or her salary. Remember wealth is measured by the goods and services it can buy, not by numerals.

> *New Ideas from Dead Economics,* 1989

Sir George Gardiner

1935–; Conservative MP 1974–97

Receiving support from Ted Heath in a by-election is like being measured by an undertaker.

David Garrick

Heart of oak are our ships
Heart of oak are our men:
We always are ready;
Steady boys, steady,
We'll fight and we'll conquer again and
  again.

> *Heart of Oak,* 1770

George V

1865–1936; King of Britain 1910–36

How is the Empire?

> Last words, January 12, 1936

Henry George

1839–1897; American Economist

What protection teaches us, is to do ourselves in time of peace what enemies seek to do to us in time of war.

> *Protection or Free Trade,* 1886

To put political power in the hands of men embittered and degraded by poverty is to tie firebrands to foxes and turn them loose amid the standing corn.

> *Progress and Poverty,* 1870

Edward Gibbon

1737–1794; Historian

It has been calculated by the ablest politicians that no State, without being soon exhausted, can maintain above the hundredth part of its members in arms and idleness.

> *Decline and Fall of the Roman Empire,* 1776–88

Corruption, the most infallible symptom of constitutional liberty.

> Ibid.

George Gilder

1939– ; American political philosopher and speech writer to Ronald Reagan

Capitalism begins with giving. Not from greed, avarice, or even self love can one expect the rewards of commerce, but from a spirit closely akin to altruism, a regard for the needs of others, a benevolent, outgoing and courageous temper of mind.

> *Wealth & Poverty,* 1981

Real poverty is less a state of income than a state of mind.

> Ibid.

A successful economy depends upon the proliferation of the rich, on creating a large class of risk-taking men who are willing to shun the easy channels of a comfortable life in order to create a new enterprise, win huge profits and invest them again.

> Ibid.

The man has the gradually sinking feeling that his role as provider, the definitive male activity from the primal days of the hunt through the

industrial revolution and on into modern life, has been largely seized from him; he has been cuckolded by the compassionate state.
Ibid.

Socialism presumes that we already know most of what we need to know to accomplish our national goals. Capitalism is based on an idea that we live in a world of unfathomable complexity, ignorance and peril, and that we cannot possibly prevail over our difficulties without constant efforts of initiative, sympathy, discovery and love.
Ibid.

Whether sorting potatoes or writing software [entrepreneurs] are movers and shakers, doers and givers, brimming with visions of creation and opportunity.
Ibid.

[Entrepreneurs] are optimists, who see in every patch of sand a potential garden, in every man a potential worker, in every problem a possible profit. Their self-interest succumbs to their deeper interest and engagement with the work beyond themselves, impelled by their curiosity, imagination, and faith.
Ibid.

Capitalism offers nothing but frustrations and rebuffs to those who wish—because of claimed superiority of birth, credentials, or ideals—to get without giving, to take without risking, to profit without sacrifice, to be exalted without humbling themselves to understand others and meet their needs.
Ibid.

Just as the sociologist requires books and free time and the bureaucrat needs arbitrary power, the capitalist needs capital.
Ibid.

Ian Gilmour

1926– ; Conservative MP, Cabinet Minister, 1979–81

Unfortunately monetarism, like Marxism, suffered the only fact that for a theory is worse than death: it was put into practice.
Dancing with Dogma

Contemporary Conservatism as practised by the leadership is, like contemporary art, seldom much admired at the time; it only achieves acceptance and admiration in retrospect.
Inside Right, 1977

Socialists may look forward to some grim utopia. Conservatives have no such illusions about the future or the past. For them there has never been a 'golden age' and there never will be. Similarly there is no fixed or golden policy to which the Conservative Party could or should turn.
Ibid.

It is certainly neither practicable nor sensible to seek consistency in Tory policy through the ages in the shallow sense of sameness. For instance the party has had the good sense to move from protection to free trade, back to protection and then again towards free trade according to the economic circumstances of the time. Again, there can be no permanent attitude to the state, since the state is continually changing.
Ibid.

Newt Gingrich

1943–; American Congressman

The welfare state kills more people in a year than private business.
1989

One of the greatest intellectual failures of the welfare state is the penchant for sacrifice, so long as the only people being asked to sacrifice are working, tax-paying Americans.
USA Today, 16 January 1995

A society that focuses on creating wealth will find itself getting very, very rich and dramatically increasing the scale of achievement, whereas the society that focuses on redistributing wealth will rapidly discourage people from creating it.

No society can survive, no civilisation can survive, with having twelve year olds having babies, with fifteen year olds killing each other, with seventeen year olds dying of AIDS, with eighteen year olds getting diplomas they can't read.
Commentary, 1994

Building the Panama Canal all of us wanted to keep? We invented a nation, built a canal, manned the canal, cured yellow fever, and had a navy to protect it.
The Heritage Foundation, April 1988

Bureaucratic rules cannot take the place of common sense.
Ibid.

Today's taxes are so high they force many mothers to work. Today's taxes are anti-child, anti-family and anti-work. Furthermore, our tax system is anti-savings, anti-investment and anti-jobs.
Ibid.

Nathan Glazer

1923– ; American sociologist

To live with the two fraternities—the fraternity of the racial and ethnic group and the fraternity of the larger American society—means to acknowledge, and to accept, differences that are not the result of discrimination but are themselves the result of a concrete group life.
Ethnic Dilemmas 1964–1982, 1983

Every contemporary society tries to reduce differences and inequalities, and ours should too. But what is problematic is the attempt to treat every difference as the result of discrimination and as a candidate for governmental action to reduce it. In a multiethnic society, such a policy can only encourage one group after another to raise its claims to special treatment for its protection.
Ibid.

[T]he rising emphasis on group differences which government is called upon to correct might mean the destruction of any hope for the larger fraternity of all Americans, in which people are tied to one another in what they feel to be a common good society, and in which the tie is close enough to allow tolerance for their range of differences.
Ibid.

Lord Glenarthur

To go round the world in a week, which
I did the other day, is very exhausting.
1988

Viscount Goderich

1782–1859; Prime Minister 1827–1828

I cannot forget that the principle of
our constitution is jealousy. It is jealous
of the Crown, jealous of the aristocracy, jealous of the democracy, and the
Roman Catholics have no right to
complain, if it is jealous of them.
> Speech in the House of Commons
> during the debate on Catholic
> emancipation, 1 March 1813

The science of Government, whether
legislative or executive, was, in fact,
neither more nor less than a perpetually recurring struggle with difficulties.
> Speech in the House of Lords

William Godwin

1756–1836; Philosopher and novelist

Government can have no more than
two legitimate purposes—the suppres-
sion of injustice within the community,
and the common defence against
external invasion.
> An Enquiry Concerning Political
> Justice, 1793

Goethe

1749–1832; German Writer

Legislators and revolutionaries who
promise liberty and equality at the
same time are either utopian dreamers
or charlatans.
> In Maxims and Reflections, No. 953

What is the best government? That
which teaches us to govern ourselves.
> Ibid.

Freedom! A fine word when rightly
understood. What freedom would you
have? What is the freedom of the most
free? To act rightly!
> Egmont, 1788

Man tue was man will. (One does what
one wishes)
> Ibid.

We do not have to visit a madhouse to
find disordered minds; our planet is the
mental institution of the universe.

Knowing is not enough; we must apply.
Willing is not enough; we must do.

There is nothing more frightful than
ignorance in action.

Everybody wants to be somebody;
nobody wants to grow.

The world is so empty if one thinks only
of mountains, rivers and cities; but to
know someone here and there who
thinks and feels with us, and though
distant, is close to us in spirit—this makes
the earth for us an inhabited garden.

He only earns his freedom and existence who daily conquers them anew.
> Prologue in Heaven

Barry Goldwater

1909–98; US Senator

The inescapable and harmful by-product
of such operations as Social Security …
has been the weakening of the individual
personality and of self-reliance.
> 1956

The conscience of the Conservative is pricked by anyone who would debase the dignity of the individual human being. Today therefore, he is at odds with dictators who rule by terror, and equally with those gentler collectivists who ask our permission to play God with the human race.
Conscience of a Conservative, 1960

If the Conservative is less likely anxious than his liberal brethren to increase Social Security benefits, it is because he is more anxious than his Liberal brethren that people be free throughout their lives to spend their earnings when and as they see fit.
Ibid.

The effect of Welfarism on freedom will be felt later on—after its beneficiaries have become its victims, after dependence on government has turned into bondage and it is too late to unlock the jail.
Ibid.

Let us, then, not blunt the noble impulses of mankind by reducing charity to a mechanical operation of the federal government … Let welfare be a private concern.
Ibid.

Extremism in the defence of liberty is no vice. Moderation in the pursuit of justice is no virtue.
16 July 1964

A government that is big enough to give you all you want is big enough to take it all away.
1964

The conservative movement is founded on the simple tenet that people have the right to live as they please, as long as they don't hurt anyone else in the process. No one has ever shown me how being gay or lesbian harms anyone else.
Atlanta Journal, July 19 1994

Hubert Humphrey talks so fast that listening to him is like trying to read Playboy magazine with your wife turning over the pages.

Teresa Gorman
1931–; Conservative MP, 1987–

Perhaps we should do something more drastic, like cutting their goolies off.
On appropriate punishments for rapists

The enemy is the old, wet Tories who think they were born to rule.
I am Florence Nightingale to the middle aged woman—St Teresa of the menopause.
On her promotion of HRT treatment

I deplore smoking, but I'm against banning smoking; it's not the substances that are at fault, but inadequate people.

I go a long way for a mild curry, but if it's too hot or strong it gives you a pain in the butt.

America changed my life. It was the first time I'd lived in a capitalist society; it was like coming out from behind the iron curtain.

I haven't taken the course of Cecil Parkinson and Peter Walker and everyone else who talks posh; I dare say some of the Tory old guard think I am quite frightful—a common, vulgar little woman and an upstart from nowhere.

I think most of the wrinkles have been ironed out.
> On hormone replacement therapy for older women, 1988

They tried to demoralise me, but as far as I am concerned they were just abusing me.
> On the Whips' pressure to vote for Maastricht, 1992

The Prime Minister has got the Parliamentary Party by the goolies.
> On John Major

Compassion is a disease for which Conservatism is the only cure.
> February 1998

Ian Gow

1937–89; Conservative MP, 1974–89

If paternity leave was granted, it would result in a direct incitement to a population explosion.
> 1979

Phil Gramm

US Senator

Balancing the budget is like going to heaven. Everybody wants to do it, but nobody wants to do what you have to do to get there.
> 16 September 1990

No great cause has ever been won under the banner of Moderation. The answer is not more government—it's more opportunity. And the path to greater opportunity for all our people will be found by controlling public spending and letting the people who do the work pay the taxes and pull the wagon keep more of what they earn.
> Republican Convention, 1992

All over the world people are rejecting government as a decision-maker. All over the world people are rejecting government as a source of wisdom, a source of prosperity or a source of efficiency. All over the world people are turning to individual freedom and free enterprise and individual initiative.
> January 31 1993

Horace Greeley

1811–72; Journalist

Go West, young man, and grow up with the country.

George Grenville

1712–1770; Prime Minister 1763–5

A wise government knows how to enforce with temper or to conciliate with dignity.
> Speech against the expulsion of John Wilkes from Parliament, 1769

Viscount Edward Grey

1862 –1933; Foreign Secretary 1905–16

The United States is like a gigantic boiler. Once the fire is lighted under it there is no limit to the power it can generate.

John Gummer

1939–; Conservative MP 1970–74, 1979–

Poverty is considered quaint in rural areas because it comes thatched.

Nobody need be worried about BSE in this country or anywhere else
> As Agriculture Minister, 1990

William Hague

1961–; Conservative MP 1989–, Cabinet Minister 1995–97, Conservative Party Leader 1997–

I can think of no single act by any government that I would welcome more than the return of capital punishment.
> 1978

I shall give high priority to learning the Welsh national anthem.
> On becoming Welsh Secretary, July 1995

Never again will we have a divided organisation; never again will the voice of our members go unheard; and never again will we allow the good name of our party to be blackened by the greed and selfishness of a few.
> First speech as leader to the Conservative Party Conference, 10 October, 1997

It is time for a change.
> Ibid.

I should like to tell you about an open Conservatism—one that is tolerant; that believes freedom is about much more than economics; and that believes freedom does not stop at the shop counter. I should like to tell you about a democratic, popular conservatism that listens and that has compassion at its core. I want to tell you about a Conservatism which is rooted in its traditions, but embraces the future. I want to tell you about a clear Conservatism that is resolute in its support for freedom, enterprise and nation.
> Ibid.

I want to tell you about a changing conservatism that acknowledges its mistakes.
> Ibid.

New Labour are for everything but nothing: tough, tender; hot, cold; soft, hard; fast slow; for you, for me; to give, to take; to stop, to start.
> Ibid.

Labour have lost their moral compass. They care most of all about what sounds good; what trips off the tongue; what plays well on the television bulletins; and what gets a headline in tomorrow's papers.
> Ibid.

Imagine if the second world war had been fought this way. You can just hear them in 1940: 'we shall review them on the beaches; we shall review them in the fields and the streets; we shall review them in the hills; we shall never publish the results'.
> Parodying New Labour's penchant for policy reviews, Ibid.

We have no intention of stooping to a new politics without conscience. Let them stoop. We will conquer.
> Ibid.

We are the only party in Britain which believes in freedom as a birthright to

be protected rather than a concession to be handed down.
Ibid.

Yet again, we have the nauseating spectacle of Labour politicians who took every advantage and opportunity for themselves and them use their power to deny the same opportunity to the generation that comes after them.
Ibid.

Compassion is not a bolt-on extra to Conservatism. It is at its very core.
Ibid.

For Conservatives … compassion does not end when you send your cheque to the Inland Revenue.
Ibid.

It is an abdication of leadership to lead the people in to the casual destruction of our constitution.
Ibid.

Europe itself is not a nation and should not aspire to be a nation.
Ibid.

… we say no to abolishing the pound for the foreseeable future.
Ibid.

It did enormous damage to the credibility of our party and we paid the price.
On the decision to join the ERM, Ibid.

I believe in freedom, enterprise, education, self-reliance, obligation to others and the nation.
Ibid.

I cannot think of a better guide to Conservatives than those famous words of Rabbi Hillel:' If I am not for myself, who should be for me … but if I am only for myself, who am I?'
Speech to Conservative Friends of Israel, 1997

It was inevitable that the *Titanic* would set sail, but that does not mean it was a good idea to be on it.
On the Single European Currency, *Daily Telegraph,* 7 January 1998

One of the reasons we lost in 1997 was that we appeared to have become the economics party, as we were shining an intense searchlight on a particular set of economic issues.
Speech on Freedom and the Family, Social Market Foundation, January 1998

… the institutions which Conservatives value flourish in the space created by limited government and a market economy. Strong families, good schools, proud cities—all need to be able to shape their own characters free from the heavy burden of intrusive and expensive government. David Willetts calls that civic Conservatism; I would call it popular Conservatism.
Ibid.

We are not just atomised individuals pursuing our own narrow economic self-interest.
Ibid.

I do not mind Conservatives learning from Maureen Lipman and showing a little bit more respect for those -ologies. There is evidence of the right way forward buried in the latest sociological research.
Ibid.

It is the political, democratic sovereignty of the people—exercised at the ballot box, expressed through the legal sovereignty of Parliament and held in stewardship by the government—which is the key to accountable government today.
> Speech to the Centre for Policy Studies, February 1998

Labour has embarked on a journey of constitutional upheaval without a route map. They have no clear idea of where the journey will take them or what the final destination will look like.
> Ibid.

The Government is now embarking on what is potentially the most damaging step of all: removing the main independent element in the House of Lords by excluding the hereditary peers.
> Ibid.

We resolutely reject proportional representation.
> Ibid.

Labour is playing Jenga.
> On Labour's plans for constitutional change, Ibid.

Tony Blair would call them Uncool Britannia.
> On the people he grew up with, Ibid.

I have no interest in leading a bunch of Blue Trotskyites trotting into the Wilderness.
> On the importance of 'One Nation' ideas, Ibid.

Our historic journey and our destination is to serve our country once more.
> Ibid.

If political integration is pushed too far, it becomes impossible to sustain accountability and democracy.
> Speech to INSEAD, France, May 1998

Perhaps the best definition of a nation is this: it is a group of people who feel enough in common with one another to accept government from each other's hands. That is why democracy functions best within nations.
> Ibid.

Lord Hailsham

1907–; Conservative MP 1963–70, Cabinet Minister 1956–64, Lord Chancellor 1970–74, 1979–87

Conservatives do not believe that the political struggle is the most important thing in life. The simplest of them prefer fox hunting—the wisest religion.
> *The Case for Conservatism*, 1946

The responsibility of a political party is in inverse proportion to its chances of getting into office.
> House of Lords, 13 February 1961

A great party is not to be brought down because of a squalid affair between a woman of easy virtue and a proved liar.
> On the Profumo affair, 13 June 1963

The moment politics becomes dull. democracy is in danger.
> 1966

Since the War, Parliament seems to me to have gone legislation-mad; we are passing too many laws, too ill-thought out, too little intelligible and too little related to the moral understanding of

the people. Let us have a little respite from new law making and spend our time in consolidating, codifying, improving and I hope so—replacing.
1975

Once human beings abandon the basic structure of morality in their commerce with one another, once they abandon the object standards of right and wrong, once they cease to control their own passions, their desire for wealth or sex or even their mere dislike of their fellow men and once they begin to rationalise and sublimate these instincts by relating them to some real or imaginary political or moral cause, once it is believed that men do evil that good might come. That end justifies the means, there really is no depth to which human nature cannot fall.
1975

By far too many publicists has political crime been defended as something honourable, the perpetrators lauded as national heroes or freedom fighters, invited to international conferences, heard with respect at international gatherings and all the time the morality of the political criminal has degenerated.
1975

Like the Bible, the law should be written in a language understood by the people and not wrapped up in a learned tongue acceptable only to a cast of priestly intimates.
1975

In a confrontation with the politics of power, the soft centre has always melted away.

A practical old bruiser with a first-class mind and very bad manners.
On Denis Healey, 2 June 1987

The English, and more latterly, the British, have the habit of acquiring their institutions by chance or inadvertence, and shedding them in a fit of absentmindedness.
Guildhall Lecture, 10 November 1987

Nations begin by forming their institutions, but in the end, are continuously formed by them or under their influence.
Ibid.

Lord Halifax

1881–1959; Conservative Politician, Foreign Secretary 1938–40

I often think how much easier the world would have been to manage if Herr Hitler and Signor Mussolini had been at Oxford.
As Foreign Secretary 1938–41

Alexander Hamilton

1755–1804; American Constitutionalist

Why has government been instituted at all? Because the passions of men will not conform to the dictates of reason and justice without constraint.
The Federalist Papers, 1788

Christine Hamilton

1949–; Wife of Neil Hamilton and media personality

I would fight the world on Neil's behalf. We have set about rebuilding our lives. We have done it before. We can do it again. We've hit a rock but we will go on.

Get those greasy reptiles off the church daffodils.

> To reporters stalking her home, 1997

Why don't you get a proper job instead of shovelling shit?

> Ibid.

Neil Hamilton

1949–; Conservative MP 1983–97

Joining the ERM is no soft option. We have a choice. Either we can use interest rates to stabilise the currency, in which case the economy will go up and down; or we can stabilise the economy, in which case the currency goes up and down. There is no way of wishing away that distinction and that choice.

> Speech to the House of Commons, May 1, 1990

I am a humble lawyer, and my only connection with the world of nuts and bolts has been the occasional throwing of a spanner into the works over the years.

> Speech to the House of Commons, December 14, 1992

Isn't it fantastic that just at the moment when we are getting rid of passports for people in Europe we are introducing them for cows and sheep?

> Speech to the House of Commons, October 4, 1993

I have always believed that a government had a limited capacity to do good and a virtually infinite capacity to do harm.

> Speech to the House of Commons, February 4, 1994

I must remember to declare it in the Register of Interests.

> Referring to a biscuit received during a factory visit, 1994

The Norwegians recently voted in a referendum not to join the European Community. That preserves the option for Britain to have a referendum to decide whether we wish to join Norway.

> Speech to North West Young Conservatives Conference, February 2, 1995

J. H. Hammond

In all social systems there must be a class to do the mean duties … It constitutes the very mudsills of society … Fortunately for the South, she found a race adapted for that purpose … We use them for that purpose and call them slaves.

> *American Senator,* 1858

Sir William Harcourt

1827–1904; Liberal MP, Chancellor of the Exchequer

The Conservatives, mark my word, never yet took up a cause without betraying it in the end.

> The *Times,* 1885

Warren Harding

1865–1923; American President 1921–3

Government, after all, is a very simple thing.

Jeffrey Peter Hart

1931– ; American Academic

Within their own environment, however, we do not seem to encounter much criticism or independence—merely a lot of people who tend to sound the same.
> On liberal academics, *Acts of Recovery*, 1989

… the traditional attitudes and ideas of Western Culture form, so to speak, the thesis, while liberalism constitutes the antithesis, the negative image. Thus, from the liberal perspective, most traditional virtues become negative qualities.
> Ibid.

In this melodrama the result is always predictable and therefore boring.
> On liberal pieties, Ibid.

The liberal converts pity into a kind of nervous tic, the habitual response to everything.
> Ibid.

Mere beauty happens to be extremely important to me.
> Responding to liberal criticism of the Carnival Queen being chosen for her mere beauty. Ibid.

Communism has been the dominant fact of the 20th century, fascism a mere blip by comparison. Perhaps a 100 million have been killed …
> *Communism, It's All Over*, June 1989

During his first term as President, Ronald Reagan said two things that aroused fury on the left. He said that the Soviet Union is an evil empire and that Communism is a vast historical mistake. He was correct on both accounts.
> Ibid.

Friedrich von Hayek

1899–1992; Austrian economist

The system of private property is the most important guarantee of freedom, not only for those who own property, but scarcely less for those who do not.
> *Road to Serfdom*, 1944

The more the state plans the more difficult planning becomes for the individual.
> Ibid.

We have progressively abandoned that freedom in economic affairs without which personal and political freedom has never existed in the past.
> Ibid.

It is now often said that democracy will not tolerate capitalism. If capitalism means here a competitive system based on free disposal over private property, it is far more important to realise that only within this system is democracy possible. When it becomes dominated by a collectivist creed, democracy will inevitably destroy itself.
> Ibid.

In any society freedom of thought will probably be of direct significance only for a small minority. But this does not mean that anyone is competent, or ought to have power, to select those to whom this freedom is to be reserved.
> Ibid.

Our freedom of choice in a competitive society rests on the fact that if one person refuses to satisfy our wishes, we can turn to another. But if we face a monopolist we are at his mercy.

Ibid.

I am certain that nothing has done so much to destroy the juridical safeguards of individual freedom as the striving after this miracle of social justice.

Economic Freedom & Representative Government, 1973

One cannot help a country to maintain its standard of life by assisting people to consume more than they produce.

Daily Telegraph, 26 August 1976

Liberty not only means that the individual has both the opportunity and the burden of choice; it also means that he must bear the consequences of his actions ... Liberty and responsibility are inseparable.

Constitution of Liberty, 1960

The greatest danger to liberty today comes from the men who are most needed and most powerful in modern government, namely, the efficient expert administrators exclusively concerned with what they regard as the public good.

Ibid.

It is of the essence of the demand for equality before the law that people should be treated alike in spite of the fact that they are different.

Ibid.

The great aim of the struggle for liberty has been equality before the law.

Ibid.

... Responsibility ... often evokes the outright hostility of men who have

been taught that it is nothing but circumstances over which they have no control that has determined their position in life or even their actions. This denial of responsibility is, however, commonly due to a fear of responsibility, a fear that necessarily becomes a fear of freedom.

Ibid.

[The] impersonal process of the market ... can be neither just or unjust, because the results are not intended or foreseen.

'Social or Redistributive Justice', in *The Essence of Hayek,* 1984

Henry Hazlitt

1894–1993; Author

[The] private sector of the economy is, in fact, the voluntary sector; and ... the public sector is, in fact, the coercive sector. The voluntary sector is made up of the goods and services for which people voluntarily spend the money they have earned. The coercive sector is made up of the goods and services that are provided, regardless of the wishes of the individual, out of taxes that are seized from him.

From *The Wisdom of Henry Hazlitt,* 1993

Edward Heath

1916– ; Conservative MP, 1950–, Prime Minister, 1970–4

I owe everything to my mother.

1950

We may be a small island but we are not a small people.

1970

This would at a stroke reduce the rise in prices, increase production and reduce unemployment.

> 16 June 1970, on proposals to reduce taxation

We will have to embark on a change so radical, a revolution so quiet and yet so total, that it will go far beyond the programme for a Parliament.

> October 1970, Speech to the Conservative Party Conference

When we came to the end of the negotiations in 1963, after the Veto had been imposed, the negotiator on behalf of India said: 'When you left India some people wept. And when you leave Europe tonight some will weep. And there is no other people in the world of whom these things can be said.' That was a tribute from an Indian to the British. But tonight when this House endorses this Motion may millions of people right across the world will rejoice that we have taken our rightful place in a truly United Europe.

> Speech to the House of Commons, 1971

We are going to build on the past but we are not going to be strangled by it.

> 1972

The unpleasant and unacceptable face of capitalism.

> On the Lonrho affair, 15 May 1973

Our problem at the moment is a problem of success.

> Six weeks before the three-day week, November 1973

I am not a product of privilege. I am a product of opportunity.

In excluding me from the Shadow Cabinet Margaret Thatcher has chosen what I believe to be the only wholly honest solution and one which I accept and welcome.

> February 1975

Let nobody think that cuts in government expenditure can be made easily or painlessly because they cannot ... Civil servants too have wives and families, and civil servants too have to have consideration.

> 1976

Britain has now come to the end of the present road. The rest of the world knows it. The rest of the world is very sorry, but the rest of the world regrets that it is unable to oblige any longer.

> 1976

Please don't applaud—it may irritate your neighbour.

> Conservative Party Conference, Blackpool, October 1981

I think Churchill would be appalled at the Thatcher government.

Whatever the lady does is wrong. I do not know of a single right decision taken by her.

There's a lot of people I've encouraged and helped to get into the House of Commons. Looking at them now, I'm not so sure it was a wise thing to do.

> 1989

My mission is humanitarian. Therefore it in no way represents the British Government.

> Former Prime Minister on his mission to release Western Hostages in Baghdad, 1990

You don't have to leave Number Ten in tears.
> *Independent on Sunday,* 23 January 1990

Rejoice, Rejoice!
> Upon hearing the news of Margaret Thatcher's resignation, November 1990

Out go the estate-owners, in come the estate agents.
> September 1990

Do you know what Margaret Thatcher did in her first budget? Introduced VAT on yachts! It somewhat ruined my retirement.
> 28 November 1992

I saw him [Norman Tebbit] in the members' lobby trying to persuade new members to vote against the Government.
> 1993

Robert Heinlein

An armed society is a polite society.

Peter Hennessy

1947– ; Political Historian

He seemed like a benign and decent beached whale washed up on the harder shores of modern Conservatism.
> On R. A. Butler, 1987

Patrick Henry

1736–99; American Revolutionary Leader

Is life so dear, or peace so sweet, as to be purchased at the price of chains and slavery? Forbid it, Almighty God! I know not what course others may take; but as for me, give me liberty or give me death.
> Speech, March 23 1775

The constitution is not an instrument for government to restrain the people, it is an instrument for the people to restrain the government — lest it come to dominate our lives and interests.

We are not weak, if we make proper use of those means which the God of nature hath placed in our power ... The battle, sir, is not to the strong alone; it is to the vigilant, the active, the brave.

I have disposed of all my property to my family. There is one thing more I wish I could give to them, and that is the Christian religion. If they had that and I had not given them one cent, they would be rich. If they have not that, and I had given them the world, they would be poor.

Auberon Herbert

If government half a century ago had provided us with all our dinners and breakfasts, it would be the practice of our orators today to assume the impossibility of our providing for ourselves.

Joseph Hergesheimer

No one can walk backwards into the future.
> *The Three Black Pennies*

Michael Heseltine

1933– ; Conservative MP 1970–, Cabinet Minister 1979–86, 1990–97

The Red Flag was never flown throughout these islands yet, nor for a

thousand years has the flag of any other alien creed.
1976

Our way depends on exhortation, incentive, encouragement and reward in a free society. Labour's way depends on control, constraint, compulsion in a command economy. In our society you persuade people to give of their best. In their society a sulky, resentful, bitter people comply, as their choice to do otherwise dies with the crushing of their hopes. Our way throughout history has powered a great and free society. Their way has powered the tyrannies. The Labour way gives power to the state, trusts no one, offers no faith. Our way puts faith in people, leaves power with the people, and therefore, trusts the people.
1976

You cannot restore our cities while running down our countryside.
1977

When Michael Foot decries the judges, does he wonder that the young criminal gets the message? Are Labour Cabinet Ministers who stand shoulder to shoulder in the picket lines really free from all guilt when violence later erupts around the heads of our long suffering police?
1977

Throughout history under every system those who exercised power and responsibility enjoyed privileges beyond the means of the people at large. The only distinction that I would draw is that in a free enterprise system

those who enjoy the privileges expect to pay for them themselves, whilst under a Socialist system those who enjoy the privileges are expert at finding someone else to pay for them.
1977

I knew that 'He who wields the knife never wears the crown'.
1986

The market has no morality.
27 June 1988

Polluted rivers, filthy streets, bodies bedded down in doorways are no advertisement for a prosperous or caring society.
Conservative Party Conference, 10 October 1989

The Tory recognises the contrast between laissez-faire and noblesse oblige.
The *Observer*, 18 March 1990

I am persuaded that I now have a better prospect than Mrs Thatcher of leading the Conservatives to a fourth electoral victory and preventing the calamity of a Labour Government.
November 14 1990

She has made a remarkable contribution to Britain's history and has led this country with great distinction in the 1980s.
BBC TV News, 22 November 1990

The essence of being a Prime Minister is to have large ears.
Interview on Radio 4, 1990

I went up the greasy pole of politics step by step.
After his challenge for leadership of the Conservative Party, 1990

If I have to intervene to help British companies, I'll intervene before breakfast, before lunch, before tea and before dinner. And I'll get up the next morning and I'll start all over again.

> Conservative Party Conference, 7 October 1992

The self-appointed king of the gutter.

> On Neil Kinnock

A one-man band who has transformed a party without a leader into a leader without a party ... And he was a leader with more answers than there were questions, and more news conferences than there were newspapers.

> On Paddy Ashdown, 1992

Karl Hess

Libertarian

Libertarianism is the view that each man is the absolute owner of his own life, to use and dispose of it as he sees fit; that all man's social actions should be voluntary and that respect for every other man's similar and equal ownership of life and, by extension, the property and fruits of that life, is the ethical basis of a humane and open society. In this view, the only function of law or government is to provide the sort of self-defence against violence that an individual, if he were powerful enough, would provide for himself.

> Karl Hess, quoted in *Radical Libertarianism* by J. Tuccille, 1970

Gertrude Himmelfarb

1922– ; Political Philosopher

Liberals have always known that power tends to corrupt and absolute power

tends to corrupt absolutely ... [We] are now discovering that absolute liberty also tends to corrupt absolutely.

> *On Looking into the Abyss*, 1994

A liberty that is divorced from tradition and convention, from morality and religion, that makes the individual the sole repository and arbiter of all values and puts him in an adversarial relationship to society and the state—such a liberty is a grave peril to liberalism itself. For when that liberty is found wanting, when it violates the moral sense of the community or is incompatible with the legitimate demands of society, there is no moderating principle to take its place, no resting place between the wild gyrations of libertarianism and paternalism.

> Ibid.

Thomas Hobbes

1588–1679; Philosopher

How could a state be governed ... if every individual remained free to obey or not to obey the law according to his private opinions?

> *Leviathan*, 1651

Liberties depend on the silence of the law.

> Ibid.

Intemperance is naturally punished with diseases; rashness, with mischance; injustice, with violence of enemies; pride, with ruin; cowardice, with oppression; and rebellion, with slaughter.

> Ibid.

For the laws of nature (as justice, equity, modesty, mercy, and, in sum,

doing unto others as we would be done to) of themselves, without the terror of some power, to cause them to be observed, are contrary to our natural passions, that carry us to partiality, pride, revenge and the like.
Ibid.

[in a state of nature] No arts; no letters; no society; and which is worst of all, continual fear and danger of violent death; and the life of man, solitary, poor, nasty brutish and short.
Ibid.

Eric Hoffer

1902–1983; American Author

We clamour for equality chiefly in matters in which we cannot ourselves hope to obtain excellence.
The Passionate State of Mind, 1955

No matter how noble the objectives of a government, if it blurs decency and kindness, cheapens human life, and breeds ill will and suspicion—it is an evil government,
Ibid.

We cannot win the weak by sharing our wealth with them. They feel our generosity as oppression.
The Ordeal of Change, 1963

There can be no freedom without freedom to fail.
Ibid.

I doubt if the oppressed ever fight for freedom. They fight for pride and power: the power to oppress others. The oppressed want above all to imitate their oppressors; they want to retaliate.
The True Believer, 1951

It is to escape the responsibility for failure that the weak so eagerly throw themselves into grandiose undertakings.
Ibid.

Douglas Hogg

Conservative MP, Cabinet Minister

Beef is a perfectly safe and a good product.
As Agriculture Minister, 1995

Oliver Holmes

The life of the law has not been logic; it has been experience. The law embodies the story of a nation's development through many centuries, and it cannot be dealt with as if it contained the axioms and corollaries of a book of mathematics.
The Common Law, 1881

Alec Douglas-Home

1903–95; Conservative MP 1963–70, Foreign Secretary 1960–63, 1970–74, Prime Minister 1963–64

Patriotism in the twentieth century is still a noble thing if one thinks of our flag … as a banner proclaiming the image of the kind of life and the values in which British people believe.

I could never be Prime Minister. I do my sums with matchsticks.
1962

When I have to read economic documents I have to have a box of matches and start moving them into position to simplify and illustrate the points to myself.
The *Observer,* 16 September 1962

As far as the Fourteenth Earl is concerned, I suppose Mr Wilson, when
you come to think of it, is the fourteenth Mr Wilson.
Daily Telegraph, 22 October 1963

There are two problems in my life. The
political ones are insoluble and the
economic ones are incomprehensible.
1964

I am a fan of television as far as sport
and ceremonial are concerned. I think
it less suited to politics than to anything else. You are dealing with the
most complicated issues in a very short
time and it is bound to be superficial.
1988

Caroline Douglas Home

He is used to dealing with estate
workers. I cannot see how anyone can
say he is out of touch.
On her father becoming Prime
Minister, 1963

Homer

c.8th century BC; Greek Poet

Without a sign, his sword the brave
    man draws
And asks no omen but his country's
    cause.
    Iliad

For a better and higher gift than this
there cannot be, when with accordant
aims man and wife have a home. Great
grief is it to foes and joy to friends; but
they themselves know its meaning.
    Odyssey

Sidney Hook

Social Philosopher

To silence criticism is to silence freedom.
    New York Times, September 30 1951

Sir John Hoskyns

1927–; Businessman

The Tory Party never panics, except in
a crisis.
    Sunday Times, 19 February 1989

Michael Howard

1941–; Conservative MP, 1983–, Cabinet
Minister, 1990–97

To spend many years in prison for a
crime you did not commit is both a
terrible thing and one for which
release from prison and financial
recompense can make amends. Even
this injustice cannot be compared to
the icy comfort of a posthumous
pardon. We cannot but be relieved that
the death penalty was not available
when we consider the irreparable
damage which would have been
inflicted on the criminal justice system
in this country had innocent people
been executed.
    1994

Sir Geoffrey Howe

1926– ; Conservative MP 1964–66, 1970–
92, Chancellor of the Exchequer, 1979–83,
Foreign Secretary 1983–89, Leader of the
House of Commons 1989–90

Britain is poised today on the brink of
hyper-inflation. It could destroy our
society, as it did in Germany in the

1920s. There is only a wafer-thin majority of error between our present condition and British inflation of 50 and 100 per cent a year … that is why it is of such paramount importance for us to come to grips with this present inflation.
> 1975

Phrases like 'catching up' and 'cost of living increase' which trip off the tongue of many negotiators should be on the way out. In the not too distant future, the notion of automatic pay increase must become as exceptional as it was novel a generation ago.
> As Chancellor of The Exchequer, 1982

Inflation is a great moral evil. Nations which lose confidence in their currency lose confidence in themselves.
> The *Times*, July 1982

The British disease is considering others more responsible than ourselves.
> As Chancellor of The Exchequer, 1986

The future, where most of us are destined to spend the rest of our lives.
> Interview for *A Week in Politics*, Channel 4, 1986

I believe both the Chancellor and the Governor are cricketing enthusiasts so I hope there will be no monopoly of cricketing metaphors. It's rather like sending your opening batsmen to the crease only for them to find that before the first ball is bowled, their bats have been broken by the team captain. The time has come for others to consider their own response to the tragic conflict of loyalties with which I have myself wrestled for perhaps too long.
> Resignation Speech to the House of Commons, 13 November 1990

Margaret Thatcher was beyond argument a great Prime Minister. Her tragedy is that she may be remembered less for the brilliance of her many achievements than for the recklessness with which she later sought to impose her own increasingly uncompromising views.
> 1994

David Howell

Conservative MP

That speech must have affected every thinking Conservative MP and many others as well.
> On Geoffrey Howe's resignation speech, precipitating Margaret Thatcher's downfall, 1990

Elbert Hubbard

Every tyrant who has lived has believed in freedom—for himself.

David Hume

1711–76; Philosopher

Nothing appears more surprising to those who consider human affairs with a philosophical eye, than the ease with which the many are governed by the few.
> *Essays: First Principles of Government*

Ted Hunt

The Conservatives conserve what you've got, the Liberals are liberal with it and Labour gives it all away.

Douglas Hurd

1930–; Conservative MP 1974–97, Cabinet
Minister 1985–96

The United Nations should not be
called on to deal with every situation
regardless of the circumstances or the
prospects of success ... The way to
build up its reputation is to encourage
it to take on those activities it can do,
and refuse those things which are at
present beyond its power.

The UN, A Conservative Analysis,
CPC, 1967

There is a market for medical services
as far as for any other commodity. We
must let the demand find its own level
by the free play of the market.

Character in *Smile on the Face of the
Tiger,* Hurd & Osmond

It will be a long road back.

After the February 1974 General
Election

There's so much more to nick.

As Home Secretary, giving his
explanation for increases in crime

The low price and high purity of the
drugs being peddled on London streets
are grim indications of the amount of
drugs still reaching this country and
there are no signs of crack being widely
used in London yet.

1986

There's a lot of overcrowded prisons in
the south, and we're planning a new one.

As Home Secretary, 1988

The family is our first defence against
crime. For too long in this country we
have pushed parental responsibility to
the sidelines.

As Home Secretary, 1989

This is the last speech in the last debate
on the Maastricht treaty.

As Foreign Secretary closing the
debate on Maastricht, 1992

The survival of the Conservative
Government is not at stake, what is at
stake is the survival of a credible
foreign policy.

As Foreign Secretary on the
Maastricht Treaty, 1992

To expect the Liberals to control
Labour would be like asking Dad's
Army to restrain the Mongol hordes.

1992

Because you can't help everybody, it
doesn't mean you can't help somebody.

On the decision to bring a wounded
five-year old girl from Sarajevo to
London for treatment

There is I think a real danger that,
egged on by the media, all parties in
this House, all of us, may play out the
old play, not realising that beyond the
footlights half the audience has crept
away and the other half is sitting there
in mounting irritation.

15 November 1995

Henry Hyde

American Republican Congressman

Abortion is the killing of an innocently
inconvenient human life.

US News & World Report, May 4
1981

Balancing the budget is a fundamental
condition of governing. For most of
the nation's history, balancing budgets
in peacetime was assumed as a normal
operating procedure.

USA Today, January 26 1995

Michael Ivens

1924–; Business Leader

I believe that Conservatism suffers great damage if it identified with an illiterate pseudo-Darwinism of competitive nature, red in tooth and claw.

1988

Andrew Jackson

1767–1845; US President 1828–36

Peace, above all things, is to be desired, but blood must sometimes be spilled to obtain it on equable and lasting terms.

James VI & I

1566–1625; King of Scotland 1567 and England and Wales 1603

I will govern according to the commonweal but not according to the common will.

Address to the House of Commons
1621

Thomas Jefferson

1743–1826; American President 1801–09

It is error alone which needs the support of government. Truth can stand by itself.

1804

To compel a man to subsidise with his taxes the propagation of ideas which he disbelieves and abhors is sinful and tyrannical.

Never spend your money before you have it.

The price of liberty is eternal vigilance.

A little rebellion now and then ... is a medicine necessary for the sound health of government.

The man who never looks into a newspaper is better informed than he who reads them, inasmuch as he who knows nothing is nearer to truth than he whose mind is filled with falsehoods and errors.

1807

I place economy among the first and most important virtues, and public debt as the greatest of dangers ... We must make our choice between economy and liberty, or profusion and servitude. If we can prevent the government from wasting the labours of the people under the pretence of caring for them, they will be happy.

All authority belongs to the people.

I swear upon the altar of God, eternal hostility to every form of tyranny over the mind of man.

Experience hath shewn, that even under the best forms [of government] those entrusted with power have, in time, and by slow operations, perverted it into tyranny.

The legitimate powers of government extend to such acts only as they are injurious to others.

Nothing ... is unchangeable but the inherent and unalienable rights of man.

I would rather be exposed to the inconveniences attending too much liberty than to those attending too small a degree of it.

The constitutions of most of our States assert that all power is inherent in the people; that ... it is their right and duty to be at all times armed.
> Letter to John Cartwright, 1824.

We must make our election between economy and liberty, or profusion and servitude.
> Letter to Samuel Kercheval, 1816.

I am not a friend to a very energetic government. It is always oppressive.
> Letter to James Madison, 1787.

The freedom and happiness of man ... are the sole objects of all legitimate government.

The tree of liberty must from time to time be refreshed with the blood of tyrants and patriots. It is its natural manure.

Whenever a man has cast a longing eye on offices, a rottenness begins in his conduct.

I have no ambition to govern men. It is a painful and thankless office.

It is the trade of lawyers to question everything, yield to nothing and to talk by the hour.

Delay is preferable to error.
> Letter to George Washington, 1792

Douglas Jerrold

Dogmatism is puppyism come to its full growth.
> *Wit & Opinions,* 1858

Dr Samuel Johnson
1709–1784; Lexicographer

A man is never more innocently involved than in the making of money. It is better that some should be unhappy than that none should be happy, which would be the case in a general state of equality.
> *Life of Samuel Johnson,* April 1776

Your levellers wish to level down as far as themselves; but they cannot bear levelling up to themselves.
> Ibid. 1791

Most of the misery which the defamation of blameless actions or the obstruction of honest endeavours brings upon the world is inflicted by men that propose no advantage to themselves but the satisfaction of poisoning the banquet which they cannot taste, and blasting the harvest which they have no right to reap.
> *The Rambler,* 1751

That man is little to be envied whose patriotism would not gain force upon the plain of Marathon, or whose piety would not grow warmer among the mists of Iona.
> *Journey to the Western Isles of Scotland,* 1775

Robert Jones
1950–; Conservative MP, 1983–97

Margaret Thatcher and Ted Heath both have a great vision. The difference is that Margaret Thatcher has a vision that Britain will one day be great again, and Ted Heath has a vision that one day Ted Heath will be great again.

Keith Joseph

1918–94; Conservative MP, 1956–87, Cabinet Minister 1970–74, 1979–86

Problems reproduce themselves from generation to generation. I refer to this as a cycle of deprivation.
1972

Incomes policy alone as a way to abate inflation caused by excessive money supply is like trying to stop water coming out of a leaky hose without turning off the tap.
Speech in Preston, 5 September 1974

People who could not tell a lathe from a lawnmower and have never carried the responsibilities of management never tire of telling British management off for its alleged inefficiency.
The *Times*, 9 August 1974

The balance of our population, our human stock, is threatened. A high and rising proportion of children are being born to mothers least fitted to bring children into the world and bring them up.
Speech in Birmingham, 19 October 1974

We need more inequality in order to eliminate poverty.
1975

Our human stock is threatened ... These mothers ... single parents from classes four and five are now producing

a third of all births. If we do nothing, the nation moves towards degeneration.
1975

Conservatism, like selfishness, is inherent in the human condition.
New Statesman, 1975

Our opponents are driven by their vision, a messianic vision of the perfectibility of man. It may have been conceived with fine intentions; it may have been born of a passion, but it has become an engine of tyranny, impoverishment and unemployment.
1976

Socialist short-cuts to Utopia only turn into blind alleys. Slum and slump and siege.
1976

The idea that all the ills of mankind—greed, violence, corruption, cruelty, poverty—all stemmed from the institution of private property and would disappear if the state owned all, or nearly all, is against history, common sense and human nature. These ills are as old as mankind. They are at their worst where the state is strongest.
1976

Oil will not save us, because by overmanning we are blunting our competitiveness faster than oil will make good. Unless overmanning is halted and corrected, no subsidies, no forced investment, no sector linking parties, nothing will rescue us from a stagnant and declining standard of living and unemployment.
1977

Without competition the pursuit of profit is immoral and mere exploitation.
1978

If we are going to be prosperous we need more millionaires and more bankrupts.
House of Lords, 19 February 1988

There are no illegitimate children—only illegitimate parents.
1991

How on earth do the birds know it's a sanctuary?

E. Kedourie

If, making use of William James's distinction, we were to divide Conservatives into those who are tender-minded and those who are tough-minded, it is the latter whom Salisbury may be said to represent and exemplify. And if, today, he seems to us a very remote figure, this is not only because the assumptions and conditions of British politics have changed utterly since his day, but also because, during Baldwin's ascendancy and afterwards, it is largely a tender-minded Conservatism which has set the tone and dominated the Party's rhetoric.
Encounter, 1972

Conservatism follows and does not precede the existence of a Conservative party. It is a natural attempt by a body with a long continuous existence to articulate and make intelligible to itself its own character.
1984

Jack Kemp

US Congressman

There are no limits on our future if we don't put limits on our people.
April 6 1987

We don't believe children are just mouths to feed. They are hearts, minds, and souls for our future. And they deserve our protection not only after their birth, but before they are born.
Republican Convention 1992

John Fitzgerald Kennedy

1917–63; US President 1960–63

Those who make peaceful revolution impossible will make violent revolution inevitable.

If a free society cannot help the many who are poor, it cannot save the few who are rich.
Inaugural speech, 20 January 1961

Let us never negotiate out of fear. But let us never fear to negotiate.
Ibid.

Ask not what your country can do for you. Ask what you can do for your country.
Ibid.

Liberty without learning is always in peril and learning without liberty is always in vain.
18 March 1963

Alan Keyes

Affirmative action is a betrayal of the principles of the civil rights movement.

Martin Luther King jr

1929–68; American Civil Rights Leader

The time is always right to do what is right.

Nothing in all the world is more dangerous than sincere ignorance and conscientious stupidity.
Strength to Love, 1963

Injustice anywhere is a threat to justice everywhere.
Ibid.

The ultimate measure of a man is not where he stands in moments of comfort and convenience, but where he stands at times of challenge and controversy.
Ibid.

I have a dream that one day on the red hills of Georgia the sons of former slaves and the sons of former slave-owners will sit down together at the table of brotherhood.
Washington DC 1963

Rudyard Kipling

1856–1936; Poet and writer

Take up the White Man's Burden.
1899

Politicians. Little tin gods on wheels.

Russell Kirk

Privilege, in any society, is the reward of duties performed.
Enlivening the Conservative Mind, 1953

The intelligent conservative combines a disposition to preserve with an ability to reform.
Intelligent Woman's Guide to Conservatism, 1957

Equality in the sight of God, equality before the law, security in what is one's own, participation in the common activities and consolations of society—these are the true natural rights.
The Conservative Mind, 1953

The twentieth-century Conservative is concerned, first of all, for the regeneration of spirit and character—with the perennial problem of the inner order of the soul, the restoration of the ethical understanding, and the religious sanction upon which any life worth living is founding. This is conservatism at its highest.
The Conservative Mind, 1953

The better natures among us, surely, will be hard put … to love America if it becomes a nation wholly mannerless, an incivil society, in which generosity and charity are scorned as weakness, in which all great literature, and charity are scorned as weakness, in which all great literature, and the whole stock of the moral imagination, is rejected out of a lust for the gratification of carnal appetites and a taste for second-hand violence and concupiscence.
Prospects for Conservatives, 1989

The conservative of reflection will not be afraid to defend the manners and tastes of a gentle and generous nature … in this industrial age.
Prospects for Conservatives, 1989

Henry Kissinger

1923–; American Secretary of State

Of all the men running, Richard Nixon is the most dangerous to have as President. I would never work for that man. That man is a disaster.

> During presidential election campaign, 1968

There cannot be a crisis next week. My schedule is already full.

> 1969

Power is the great aphrodisiac.

> 1971

You can't win through negotiations what you can't win on the battlefield.

> 1973

No foreign policy, no matter how ingenious, has any chance of success if it is borne on the minds of a few and carried in the hearts of none.

> August 1973

We must learn to distinguish morality from moralising.

> 1976

The illegal we do immediately. The unconstitutional takes a little longer.

> Attributed, 1977

History knows no resting places and no plateaux.

> *White House Years*, 1979

The management of a balance of power is a permanent undertaking, not an exertion that has a foreseeable end. The statesman's duty is to bridge the gap between his nation's experience and his vision.

> *Years of Upheaval*, 1982

In crises the most daring course is often the safest.

> Ibid.

An Iranian moderate is one who has run out of ammunition.

> 1987

History has so far shown us only two roads to international stability: domination and equilibrium.

> 1991

Statesmen who base their policy on the expectation of recurrent miracles usually suffer shipwreck.

> *Newsweek*, September 27 1993

The main advantage of being famous is that when you bore people at dinner parties they think it is their fault.

> Atrributed, 1995

Dame Jill Knight

1923–; Conservative MP, 1966–97

Anyone in his position needs to be whiter than white.

> On Nelson Mandela, Radio Ulster, 1990

William Knudson

Germany has been transformed since my last visit several years ago … the Reich is the miracle of the twentieth century.

> As President of General Motors, 1938

Helmut Kohl

1930– ; German Chancellor

I have been underestimated for decades. I have done very well that way.

> 1987

We Germans now have the historic chance to realise the unity of the Fatherland.
1990

Irving Kristol

A welfare state, properly conceived, can be an integral part of a conservative society.
American Spectator, 1977

People need religion. It's a vehicle for a moral tradition. A crucial role. Nothing can take its place.
Two Cheers for Capitalism, 1979

... new conservatism is antiromantic in substance and temperament. Indeed, it regards political romanticism—and its twin, political utopianism—of any kind as one of the plagues of our age. This is but another way of saying it is a philosophical–political impulse rather than a literary–political impulse. Or, to put it still another way: its approach to the world is more 'rabbanic' than 'prophetic'.
Reflections of a Neoconservative, 1983

Neo-conservatives are unlike old conservatives because they are utilitarians, not moralists, and because their aim is the prosperity of post-industrial society, not the recovery of a golden age.
Times Higher Educational Supplement, 1987

Norman Lamont

1942– ; Conservative MP, 1972–97, Cabinet Minister, 1989–93, Chancellor of the Exchequer 1990–93

There is plenty of scope for the House of Commons to fulfil its traditional functions of scrutinising and amending legislation.
Defending entry to the EEC, 1973

The turn of the tide is sometimes difficult to discern. What we are seeing is the return of that vital ingredient, confidence. The green shoots of economic spring are appearing once again.
Speech at the Conservative Party Conference, 9 October 1991

A price worth paying.
Answering criticism on the level of unemployment, 16 May 1991

Je ne regrette rien.
Following UK withdrawal from the ERM, 1992

The Exchange Rate Mechanism is not an optional extra, an add-on to be jettisoned at the first hint of trouble. It has been and will remain at the heart of our macro-economic policy.
1992

All I want to say, particularly to our partners ... is don't push it, don't push it , because that isn't going to help us get it through.
On the Maastricht Treaty, 1992

We give the impression of being in office but not in power.
House of Commons, 9 June 1993

Our ability to make our own laws without outside interference has gone.
1996

Ian Lang

1940–; Conservative MP, 1979–97, Cabinet
Minister, 1990–97

Karaoke Kinnock, the man who'll sing
any song you want him to.
1992

Too many people have forgotten that it
was he who led us to an election
victory last year that many thought
impossible.
On John Major, 1993

Job insecurity is a state of mind.
As President of the Board of Trade,
1995

Ivan Lawrence

1936–; Conservative MP, 1974–97

This is a man who will stoop at
nothing.
On Saddam Hussein during the Gulf
Crisis, 1990

Nigel Lawson

1932– ; Conservative MP, 1974–92, Chancellor of the Exchequer 1983–89

The Conservative Party has never
believed that the business of government is the government of business.
10 November 1981

I shall resist the tempatation to dwell
on the golden age of the '50s and '60s
when I was a financial journalist. But I
must say I am struck by the modern
obsession with inevitably speculative
forecasts of the short-term future, at
the expense of informing the reader
about what is actually happening in the
present.
As Chancellor of the Exchequer, 1984

One of the important things this
government has tried to do is rehabili-
tate the idea of profit in political
discourse. I don't think the man in the
street ever thought that profit was a
dirty word, but it had almost become a
dirty word among the intelligentsia.
As Chancellor of the Exchequer, 1986

In the next Parliament, we aim to
eliminate inflation altogether.
As Chancellor of the Exchequer, 1986

I would not take too much notice of
teenage scribblers in the City who
jump up and down in an effort to get
press attention.
As Chancellor of the Exchequer,
responding to economists gloomy
economic predictions.

You don't make the poor rich by
making the rich poor.
As Chancellor of the Exchequer
(quoting Barin Bauer, economist),
1987

The sharp deterioration has now come
to an end.
As Chancellor of the Exchequer, 1989

Inflation is a disease of money.
1989

He has an infallible knack for getting
the wrong end of every stick.
On Neil Kinnock

I think we've been treated to a dose
of the sort of sanctimonious humbug
which is characteristic of sections of
the British press. It is the politics of
envy and an awful lot of humbug.
Everybody knows that people get
paid all different salaries, that newspaper editors don't do all that badly,

but it's a sort of nauseating form of demagoguery.

> Responding to criticisms of the directorships he accepted immediately after leaving office.

I was a very convenient scapegoat for many people in the party because I had resigned and was expendable.

> In a television interview, 1992

Peter Lilley

1943–; Conservative MP, 1983–

Of course nobody likes the Conservatives. They only vote for us because they think we are right.

Rush Limbaugh

US Political Commentator

Poverty and suffering are not due to the unequal distribution of goods and resources, but to the unequal distribution of capitalism.

I prefer to call the most obnoxious feminists what they really are: feminazis.

> The Way Things Ought to Be, 1992

Abraham Lincoln

1809–75; American President 1861–5

No man is good enough to govern another man without that other's consent.

> 16 October 1854

Those who deny freedom to others, deserve it not for themselves.

> 1856

What is conservatism? Is it not adherence to the old and tried, against the new and untried?

> 27 February 1860

Any people anywhere being inclined and having the power have the right to rise up and shake off the existing government, and force a new one that suits them better.

The probability that we may fail in the struggle ought not to deter us from the support of a cause we believe to be just.

Property is the fruit of labour; property is desirable; it is a positive good in the world. That some should be rich shows that others may become rich, and, hence, is just another encouragement to industry and enterprise.

I will say then that I am not, nor have ever have been in favour of bringing about in any way the social and political equality of the white and black races.

> Campaigning for President, 1958

Even when you cease to be slaves, you are yet far removed from being placed on an equality with the white race. You are cut off from many of the advantages which the other race enjoys. It is better for us both to be separated.

> As President in a meeting with free Negro leaders, 1862

If my name ever goes into history, it will be for this act, and my whole soul is in it.

> Signing the Emancipation Proclamation, 1863

The central act of my administration, and the great event of the nineteenth century … It is a momentous thing to be the instrument … of the liberation of a race.

> Referring to the Emancipation
> Proclamation, 1862

In all that the people can individually do well for themselves, the government ought not to interfere.

Discourage litigation. Persuade your neighbour to compromise whenever you can. As a peacemaker the lawyer had a superior opportunity of being a good man. There will still be business enough.

Walter Lippmann

Where all men think alike, no one thinks very much.

No a priori reasoning can anticipate the precise formulae which will reconcile the varied interests of men … Thus in Plato's great scheme each man was assigned his station and his duties; any architectural plan is necessarily based on the same presumption. But Plato's scheme only worked in Plato's imagination; never in the real world … For the scheme, implies that men will remain content in the station which the visionary has assigned to them. To formulate such plans is not to design a society for real men. It is to re-create men to fit the design.

> *The Good Society,* 1937

Lord Liverpool

1770–1828; Prime Minister 1812–1827

On peace our greatness as a nation completely and almost wholly depends.

> 29 February 1792

Not to protect the agricultural interest would be in reality to discourage it.

> 15 March 1815

Selwyn Lloyd

1904–78; Conservative MP, 1945–76, Cabinet Minister 1955–63, Speaker of the House of Commons 1971–76

I do not speak any foreign language. Except in war, I have never visited any foreign country. I do not like foreigners.

> 1978

John Locke

1632–1704; Philosopher

Wherever law ends, tyranny begins.

> Two Treatises of Government, 1690

I have always thought the actions of men the best interpreters of their thoughts.

The Care therefore of every man's Soul belongs unto himself, and is to be left unto himself. But what if he neglect the Care of his Soul? I answer, What if he neglects the Care of his Health, or of his Estate, which things are nearly related to the Government of the Magistrate than the other? Will the magistrate provide by an express Law, That such an one shall not become poor or sick? Laws provide, as much as is possible, that the Goods and Health of Subjects be not injured by the Fraud and Violence of others; they do not guard them from the Negligence or Ill-husbandry of the Possessors themselves.

A Letter Concerning Toleration, 1689

Whenever the Legislators endeavour to take away, and destroy the Property of the People, or to reduce them to Slavery under Arbitrary Power, they put themselves into a state of War with the People, who are thereupon absolved from any farther Obedience ... [Power then] devolves to the People, who have a Right to resume their original Liberty, and, by the Establishment of a new Legislative (such as they shall think fit) provide for their own Safety and Security, which is the end for which they are in Society.

Second Treatise of Civil Government, 1690

The freedom of men under government is to have a standing rule to live by, common to every one of that society, and made by the legislative vested in it; a liberty to follow my own will in all things, when the rule prescribes not, and not to be subject to the inconsistent, uncertain, unknown arbitrary will of another man.

On Government

Lord Lothian

After all, they are only going into their own back garden.

On Hitler's remilitarisation of the Rhineland

Douglas MacArthur

1880–1964; American General

No man is entitled to the blessings of freedom unless he be vigilant in its preservation.

Speech in Japan, May 3 1948

It is fatal to enter any war without the will to win it

Republican National Convention, 1952

Thomas Babington Macaulay

1800–59; Historian and critic

An acre in Middlesex is better than a principality in Utopia.

Lord Bacon, 1837

Free Trade, one of the greatest blessings which a government can confer on a people, is almost in every country unpopular.

On Mitford's *History of Greece*

The science of government is an experimental science and like all other experimental sciences it is generally working itself clearer and clearer and depositing impurity after impurity. I have long been convinced that institutions purely democratic must, sooner or later, destroy liberty or civilisation or both.

Letter to H. S. Randall, 1857

Those who compare the age in which their lot has fallen with a golden age which exists only in imagination, may talk of degeneration and decay; but no man who is correctly informed as to the past will be disposed to take a morose or desponding view of the present.

History of England 1841–61

David Maclean

1953–; Conservative MP, 1987–

Most [street beggars] are Scottish and I've never met one yet who politely and gently asked for money … There are no genuine beggars. Those who are in need have got all the social benefits they require … Beggars are doing so out of choice because they find it more pleasant … I always give them some-thing—I give them a piece of my mind.

> As a Home Office minister, 1997

Iain Macleod

1913–70; Conservative MP, 1950–70, Cabinet Minister 1952–63, 1970

The Conservative Party always in time forgives those who were wrong. Indeed, often, in time, they forgive those who were right.

> The *Spectator,* 21 February 1964

Revolutions in this country, and especially within the Tory Party, are rarely plotted. They just happen.

> The *Spectator,* 30 July 1965

He is a waste paper basket, filled with lightly given promises and pledges.

> On Harold Wilson

John F. Kennedy has described himself as an idealist without illusions. Harold Wilson is an illusionist without ideals.

Harold Macmillan

1894–1986; Conservative MP, 1924–29, 1931–45, 1945–64, Prime Minister 1957–63

Housing is not a question of Con-servatism or Socialism. It is a question of humanity.

> September 1925

He enjoys prophesying the imminent fall of the capitalist system, and is prepared to play a part, any part, in its burial, except that of mute.

> On Aneurin Bevan, Speech in the House of Commons, 1934

Toryism has always been a form of paternal socialism.

> 1936

He is forever poised between a cliché and an indiscretion.

> On Anthony Eden

Indeed, let's be frank about it, some of our people have never had it so good.

> Speech at Bedford, 20 July 1957

I thought the best thing to do was settle up these little local difficulties, and then turn to the wider vision of the Commonwealth.

> The *Times,* 8 January 1958 following the resignation of three Cabinet Ministers

The wind of change is blowing through this continent whether we like it or not, this growth of political consciousness is a political fact.

> Speech to South African Parliament in Cape Town, 3 February 1960

As usual the Liberals offer a mixture of sound and original ideas. Unfortunately, none of the sound ideas is original and none of the original ideas is sound.

> 1961

Events, dear boy, events.

The only reason Harold Wilson as a child had to go to school without boots on, was that his boots were probably to small for him.

> (attrib.)

First of all the Georgian silver goes, and then all that nice furniture that used to be in the saloon. Then the Canalettos go.

> Speech to the Tory Reform Group mocking privatisation, 8 November 1985

Selling the family silver.

> Referring to the privatisation of profitable nationalised industries, 1986

Joseph McCarthy

American Senator

It's the most unheard-of thing I've ever heard of.

> 1950s

McCarthyism is Americanism with its sleeves rolled.

> 1952

I have here in my hand a list of 205 … members of the Communist Party and whom nevertheless are still working and shaping policy in the State Department.

> 1950

I think it is a shoddy, unusual thing to do to use the floor of the Senate to attack your opponent without any proof whatever.

> Responding to criticism, 1956

Robert McNamara

The major part of the US military task [in Vietnam] can be completed by the end of 1965.

> As US Defence Secretary, 1962

James Madison

1751–1836; American President 1809–17

I believe there are more instances of the abridgement of the freedom of the people by gradual and silent encroachments of those in power than by violent and sudden usurpations.

Magna Carta

1215

No freeman shall be taken, or imprisoned, or outlawed, or exiled, or in anyway harmed, nor will we go upon him, nor will we send upon him, except by the legal judgement of his peers or by the laws of the land.

To none will we sell, no none deny or delay, right or justice.

Henry Sumner Maine

1822–1888; British legal scholar

[A] formidable conception bequeathed to us by Rousseau is that of the omnipotent democratic State rooted in natural right; the State which has at its disposal everything which individual men value, their property, their persons, and their independence; the State which is bound to respect neither precedent not prescription; the State which may make laws for its subjects ordaining what they shall drink or eat, and in what way they shall spend their earnings; the State which can confiscate all the land of the community, and which, if the effect on human motives is what may be expected to be, may force us to labour on it when the older

incentives to toil have disappeared. Nevertheless this political speculation, of which the remote and indirect consequences press us on all sides, is of all speculations the most baseless. The natural condition from which it starts is a simple figment of the imagination.
Popular Government (1886)

Compte Joseph Marie de Maistre

The more you examine the part human action plays in the formation of political constitutions, the clearer it becomes that it is effective only in an extremely subordinate role or as a simple instrument …

The fundamentals of political constitutions exist before all written laws.

Lady Olga Maitland

Conservative MP, 1992–97

Of course we are not patronising women. We are just going to explain to them in words of one syllable what it is all about.

John Major

1941–; Conservative MP 1979–, Cabinet Minister 1987–90, Prime Minister 1990–97

Conservatives should welcome controls on prices and incomes, even as a permanent feature of the economy.
1973

His idea of policy is to spend, spend, spend. He is the Viv Nicholson of politics.
Comparing Michael Foot to the 1960s Pools winner

If the policy isn't hurting, it isn't working.
27 October 1989

It will take some time, it always does, to change the economy. It's like turning the *Titanic* round, as you know.
As Chancellor of the Exchequer, 1990

'If' is a very large preposition.
1990

Sustainable growth that is sustainable.
1990

I believe in the next ten years we will have to continue to make changes that will genuinely produce across the whole of this country a genuinely classless society.
November 23 1990

I'm not running as Son of Margaret Thatcher, I'm running as myself on my own priorities and my own programme.
Interview on *Walden,* 25 November 1990

I'm my own man.
On becoming Prime Minister, 1990

You can't influence Europe's future from the terraces. You have to be on the pitch and playing hard.
Altrincham, November 29 1990

Gentlemen, I think we had better start again somewhere else.
Following the IRA attack on Downing Street, 7 February 1991

My aim for Britain in the Community can be simply stated. I want us to be where we belong. At the very heart of Europe.
Speech in Bonn, 11 March 1991

I've got it, I like it and with your help, I'm going to keep it.

> On the Premiership, Conservative Party Conference, 11 October 1991

We are not wholly an island, except geographically.

> 1992

The chameleon of politics consistent only in his inconsistency.

> On Neil Kinnock, 1992

The matter of the timing of the Maastricht treaty is now and will remain a matter for the British parliament and for no-one else.

> Edinburgh summit, 1992

Not tonight Josephine, we'll debate it at some other time.

> To John Smith, Leader of the Labour Party, during the Maastricht debate, 1992

This is becoming more fun than I had imagined.

> During the Maastricht debate, 1992

That part of it is behind us now ... I'm drawing a line under the sand.

> Seeking to heal party divisions after the ratification of the Maastricht Treaty, 1992

I was under no illusions when I took Britain into the ERM. I said at the time that membership was no soft option. The soft option, the devaluer's option, the inflationary option, would be a betrayal of our future ... there is going to be no devaluation, no realignment.

> 10th September, 1992, six days before Britain pulled out of the ERM

We secured stable exchange rates in the ERM—and we'll keep our position there.

> 1992

I respect and accept your decision not to stay on.

> In his letter to the resigning chancellor, Norman Lamont

One week before the election, the Labour Party start cuddling up to the Liberal Democrats for support. It is like leaning on candy-floss.

> 1992

The Liberal Democrats are a Trojan Horse to the Labour Party.

> 1992

Society needs to condemn a little more and understand a little less.

> *Mail on Sunday,* 21 February 1993

Fifty years from now, Britain will still be the country of long shadows on county cricket grounds, warm beer, invincible green suburbs, dog lovers, and—as George Orwell said—old maids bicycling to Holy Communion through the morning mist.

> 22 April 1993

I was in short trousers; we had ration cards; Hitler had been dead for only seven years. They were, I remember, happy days.

> On the year *The Mousetrap* opened, 1993

I'm fit, I'm well, I'm here and I'm staying.

> Speech to the Conservative Womens' Conference, 4 June 1993

It is time to get back to basics: to self-discipline and respect for the law, to consideration for others, to accepting responsibility for yourself and your family, and not shuffling it off on to the State.
> Conservative Party Conference, 8 October 1993

We don't want three more of the bastards out there spreading poison.
> On why he chose not to sack the Eurosceptic ministers in his party, 1994

I see public service as a duty and if you can serve, I believe you have an obligation to do so.
> Resignation statement, July 1995

In short, it is time to put up or shut up.
> Ibid.

Do I look nervous?

With the retirement of 'Dickie' Bird, something sad will have gone out of English cricket.
> 1996

He made a great contribution to public life, especially in France.
> At the funeral of President Mitterrand, 1996

Something that I was not aware had happened turned out to have happened.
> On the arms to Iraq scandal, 1996

Events made a monkey of us.
> Referring to the decision to join the ERM

A soundbite never buttered a parsnip.
> April 1997

He behaves like an agitated parrot with constipation. He is more funny than wise.
> On Frank Dobson

Like me or loathe me—please don't bind my hands.
> Appealing for unity in the Conservative Party, April 1997

Well, it's over, we lost.
> May 2, 1997

When the curtain falls it is time to get off the stage.
> Resignation Statement, May 2 1997

I hope to get to the Oval in time for lunch.
> Last words as Prime Minister, May 2 1997

In retrospect I think her behaviour was intolerable.
> On Margaret Thatcher's behaviour during his Premiership, August 10, 1999

Earl of Malmesbury

I very much doubt whether many persons will be found to seek for the honour of a life peerage, for it seems to me that it would amount I will not say to an insult but to a very humiliating slight to offer a gentleman a peerage and at the same time to tell him that the title and dignity conferred upon him shall not descend to his son.
> On the first plan to introduce life peers, 1869

Lord Mancroft

All men are born equal but quite a few eventually get over it.
> 1967

Jose Marti

The spirit of a government must be that of the country. The form of the government must come from the make-up of the country. Government is nothing but the balance of the natural elements of a country.
Our America, 1891

Allan Massie

Author

Mrs Thatcher gained power at a time when it seemed that the collective was depriving the individual of responsibility for his own life. Even crime was no longer an individual act: it was a response to social conditions (a view which insulted all decent people living in the same conditions but abstaining from criminal activity). She disagreed … To dramatise this, she insisted 'society did not exist', though it was against an exaggerated view of society that she was reacting. Nothing she said would have been denied by Protestant churchmen before this century.
Allan Massie, *Sunday Times*, 1989

Michael Mates

1934–; Conservative MP, 1974–

If one cannot come to the House of Commons and tell them what is wrong with the system if one cannot speak in this place, not about innocence or guilt, not about trials, not about sub judice, but what is wrong with the system, then what is the point of being here?
On alleged attempts by the Serious Fraud Office to pervert the course of justice.

Brian Mawhinney

1940–; Conservative MP, 1979–

And in Frank Dobson's Camden, would you believe, they gave a grant to the Camden Hopscotch Asian Women's Group.
As Conservative Party Chairman, condemning a Home Office-funded community project, 1995

Reginald Maudling

1917–79; Conservative MP 1950–79, Cabinet Minister, 1955–64

There comes a time in every man's life when he must make way for older men.
On being replaced by John Davies as Shadow Foreign Secretary, November 1976

The broad stream of British foreign policy should not be sharply diverted with every change of government, for the national interest does not change much as it needs to adapt to external circumstances. In these circumstances the primary function of Opposition is to exercise vigilance, to keep a critical eye on the performance of the government, to chide when it displays tardiness or lack of vision, to suggest when new ideas are needed and openly support where support is justified and necessary.
The *Times*, 1976

David Maxwell-Fyfe

1900–67; Conservative MP

Gratitude is not a normal feature of political life.

Loyalty is the Tory's secret weapon.

Patrick Mayhew

1929–; Conservative MP 1974–97, Cabinet Minister 1990–97

Well, nobody is dead. At the end of this opera, everybody's dead.
>   On being told that nearly thirty people had been injured in a Belfast explosion, while at the opera.

Michael Medved

1948–; Film Critic

The days when Hollywood captured the imagination of the entire world with stirring accounts of our heroic history have given way to an era of self-flagellation and irresponsible revisionism—with a series of preachy, politically correct, propagandistic presentations of our country's many crimes and misdemeanours.
>   *Hollywood vs. America,* 1992

Edwin Meese

1931– ; US Attorney General 1985–1988

The protests in Beijing should be taken as a stinging rebuke to the notion of cultural relativism, and specifically of the idea that political freedom is a Western idea not universally acceptable.
>   *Communist Nations are Thirsty For Freedom,* June 1989

What is happening in Beijing gives lie to the notion that freedom is divisible; that one can have economic freedom without political freedom, or vice-versa. After all, it was Deng's free market economic reforms, established out of necessity, that created the political climate which led to the democratic protests.
>   Ibid.

David Mellor

1949–; Conservative MP, 1979–97

Nick Ross (interviewer): It does boil down to a barrel of oil at the end of the day.
David Mellor: Well, I think that's a crude way of putting it.
>   Exchange on the Iran-Iraq war, 1987

In the National Health Service, for years there has been a sterile political debate.
>   As junior health minister, 1989

To the man in the street, a number of people he has barely heard of are replaced by a number of people he has never heard of.
>   On the Cabinet reshuffle, 1993

When I should like to have been seen as a tower of strength, I am perceived by some as a point of weakness.
>   In his resignation letter to John Major

Henry Louis Mencken

1880–1956; American Satirist and Newspaper Editor

When a new source of taxation is found it never means in practice, than an old source is abandoned. It merely means that the politicians have two ways of milking the taxpayer whereas previously they had one.
>   1925

I do not have [Thomas Jefferson's] confidence in the wisdom and rectitude of the common man, but I go with him in his belief that the very commonest of common men have certain inalienable rights.
>   1927

Frank Meyer

Unless men are free to be vicious they cannot be virtuous.

> *In Defense of Freedom: A Conservative Credo,* 1962

The state must be limited to its proper function in order of preserving order. But this will only be possible when the person is considered as the central moral entity, and society as but a set of relations between persons, not as an organism superior to persons.

> Ibid.

If ultimate moral righteousness rests in society, it is justified in enforcing its righteousness, and the state which is its arm cannot be limited by any rights inherent in individual persons.

> Ibid.

John Stuart Mill

1860–73; Philosopher

The only freedom which deserves the name, is that of pursuing our own good in our own way, so long as we do not attempt to deprive others of theirs or impede their efforts to obtain it.

> *On Liberty,* 1859

The liberty of the individual must be this far limited; he must not make himself a nuisance to other people.

> Ibid.

The sole end for which mankind are warranted, individually or collectively in interfering with the liberty of action of any of their number, is self-protection.

> Ibid.

If all mankind minus one were of one opinion, and only one person were of the contrary opinion, mankind would be no more justified in silencing that one person, than he, if he had the power, would be justified in silencing mankind.

> Ibid.

Over himself, over his own body and mind, the individual is sovereign.

> Ibid.

The Conservatives, being by the law of their existence the stupidest party.

> *Considerations of Representative Government,* 1861

Lord Milner

1854–1925; Imperialist

You have been born an Englishman and as such have come first in the lottery of life.

> House of Commons

John Milton

1608–1674; Poet

As good almost kill a man as kill a good book; who kills a man kills a reasonable creature, God's image; but he who kills a good book, kills reason itself.

> *Areopagitica,* 1644

Give me the liberty to know, to utter, and to argue freely according to conscience, above all liberties.

> Ibid.

… though all the winds of doctrine were let loose to play upon the earth, so Truth be in the field, we do injuriously by licensing and prohibiting to misdoubt her strength. Let her and Falsehood grapple; who ever knew Truth put to the worse in a free and open encounter?

> Ibid.

Ludwig von Mises

1881–1973; Austrian Economist

A nation is the more prosperous today the less it has tried to put obstacles in the way of the spirit of free enterprise and private initiative.

The Anti-Capitalist Mentality, 1956

Nobody is needy in the market economy because of the fact that some people are rich. The riches of the rich are not the cause of the poverty of anybody. The process that makes some people rich is, on the contrary, the corollary of the process that makes many people's satisfaction.

Ibid.

What is wrong with our age is precisely the widespread ignorance of the role which ... policies of economic freedom played in the technological evolution of the last two hundred years.

Human Action, 1949

It is always the individual who thinks. Society does not think any more than it eats or drinks.

Ibid.

It is ... wrong to assume that there prevails within a market economy, not hampered and sabotaged by government interference, a general tendency towards the formation of monopoly. It is a grotesque distortion of the true state of affairs to speak of monopoly capitalism instead of monopoly interventionism and of private cartels instead of government cartels.

Ibid.

Moliere

French Dramatist

Of all human follies there's none could be greater than trying to render our fellow men better.

Thomas Molnar

1921– ; Hungarian-born author

Passion for equality blinds the utopian to the fact that society, as a whole, is based on inequality of men in two respects: the inventor, the innovator, the exceptional man creates something new and insures continuous progress; the others emulate his work or merely improve their own lot by benefiting from his creativity.

Utopia: The Perennial Heresy, 1967

No more eloquent funeral oration could be pronounced over the tomb of an ideology that has failed its believers because they despised the true nature of man.

On the failed utopia of the Soviet Union, Ibid.

Lord Robert Montague

To give education gratuitously will only degrade the education so given in the estimation of the parents.

Opposing free education, 1870

Montesquieu

1689–1755; French Jurist and Philosopher

It is true that in democracies the people seem to act as they please.

But political liberty does not consist simply in doing whatever one wishes. In governments, that is, in societies directed by laws, liberty can consist only in the power of doing what we ought to do, without being constrained from doing what we ought not to do. We must distinguish freedom from liberty. Again, liberty is the right to do everything the law permits. If a citizen does what the law prohibits, he sacrifices his liberty.

The Spirit of the Laws, 1748

But constant experience shows us that every man invested with power is apt to abuse it, and to carry his authority as far as it will go.

Ibid.

Commerce is a cure for the most destructive prejudices.

Ibid.

Peace is the natural effect of trade.

Ibid.

Useless laws weaken the necessary laws.

Ibid.

Lord Montgomery

There was universal support for it and very little opposition.

Describing the reform of the drink licensing laws, 1987

Thomas Moore

If I may judge from my personal knowledge of Herr Hitler, peace and justice are the key-words of his policy.

1933

Oswald Mosley

1896–1980; Member of Parliament ,1918–31

I am not and have never been a man of the right. My position was on the left and is now in the centre of politics.

1968

Lord Mountbatten

Actually, I vote Labour, but my butler's a Tory.

1945

Malcolm Muggeridge

1903–1990; Social Commentator

Searching in my mind for an appropriate name for the seventies, I settle for the Decade of the Great Liberal Death Wish. It seems to me that this process of death wishing, in the guise of liberalism, has been eroding the civilisation of the west for a century and more, and is now about to reach its apogee.

Things Past, 1978

Previous civilisations have been overthrown without by the incursion of barbarian hordes; ours has dreamed up its own dissolution in the minds of its own intellectual elite.

Ibid.

Liberalism will be seen historically as the great destructive force of our time; much more so than communism, fascism, Nazism, or any of the other lunatic creeds which make such immediate havoc …

Ibid.

There is no snobbishness like that of professional egalitarians.

Chronicles of Wasted Time, 1978

Charles Murray

We believe that human happiness
requires freedom and that freedom
requires limited government.
*What It Means to Be a Libertarian: A
Personal Interpretation*, 1997

Richard Needham

1942–; Conservative MP 1979–97

I wish that old cow would resign.
Caught out on a mobile phone
talking about Margaret Thatcher,
1990—he later said sorry.

Godfrey Nicholson

A platitude is a truth we are tired of
hearing
House of Commons, 10 July 1933

Harold Nicolson

… the mind and manners of a clothes
brush.
On Austen Chamberlain, Diary, 6
June 1936

I think it is a combination of real
religious fanaticism with spiritual
trickiness which makes one dislike Mr
Chamberlain so much. He has all the
hardness of a self-righteous man, with
none of the generosity of those who
are guided by durable moral standards.
On Neville Chamberlain, Diary, 26
April 1939

Attlee is a charming and intelligent
man, but as a public speaker he is,
compared to Winston [Churchill], like
a village fiddler after Paganini.
Diary, 10 November 1947

Friedrich Nietzsche

1844–1900; Philosopher

Every tradition grows ever more
venerable—the more remote its origin,
the more confused that origin is. The
reverence due to it increases from
generation to generation. The tradition
finally becomes holy and inspires awe.
Human, all too Human, 1878

Robert A. Nisbet

1913–; American Sociologist

I cannot help thinking that what we
need above all else in this age is a new
philosophy of laissez-faire. The old
laissez-faire failed because it was based
on erroneous premises regarding
human behaviour … because it mis-
took for ineradicable characteristics of
individuals characteristics that were in
fat inseparable from social groups …
Far from proving a check upon the
growth of the omnicompetent State,
the old laissez-faire actually accelerated
its growth. Its indifference to every
form of community and association left
the State as the sole area of reform and
security … To create conditions in
which the autonomous individuals
could prosper, could be emancipated
from the binding ties of kinship, class
and community, was the objective of
the older laissez-faire. To create conditions within which autonomous
groups may prosper must be, I believe,
the prime objective of the new laissez-
faire.
The Quest for Community, 1953

Richard Nixon

1913–94; American President 1969–74

I also believe that academic freedom should protect the right of a professor or student to advocate Marxism, Socialism, Communism or any other minority viewpoint—no matter how distasteful to the majority.

What are our schools for if not indoctrination against communism?

The successful leader does not talk down to people. He lifts them up.

A man is not finished when he is defeated. He is finished when he quits.
December 10 1978

Once you get into this great stream of history, you can't get out.

If you want to make beautiful music, you must play the black and the white notes together.

I have impeached myself by resigning.

By taking this action, I hope that I will have hastened the start of the healing.

While technically I did not commit a crime, an impeachable offence … these are legalisms, as far as the handling of this matter is concerned; it was so botched up, I made so many bad judgements. The worst ones, mistakes of the heart, rather than the head. But let me say, a man in that top job—he's got to have a heart, but his head must always rule his heart.

I've analysed the best I can … and I have not found an impeachable offence, and therefore resignation is not an acceptable course.

We are all in it together. This is a war. We take a few shots and it will be over. We will give them a few shots and it will be over.

I can see clearly now … that I was wrong in not acting more decisively and more forthrightly in dealing with Watergate …

I gave 'em a sword. And they stuck it in, and they twisted it with relish. And I guess if I had been in their position, I'd have done the same thing.

You must pursue this investigation of Watergate even if it leads to the president. I'm innocent. You've got to believe I'm innocent. If you don't, take my job.

I can take it … The tougher it gets, the cooler I get …

When the president does it, that means it is not illegal.

I was under medication when I made the decision to burn the tapes.

This is the greatest week in the history of the world since the creation.
On the first landing on the moon

Steven Norris

1945–; Conservative MP, 1983–97

It's like a vasectomy—you can have all of the fun without any of the responsibility.
On the benefits of a Peerage

You have your own company, your own temperature control, your own music and you don't have to put up with dreadful human beings sitting alongside you.
On the benefits of commuting by car rather than public transport, as Minister of Transport, 1995

Lord North

1732–1792; Prime Minister 1770–1782

Men may be popular without being ambitious, but there is hardly an ambitious man who does not try to be popular.

The American Disputes are settled and there is nothing to interrupt the peace and prosperity of the nation.
1771

I never should be so presumptuous as to think myself capable of directing the departments of others ... I do not think our constitution authorises such a character as that animal called a Prime Minister.
1778

[Affairs of state] can hardly be well conducted unless there is person in the Cabinet capable of leading, of discerning between opinions, of deciding quickly and confidently, and connecting all the operations of government...
To King George III, 1778

Oliver North

American National Security Staff and Author

I remember watching on television as the Berlin Wall came down. I had tears in my eyes ... I felt that way again in 1990, when, for the second time in eleven years, the people of Nicaragua rejected a brutal and corrupt regime. And yet again in 1991, watching Boris Yeltsin stop a Soviet tank during the second Russian Revolution.
Under Fire, 1991

Michael Novak

1933– ; American Philosopher

It is an analytical mistake to hold that socialism respects the social nature of humans, while democratic societies are characterised by 'progressive individualism.' In actual history, exactly the reverse happens. One may test this proposition empirically. In which actual nations do voluntary associations and co-operative habits actually thrive, and in which do they wither?
Confessions of a Catholic, 1983

P. J. O'Rourke

American political satirist

You can't get rid of poverty by giving people money.

Giving money and power to government is like giving whiskey and car keys to teenage boys.

There is only one basic human right, the right to do as you damn well please.
Speech to the Cato Institute, 1993

There are just two rules of governance in a free society: Mind your own business. Keep your hands to yourself.

When buying and selling are controlled by legislation, the first things to be bought and sold are legislators.

The American political system is like fast food—mushy, insipid, made out of disgusting parts of things and everybody wants some.

Matthew Oakeshott

1901–1990; Philosopher

To be a Conservative is to prefer the tried to the untried, the fact to the mystery, the actual to the possible, the limited to the unbounded, the near to the distant, the sufficient to the super-abundant, the convenient to the perfect present, laughter to utopian bliss.

Rationalism in Politics

To be conservative is not merely to be averse from change, which may be an idiosyncrasy: it is also a manner of accommodating ourselves to changes, an activity imposed upon all men. For a change is a threat to identity and any change is an emblem of extinction.

Ibid.

Reginald Paget

Conservative MP

From Lord Hailsham we have had a virtuoso performance in the art of kicking a fallen friend in the guts. When self-indulgence has reduced a man to the shape of Lord Hailsham, sexual continence requires no more than a sense of the ridiculous.

Defending Harold Macmillan over Profumo, 1963

Lord Palmerston

1784–1865; Prime Minister 1855–65

I object to it because I think it at variance with the national character ... I think a true Englishman hates doing a thing in secret or in the dark. I do not believe that a majority of Englishmen would consent to give their votes in secret even if the law permitted them to do so ... I say that for men who are charged with the high and important duty of choosing the best men to represent the country in Parliament to go sneaking to the ballot-box and poking in a piece of paper, looking round see that no one could read it, is a course which is unconstitutional and unworthy of the character of straight-forward and honest Englishmen.

At the General Election of 1852

An ancient sage said there were two things over which the gods them-selves had no power—past events and arithmetic.

Your Lordship is like a favourite footman on easy terms with his mis-tress. Your dexterity seems a happy compound of the smartness of an attorney clerk and the intrigue of a Greek lower empire.

On Peel

His life has been one great appropria-tion clause. A burglar of others' intel-lect—there is no statesman who has committed political larceny on so grand a scale.

On Peel

The Right Honourable Gentleman is reminiscent of a poker. The only difference is that a poker gives off occasional signs of warmth.

On Peel

I say yield today that which is reasonably asked and resist tomorrow that which you will be borne out in resisting; but do not let us put ourselves in the wrong today merely for fear that we may find ourselves in the right tomorrow.

Robert Parker

US Supreme Court Justice, Chief Prosecutor for the USA at the Nuremberg Trials

It is not the function of the government to keep the citizen from falling into error; it is the function of the citizen to keep the government from falling into error.

Cecil Parkinson

1931–; Conservative MP, 1970–92, Cabinet Minister, 1981–83, 1987–90

I have my own Parkinson's Law: in politics people give you what they think you deserve and deny you what they think you want.

The cost of the Eurotunnel project has risen, but it is usual in these projects and the Anglo-French consortium is looking into ways to bridge the gap
As Transport Secretary, 1989

I'm a great believer in leaving politics when you've reached your ceiling. (Pause) Though I did lower the ceiling somewhat ...
On leaving the Commons, 1992

I'm very pleased we've won another seat ... I was actually thinking John Major was going to remain leader of the party and the only Conservative Member of Parliament.
On hearing on of a second Tory victory, 1 May 1997

Christopher Patten

1944–; Conservative MP, 1979–92, Governor of Hong Kong, 1993–97

A kind of walking obituary for the Labour Party.
On Michael Foot

John Stuart Mill, rewritten by Ernest Hemingway
On David Owen

I've always had a great respect and been very candid with her, and I hope the reverse is the case.
On Margaret Thatcher, 1989

The argument about Labour destroying any prospects of recovery may be *deja-vu* here ... It's certainly not *deja-vu* in the country. It's very much *vu*. It's very much what er ... It's very much er ... shows what sort of an education I had.
1992

The Liberal Democrats couldn't survive a moment's scrutiny of their policies. At local level they back four routes for a bypass—North, South, East and West. At national level they are just as bad.
1992

John Patten

1945–; Conservative MP, 1979–97, Cabinet Minister 1992–95

There are three prongs to our anti-crime drive: stronger sentences, more police on the beat and prevention.
1987

Robert Peel

1788–1850; Prime Minister 1834–5, 1841–6

I may be a Tory—I may be an illiberal—but the fact is undeniable, that when I first entered upon the duties of the Home Department, there were laws in existence which imposed upon the subjects of this realm unusual and extraordinary restrictions.
Following his resignation as Home Secretary, 1 May 1827

I am very far from being prepared to admit that the improvement of the situation of a common police constable by giving him more money would increase the efficiency of the establishment.
> 1829

The longer I live, the more clearly do I see the folly of yielding a rash and precipitate assent to any political measure.
> 1830

We are here to consult the interests and not to obey the will of the people if we honestly believe that they will conflict with those interests.
> Third Reading of the Reform Bill, 1831

The mere interest of the occupying tenants, important as they are, are subordinate to the great question— what is calculated to increase the comforts, to improve the condition and elevate the social character of millions who subsist by manual labour whether they are engaged in manufactures or manual labour?
> Speech on repeal of the Corn Laws, 1846

But it may be that I shall leave a name sometimes remembered with expressions of good will in the abodes of those whose lot it is to labour, and to earn their daily bread by the sweat of their brow, when they shall recruit their exhausted strength with abundant and untaxed food, the sweeter because it is no longer leavened by a sense of injustice.
> On his resignation as Prime Minister, 29 June 1846

Constitutional liberty will be best worked out by those who aspire to freedom by their own efforts.
> Last speech on foreign policy in the House of Commons, 28 June 1850

It was impossible for me to reconcile the repeal of the Corn Laws by me with the keeping together of the Conservative Party, and I had no hesitation in sacrificing the subordinate object and with it my own political interests.
> *Memoirs*

Spencer Perceval

1762–1812; Prime Minister 1809–12

I have nothing to say to the nothing that has been said.
> During a debate on corrupt electoral practices

Inadvertence is certainly never felt by me as an excuse.
> Letter to Wilberforce

Ross Perot

Independent American Presidential candidate

An empty suit that goes to funerals and plays golf.
> On Dan Quayle, 1992

John Peyton

1919–; Conservative MP, 1951–79

We are a Party which can never forget its historic links with the land and its deep commitment to those who live and work in the countryside.
> On the Conservative Party, 1977

William Pitt (the elder)

1708–1778; Secretary of State 1757–61, Prime Minister 1766–8

The atrocious crime of being a young man, which the honourable gentleman had with such spirit and decency charged upon me, I shall attempt neither to palliate nor to deny, but content myself with wishing that I shall be one of those whose follies shall cease with their youth, and not of that number who are ignorant in spite of experience.

> Answering the criticism of Robert Walpole, 1741

Unlimited power is apt to corrupt the minds of those who possess it.

There is something behind the throne greater than the king himself.

> 1770

If I were an American, as I am an Englishman, while a foreign troop was landed in my country, I never would lay down my arms, never—never—never!

> 1777

William Pitt (the younger)

1759–1806; Prime Minister 1783–1801, 1804–1806

Necessity is the plea for every infringement of human freedom. It is the argument of tyrants; it is the creed of slaves.

> House of Commons, 18 November 1783

There is no principle of the law of nations clearer than this, that, when in the cause of war any nation acquires new possessions, such nation has only temporary right to them, and they do not become property till the end of the war.

> House of Commons, 30 December 1796

We must recollect … what it is we have at stake, what it is we have to contend for. It is for our property, it is for our liberty, it is for our independence, nay, for our existence as a nation; it is for our character, it is for our very name as Englishmen, it is for everything dear and valuable to man on this side of the grave.

> 22 July 1803

England has saved herself by her exertions, and will, I trust, save Europe by her example.

> Guildhall, London, 9 November 1805

Plutarch

c.46–120; Roman Historian

Men, stirred by popular applause, though they bear the name of governors, are in reality the mere underlings of the multitude. The man who is completely wise and virtuous has no need at all of glory, except so far as it disposes and eases his way of action by the greater trust that it procures him.

> *Lives*

Scilurus on his death bed, being about to leave four-score sons surviving, offered a bundle of darts to each of them and bade them break them. When all refused, drawing out one by one, he easily broke them, thus teaching them that if they held together, they would continue strong; but if they fell out and were divided they would become weak.

> *Apolothegius of Kings and Great Commanders: Scilurus*

Polybius

c. 2nd Century BC; Roman Historian

For peace, with justice and honour, is the fairest and most profitable of possessions, but with disgrace and shameful cowardice it is the most infamous and harmful of all.

> *Histories*

Karl Popper

1902–94; Philosopher

Individualism was part of the old intuitive idea of justice. That justice is not, as Plato would have it, the health and harmony of the state, but rather a certain way of treating individuals, is emphasised by Aristotle ... when he says justice is something that pertains to persons.

> *Individualism versus Collectivism,* 1945

Michael Portillo

Conservative MP, Cabinet Minister

Three letters send a chill down the spine of the enemy—SAS. Those letters spell out one clear message. Don't mess with Britain!

> Conservative Conference 1995

The European Commission might want to harmonise uniforms and cap badges, or even to metricate them. The European Court would probably want to stop our men fighting for more than

forty hours a week. They would send half of them home on paternity leave.

> Explaining why a common European defence policy would never work

If any of you have got an A-Level, it is because you have worked for it. Go to any other country, and when you have got an A-Level, you have bought it.

> Speech to Southampton students

Anyone, they say, is entitled to change his mind. Not about the defence of Britain, you're not. You either feel it in your heart, in your bones, in your gut, or you don't!

Returning Officer: Everyone happy?
Portillo: Ecstatic.

> May 2 1998

For those that wanted the Conservatives out, my defeat was a highlight. I am better at politics than I am at anything else.

> 17 November 1998

I regard the leadership thing as closed forever. I got quite close to it, but the moment passed .. I think it would be interesting to go back as a backbencher ... People thought I was too ambitious, maybe I brought some of it on myself ... I think I'm a more humble person, yes. I think I was always more humble than I was made out to be.

> The *Guardian,* 16 August 1998

The party would cheerfully engage in fighting one another over Europe, as though we were a college debating society rather than a government a week from polling day. We displayed the disciplinary qualities of a rave party rather than a political one.

> The *Spectator,* 9 August 1998

Enoch Powell

1912–96; Conservative MP 1950–74, Ulster Unionist MP 1974–87

In politics it is more blessed not to take than to give.
Daily Telegraph, 31 January 1964

History is littered with the wars which everybody knew would never happen.
Conservative Party Conference, 19 October 1967

We must be mad, literally mad, as a nation to be permitting the annual inflow of some 50,000 dependents of immigrants ... As I look ahead, I am filled with foreboding. Like the Roman, I seem to see the River Tiber foaming with much blood.
20 April 1968

Helping industry is the elephant's pit of socialism, a deep hole with sharp spikes at the bottom, covered over with twigs and fresh grass.
24 September 1969

Inflation is no mere monetary inconvenience. It is a social evil, an injustice between man and man and a moral evil, a dishonesty between government and people, between class and class ... The highest national interest, overtopping all others in the economic sphere is honest money—money that holds its value. Growth, full employment, expanding public services—all these are worth nothing unless that first and great condition is fulfilled.
1973

All political lives, unless they are cut off in midstream at a happy juncture, end in failure, because that is the nature of politics and of human affairs.
1977

I do not keep a diary. Never have. To write a diary every day is like returning to one's own vomit.
1977

Take Parliament out of the history of England and that history itself becomes meaningless.
4 February 1979

The Prime Minister, shortly after she came into office, received a sobriquet as the 'Iron Lady'. It arose in the context of remarks which she made about defence against the Soviet Union and its allies; but there was no reason to suppose that the Right Honourable Lady did not welcome and, indeed, take pride in that description. In the next week or two this House, the nation and the Right Honourable Lady herself, will learn of what metal she is made.
House of Commons, 3 April 1982

I don't really think I have ever made a mistake.
Any Questions, BBC Radio 4, 1982

Politicians who complain about the press are like ship's captains who complain about the sea.
(attrib.)

It shows that the substance under test consists of ferrous metal of the highest quality. It is of exceptional tensile strength, resistant to wear and tear, and may be used with advantage for all national purposes.

> Explaining how Margaret Thatcher had stood up to the tests of the Falklands crisis

A Tory is someone who thinks institutions are wiser than those who operate them.

> *Daily Telegraph,* 31 March 1986

Above any other position of eminence, that of Prime Minister is filled by fluke.
> 1987

To pretend that you cannot exchange goods and services freely with a Frenchman or an Italian, unless there is an identical standard of bathing beaches or tap water in the different countries is not logic. It is naked aggression.

> The *Guardian,* 22 May 1990

If Toryism includes stealing from dukes, it is a Tory measure.

> On leasehold land reform plans, 1990

James Prior

1927–; Conservative MP, 1959–87, Cabinet Minister 1970–74, 1979–84

Why does he always talk about the working people as if they were a section of society apart from the rest? Perhaps the second Lord Stansgate still believes that the only way to rally the faithful is to use the class slogans of the aristocracy. Mr Benn, I have news for you. Most of us are working people.

> 1976

When Mrs Thatcher said 'We are a grandmother,' she was including Denis in her remarks.

> 1989

Francis Pym

1922–; Conservative MP, 1961–87, Cabinet Minister 1970–74, 1979–83

Stale claret in new bottles—it is a confidence trick not to be mistaken for the elixir of life.

We've got a corporal at the top, not a cavalry officer.

> On Margaret Thatcher 1982

Landslides, on the whole, don't produce successful governments.

> 1983

Dan Quayle

American Vice President 1988–92

We're going to have the best educated American people in the world.

One word sums up probably the responsibility of any Vice-President. And that one word is, 'to be prepared'

[Republicans] understand the importance of bondage between parent and child.

> He meant to say 'bonding', 1988

The Nazi holocaust was an obscene period in our country's history ... well, not our country's history, this century's history ... we all lived in this century; I didn't live in this century ...

> 1988

There's a lot of uncharted waters in space.

> 1989

What a waste it is to lose one's mind—
or not to have a mind.
> 1989

The only regret I have was that I didn't
study Latin harder in school so I could
converse with those people.
> On visit to Latin America, 1989
> (attrib.)

There is an irreversible trend to freedom and democracy in Eastern Europe. But this may change.
> 1990

If we do not succeed, then we run the
risk of failure.
> 1990

If you elect Bill Clinton and Al Gore
you can say goodbye to water, goodbye
to food and goodbye to your jobs.
> 1992

The intergenerational poverty that
troubles us so much today is pre-
dominantly a poverty of values. Our
inner cities are filled with children
having children having children, with
people who have not been able to
take advantage of educational opportunities, with people who are dependent on drugs or the narcotic of
welfare.
> Speech, Commonwealth Club, May
> 19, 1992

Ultimately ... marriage is a moral issue
that requires cultural consensus, and
the use of social sanctions. Bearing
babies irresponsibly is, simply, wrong.
Failing to support children one has
fathered is wrong.
> Ibid.

Ayn Rand
1905–1982; Political philosopher

The secret dread of modern intellectuals, liberals and conservatives alike, the
unadmitted terror at the root of their
anxiety, which all their current irra-
tionalities are intended to slave off and
disguise, is the unstated knowledge that
Soviet Russia is the full, actual, literal,
consistent embodiment of the morality
of altruism, that Stalin did not corrupt
a noble ideal, that this is the only way
altruism has had to be or can ever be
practised.
> *Faith and Force: The Destroyers of the
> Modern World,* 1960

Nancy Reagan
Wife of Ronald Reagan

He doesn't make snap decisions, but he
doesn't overthink either.

I believe that people would be alive
today if there were a death penalty.

Ronald Reagan
American President 1980–88

Government is just like a big baby—an
alimentary canal with a big appetite at one
end and no responsibility at the other.
> 1965

Welfare's purpose should be to eliminate, as far as possible, the need for its
own existence.
> *Los Angeles Times,* 7 January 1970

Government does not solve problems.
It subsidises them.
> 11 December 1972

Heaven help us if government ever gets into the business of protecting us from ourselves.

April 12 1973

The United States has much to offer the Third World War.

1975

I've noticed that everybody who is for abortion has already been born.

21 September 1980

No arsenal or no weapon in the arsenals of the world is so formidable as the will and moral courage of free men and women.

Inauguration Speech, 20 January 1981

It is not my intention to do away with government. It is rather to make it work—work with us, not over us; stand by our side, not ride on our back. Government can and must provide opportunity, not smother it; foster productivity, not stifle it.

Inauguration Speech, 20 January 1981

The size of the Federal Budget is not an appropriate barometer of social conscience or charitable concern.

5 October 1981

It is the Soviet Union that runs against the tide of history ... It is the march of freedom and democracy which will leave Marxism-Leninism on the ash heap of history as it has left other tyrannies which stifle the freedom and muzzle the self-expression of the people.

Speech to both Houses of Parliament, 1982

History teaches that wars begin when governments believe the price of aggression is cheap.

Address to the nation, January 16, 1984

We will always remember. We will always be proud. We will always be prepared, so we may always be free.

Normandy, 6 June 1984

The men of Normandy had faith that what they were doing was right, faith that they fought for all humanity, faith that a just God would grant them mercy on this beachhead or the next. It was the deep knowledge—and pray God we have not lost it—that there is a profound moral difference between the use of force for liberation and the use of force for conquest.

Normandy, 6 June 1984

Abraham Lincoln recognised that we could not survive as a free land when some men could decide that others were not fit to be free and should therefore be slaves. Likewise, we cannot survive as a free nation when some men decide that others are not fit to live and should be abandoned to abortion or infanticide ... there is no cause more important for preserving that freedom than affirming the transcendent right to life of all human beings, the right without which no other rights have any meaning.

Abortion and the Conscience of the Nation, 1984

Die-hard conservatives thought that if I couldn't get everything I asked for, I

would jump off the cliff with the flag flying—go down in flames. No, if I can get 70 or 80 percent of what it is I'm trying to get … I'll take that and then continue to try to get the rest in the future.
New York Times, October 6, 1985

The nine most terrifying words in the English language are, 'I'm from the government and I'm here to help'.
August 2, 1986

Recession is when your neighbour loses his job. Depression is when you lose your job. And recovery is when Jimmy Carter loses his.

When you see all that rhetorical smoke billowing up from the Democrats, well ladies and gentleman, I'd follow the example of their nominee; don't inhale.
Republican National Convention, 1992

I hope you're all Republicans.
To surgeons as he entered the operating room, March 30, 1981

We who live in free market societies believe that growth, prosperity and ultimately human fulfilment, are created from the bottom up, not the government down. Only when the human spirit is allowed to invent and create, only when individuals are given a personal stake in deciding economic policies and benefiting from their success—only then can societies remain economically alive, dynamic, progressive, and free. Trust the people. This is the one irrefutable lesson of the entire post-war period contradicting the notion that rigid government

controls are essential to economic development.
September 29, 1981

Government is the people's business and every man, woman and child becomes a shareholder with the first penny of tax paid.
Address to the New York City Partnership Association, January 14, 1982

We don't have a trillion-dollar debt because we haven't taxed enough; we have a trillion-dollar debt because we spend too much.
Address to National Association of Realtors, March 28, 1982

Let us beware that while they [Soviet rulers] preach the supremacy of the state, declare its omnipotence over individual man, and predict its eventual domination over all the peoples of the earth, they are the focus of evil in the modern world … I urge you to beware the temptation … to ignore the facts of history and the aggressive impulses of any evil empire, to simply call the arms race a giant misunderstanding and thereby remove yourself from the struggle between right and wrong, good and evil.
Speech to the National Association of Evangelicals, March 8, 1983

I call upon the scientific community in our country, those who gave us nuclear weapons, to turn their great talents now to the cause of mankind and world peace, to give us the means of rendering those nuclear weapons impotent and obsolete.
Address to the Nation, March 23, 1983

There are no such things as limits to growth, because there are no limits on the human capacity for intelligence, imagination and wonder.

> Address to the University of South Carolina, Columbia, September 20, 1983

We will never forget them, nor the last time we saw them—this morning, as they prepared for their journey, and waved good-bye, and slipped the surly bonds of earth to touch the face of God.

> Speech about the *Challenger* disaster, January 28, 1986

Government growing beyond our consent had become a lumbering giant, slamming shut the gates of opportunity, threatening to crush the very roots of our freedom. What brought America back? The American people brought us back—with quiet courage and common sense; with undying faith that in this nation under God the future will be ours, for the future belongs to the free.

> State of the Union Address, February 4, 1986

[G]overnment's view of the economy could be summed up in a few short phrases: If it moves, tax it. If it keeps moving, regulate it. And if it stops moving, subsidise it.

> Remarks to the White House Conference on Small Business, August 15, 1986

The other day, someone told me the difference between a democracy and a people's democracy. It's the same difference between a jacket and a straitjacket.

> Remarks at Human Rights Day event, December 10, 1986

How do you tell a Communist? Well, it's someone who reads Marx and Lenin. And how do you tell an anti-Communist? It's someone who understands Marx and Lenin.

> Remarks in Arlington, Virginia, September 25, 1987

Mr Gorbachev, open this gate! Mr Gorbachev, tear down this wall!

> Speech near the Berlin Wall, 1987

A friend of mine was asked to a costume ball a short time ago. He slapped some egg on his face and went as a liberal economist.

> February 11, 1988

Freedom is the right to question and change the established way of doing things. It is the continuous revolution of the marketplace. It is the understanding that allows to recognise shortcomings and seek solutions.

> Address to students at Moscow State University, May 31, 1988

The best minds are not in government. If any were, business would hire them away.

> Attributed

After watching the State of the Union address the other night, I'm reminded of the old adage that imitation is the sincerest form of flattery. Only in this case, it's not flattery, but grand larceny: the intellectual theft of ideas that you and I recognise as our own. Speech delivery counts for little on the world stage unless you have convictions, and, yes, the vision to see beyond the front row seats.

> RNC Annual Gala, Feb. 3, 1994

Although the political landscape has changed, the bold ideas of the 1980's are alive and well. Republican candidates swept every major election across the country last year ... and as a result, it seems that our opponents have finally realised how unpopular liberalism really is. So now they're trying to dress their liberal agenda in a conservative overcoat.

RNC Annual Gala, Feb. 3, 1994

Are you willing to spend time studying the issues, making yourself aware, and then conveying that information to family and friends? Will you resist the temptation to get a government handout for your community? Realise that the doctor's fight against socialised medicine is your fight? We can't socialise the doctors without socialising the patients. Recognise that government invasion of public power is eventually an assault upon your own business. If some among you fear taking a stand because you are afraid of reprisals from customers, clients, or even government, recognise that you are just feeding the crocodile hoping he'll eat you last.

October 27, 1964

Have we the courage and the will to face up to the immorality and discrimination of the progressive tax, and demand a return to traditional proportionate taxation? ... Today in our country the tax collector's share is 37 cents of every dollar earned. Freedom has never been so fragile, so close to slipping from our grasp.

October 27, 1964

However, our task is far from over. Our friends in the other party will never forgive us for our success, and are doing everything in their power to rewrite history. Listening to the liberals, you'd think that the 1980s were the worst period since the Great Depression, filled with suffering and despair. I don't know about you, but I'm getting awfully tired of the whining voices from the White House these days. They're claiming there was a decade of greed and neglect, but you and I know better than that. We were there.

RNC Annual Gala, February 3, 1994

If all of this seems like a great deal of trouble, think what's at stake. We are faced with the most evil enemy mankind has known in his long climb from the swamp to the stars. There can be no security anywhere in the free world if there is no fiscal and economic stability within the United States. Those who ask us to trade our freedom for the soup kitchen of the welfare state are architects of a policy of accommodation.

October 27, 1964

In an ironic sense, Karl Marx was right. We are witnessing today a great revolutionary crisis—a crisis where the demands of the economic order are colliding directly with those of the political order. But the crisis is happening not in the free, non-Marxist West, but in the home of Marxism-Leninism, the Soviet Union ... [Communism will be] left on the ash heap of history.

June 1982

It was leadership here at home that gave us strong American influence abroad, and the collapse of imperial Communism. Great nations have responsibilities to lead, and we should always be cautious of those who would lower our profile, because they might just wind up lowering our flag.

RNC Annual Gala, February 3, 1994

It's time we asked ourselves if we still know the freedoms intended for us by the Founding Fathers. James Madison said, We base all our experiments on the capacity of mankind for self-government. This idea that government was beholden to the people, that it had no other source of power, is still the newest, most unique idea in all the long history of man's relation to man. This is the issue of this election: Whether we believe in our capacity for self-government or whether we abandon the American Revolution and confess that a little intellectual elite in a far-distant capital can plan our lives for us better than we can plan them ourselves.

October 27, 1964

Now, as most of you know, I'm not one for looking back. I figure there will be plenty of time for that when I get old. But rather, what I take from the past is inspiration for the future, and what we accomplished during our years at the White House must never be lost amid the rhetoric of political revisionists.

RNC Annual Gala, February 3, 1994

Public servants say, always with the best of intentions, What greater service we could render if only we had a little more money and a little more power. But the truth is that outside of its legitimate function, government does nothing as well or as economically as the private sector.

October 27, 1964

Surround yourself with the best people you can find, delegate authority, and don't interfere.

Fortune, September 15, 1986

The Democrats may remember their lines, but how quickly they forget the lessons of the past. I have witnessed five major wars in my lifetime, and I know how swiftly storm clouds can gather on a peaceful horizon. The next time a Saddam Hussein takes over Kuwait, or North Korea brandishes a nuclear weapon, will we be ready to respond? In the end, it all comes down to leadership, and that is what this country is looking for now.

RNC Annual Gala, February 3, 1994

The Founding Fathers knew a government can't control the economy without controlling people. And they knew when a government sets out to do that, it must use force and coercion to achieve its purpose. So we have come to a time for choosing.

October 27, 1964

The years ahead will be great ones for our country, for the cause of freedom and the spread of civilisation. The West will not contain Communism, it will transcend Communism. We will not bother to denounce it, we'll dismiss it as a sad, bizarre chapter in human history whose last pages are even now being written.

Notre Dame Univ., May 17, 1981

They say the world has become too complex for simple answers. They are wrong. There are no easy answers, but there are simple answers. We must have the courage to do what we know is morally right. Winston Churchill said that the destiny of man is not measured by material computation. When great forces are on the move in the world, we learn we are spirits—not animals. And he said, There is something going on in time and space, and beyond time and space, which, whether we like it or not, spells duty.

October 27, 1964

We are for a provision that destitution should not follow unemployment by reason of old age, and to that end we have accepted Social Security as a step toward meeting the problem. However, we are against those entrusted with this program when they practice deception regarding its fiscal shortcomings, when they charge that any criticism of the program means that we want to end payments.

October 27, 1964

We are for aiding our allies by sharing our material blessings with nations which share our fundamental beliefs, but we are against doling out money government to government, creating bureaucracy, if not socialism, all over the world.

October 27, 1964

We need true tax reform that will at least make a start toward restoring for our children the American Dream that wealth is denied to no-one, that each individual has the right to fly as high as his strength and ability will take him ... But we cannot have such reform while our tax policy is engineered by people who view the tax as a means of achieving changes in our social structure.

October 27, 1964

Yet any time you and I question the schemes of the do-gooders, we're denounced as being opposed to their humanitarian goals. It seems impossible to legitimately debate their solutions with the assumption that all of us share the desire to help the less fortunate. They tell us we're always against, never for anything.

October 27, 1964

You and I are told we must choose between a left or right, but I suggest there is no such thing as a left or right. There is only an up or down. Up to man's age-old dream—the maximum of individual freedom consistent with order—or down to the ant heap of totalitarianism. Regardless of their sincerity, their humanitarian motives, those who would sacrifice freedom for security have embarked on this downward path. Plutarch warned, The real destroyer of the liberties of the people is he who spreads among them bounties, donations and benefits.

October 27, 1964

You and I have a rendezvous with destiny. We will preserve for our children this, the last best hope of man on earth, or we will sentence them to take the first step into a thousand years

of darkness. If we fail, at least let our children and our children's children say of us we justified our brief moment here. We did all that could be done.
October 27, 1964

For you see, my fellow Republicans, we are the change!
RNC speech, August 17, 1992

The poet called Miss Liberty's torch, the lamp beside the golden door. Well, that was the entrance to America, and it still is. And now you really know why we're here tonight.

The glistening hope of that lamp is still ours. Every promise every opportunity is still golden in this land. And through that golden door our children can walk into tomorrow with the knowledge that no one can be denied the promise that is America.

Her heart is full; her torch is still golden, her future bright. She has arms big enough to comfort and strong enough to support, for the strength in her arms is the strength of her people. She will carry on in the eighties unafraid, unashamed, and unsurpassed.

In this springtime of hope, some lights seem eternal; America's is.
RNC speech, August 23, 1984

This fellow they've nominated claims he's the new Thomas Jefferson. Well let me tell you something; I knew Thomas Jefferson. He was a friend of mine and Governor ... You're no Thomas Jefferson!
Republican National Convention, 1992

This Administration's objective will be a healthy, vigorous, growing economy.
First Inaugural Address, January 20, 1981

Cures were developed for which there were no known diseases.
Commenting on Congress and the federal budget, 1981

Government has an important role in helping develop a country's economic foundation. But the critical test is whether government is genuinely working to liberate individuals by creating incentives to work, save, invest, and succeed.
October 30, 1981

Eighty per cent of pollution is caused by plants and trees.
to National Association of Realtors, March 28, 1982

She's the best man in England.
On Margaret Thatcher

The Great Society is only great in power, in size, and in cost.

Government does not generate revenue, it merely consumes it.

Balancing the budget is like protecting your virtue—you have to learn when to say no.

I've been accused of being pro-business. Well, I just have to say: Guilty as charged.

It is old fashioned, even reactionary to remind people that free enterprise has done more to reduce poverty than all the government programs dreamed up by Democrats.

We have long since discovered that nothing lasts longer than a temporary government program.

In America, our origins matter less than our destination, and that is what democracy is all about.

A broader reading of history shows that appeasement, no matter how it is labelled, never fulfils the hopes of its appeasers.

The Constitution was never meant to prevent people from praying; its declared purpose was to protect their freedom to pray.

Republicans believe every day is the 4th of July, but Democrats believe every day is April 15th.

John Redwood

1951–; Conservative MP, 1987–, Cabinet Minister 1993–95

' ...   . '
> As Welsh Secretary singing the Welsh national anthem

No Change, No Chance.
> Leadership campaign slogan

I have always said that we need a steady nerve under fire, that we need to return to common-sense policies in health, education and Europe that brings us closer to the views of the nation. This is not lurching right but getting it right.
> *Action not Words*, 1996

We should forget all this business about right or left. The old labels have much less meaning today.
> Ibid.

Ralph Reed

US Christian Coalition

We need laws that reflect the moral law and the law of God again, what is right and what is wrong, what is just and what is unjust.

Ernest Renan

1823–92

He is very unwise who tries to shut a door against the future.

Rod Richards

Conservative MP 1992–97

They are all the same. They're short, they're fat and they are fundamentally corrupt.
> Junior Welsh Office Minister on Welsh Labour Councillors, 1995

Cardinal Richelieu

1585–1642; French Chief Minister of the Crown

Not the least of the qualities that go into the making of a great ruler is the ability of letting others serve him.
> *Political Testament*, 1687

If the poor are too well off they will be disorderly.

Nicholas Ridley

1929–93; Conservative MP, 1959–92, Cabinet Minister, 1983–90

Trees have to be cut down and re-planted.
> As Environment Secretary 1989

The [European Monetary Union] is a German racket designed to take over the whole of Europe. It has to thwarted. This rushed takeover by the Germans on the worst possible basis, with the French behaving like poodles to the Germans, is absolutely intolerable.

The *Spectator*, 14 July 1990

Seventeen unelected reject politicians with no accountability to anybody, who are not responsible for raising taxes, just spending money, who are pandered to by a supine parliament which is also not responsible for raising taxes.

On the European Commission, The *Spectator*, 14 July 1990

Pat Robertson

US Tele-Evangelist

You don't go out and kick a mad dog. If you have a mad dog with rabies, you take a gun and shoot him.

On Libyan Leader Colonel Gaddafi

A dark land teeming with Homosexuals.

On Scotland (paraphrased), 1999

John Rodgers

Conservative MP

With the coming of television [the average youth] now stays indoors three or four nights a week. Those who are worried about the problem of growing juvenile delinquency should take some comfort from the fact that here is a medium which can attract the young.

1953

Theodore Roosevelt

1858–1919; American President 1901–9

It is hard to fail, but it is worse never to have tried to succeed.

Do what you can, with what you have, where you are.

There is a homely adage which runs 'Speak softly and carry a big stick, you will go far'.

1901

Malcolm Rifkind

1946–; Conservative MP 1975–97, Cabinet Minister 1986–97

The future is not what it used to be.

On *Talking Politics*, BBC Radio 1989

Old politicians never die, they just simply wade away.

On John Stonehouse

Scotland needs the Labour Party as much as Sicily needs the Mafia.

1992

Sir Hugh Rossi

1927–; Conservative MP, 1966–87

Home ownership stabilises society, engenders pride in possessions and self-respect, and gives the individual and the family personal independence and freedom. We know that it fulfils the great desire of the vast majority of people in this country ... Their (Socialist) vision of a society amounts to a form of serfdom where people are municipal tenants with nothing to call their own, subjected to the patronage and paternalism of local political barons ... we do not have to wait for Fritz Lang's *Metropolis* or even George Orwell's *1984*. It is here and now. It is to be seen in districts of Glasgow, Sheffield, Liverpool ...

1977

Our nuclear power stations are as safe as they can possibly be, and are getting safer all the time.

As Environment Minister, 1986

Jean Jacques Rousseau

1712–1778; French Philosopher

It should be remembered that the foundation of the social contract is property; and its first condition, that every one should be maintained in the peaceful possession of what belongs to him.

A Discourse in Political Economy,
1758

Salman Rushdie

Novelist

The true conservatives of Britain are now in the Labour Party, while the radicals are all in blue.

Quoted by Brian Walden, *Sunday Times,* 1989

Viscount St. Aldwyn

In my opinion, pensions … are worse than a waste of public money they are the greatest possible incentive to the absence of self-reliance and thrift.

1907

Norman St. John Stevas

1929–; Conservative MP, 1964–87, Cabinet Minister 1979–81

The twentieth century may not be a very good thing but it is the only century we've got.

1970

It wasn't an election. It was an assumption.

On Margaret Thatcher's election as Leader of the Conservative Party, 1975

The tragedy with is that the present government are much more concerned with the use of comprehensive schools as a means of social engineering to further the egalitarian society which they favour, than they are with the educational wants or otherwise of comprehensive schools.

1976

There is another threat which is more subtle and more deadly and that is the collapse into a society which is nether communist nor conservative, but is simply valueless—an amoral rootless society, indifferent to the spiritual, contemptuous of the arts, in which pornography not religion, would be the opium of the people, and the horrors of the 'Clockwork Orange' society would be translated from fantasy to reality. There is only one answer to that we have to revivify and renew moral and religious education in our schools.

1977

But I mustn't go on singling out names. One must not be a name-dropper, as Her Majesty remarked to me yesterday …

Daily Telegraph, 1979

I have nothing against Hampstead. I used to live there myself when I was an intellectual. I gave that up when I became Leader of the House.

1980

I used to be in favour of women priests but two years in the Cabinet cured me of them.

> As an ex-member of Margaret
> Thatcher's Cabinet, 1981

Lord Salisbury

1830–1903; Prime Minister 1885–86, 1886–92, 1895–1902

No lesson seems to be so deeply inculcated by the experience of life as that you never should trust experts.

> 1877

English policy is to float lazily downstream, occasionally putting out a diplomatic boathook to avoid collisions.

> 1877

Old King Tarquin knew what he was about when he symbolised the surest way of enslaving a community by striking off the heads of the tallest poppies.

> 1883

It has always been our intention that the people in their localities should govern themselves—and that the attempt to imitate continental plans by drawing all authority from the central power, though it might produce a more scientific, a more exact, and for the moment a more effective administration, yet was destitute of the two essentials of all good government that was suited to the facts and idiosyncrasies of the particular community for whom it was designed, and did not teach the people to take that active interest in their own government which is the only training that makes a man a true and worthy citizen.

> Newport, 1885

I have four departments—the Prime Minister's, the Foreign Office, the Queen and Randolph Churchill; the burden of them increases in that order.

> 1886

We are part of the community of Europe and we must do our duty as such.

> Lord Salisbury, 10 April 1888

The perils of change are so great, the promise of the most hopeful theories is so often deceptive, that it is frequently the wiser part to uphold the existing state of things, if it can be done, even though, in point of argument, it should be utterly indefensible.

> Lord Salisbury, 1890

The federated action of Europe is our sole hope of escaping from the constant terror and calamity of war.

> 1897

The one point of similarity which distinguishes all revolutions of a democratic tendency is this, that they are invariably started with the aid of sanguine and benevolent people, who have not the slightest thought of brining about the confusion to which their efforts ultimately lead. Anyone who in 1640 should have prophesied the horrors of 1649 as the probable result of the early proceedings of the long Parliament might have been truly assured that no person could attach greater importance to the rights of the

Crown and the integrity of the Constitution than Hyde and Falkland.

A violent, isolated, artificial improvement in the institutions of a community, undertaken without regard to the condition of the other portions of the machinery in concert with which it is to work, is a danger so great that no improvement at all is almost to be preferred.

The Chamberlain family govern the country as if they were following hounds—where according to hunting conventions it is mean-spirited to look before you leap.

Letter to A. J. Balfour, 1904

The Cabinet is the creature of the House of Commons. It springs from the House of Commons and dwells in the House of Commons. It is checked and corrected by the House of Commons and by the shrug of the shoulders of the private members of the House the Cabinet can be shattered In the collective deliberations of any body of men, reason gains the mastery over passion exactly in proportion as they are educated and they are few. Passion is fostered equally by the two main characteristics of the democratic sovereign—ignorance and numbers. Moderation especially on the matter of territory, has never been characteristic of democracy. Where it has had free play, in the ancient world or the modern, a thirst for empire, and a readiness for aggressive war has always marked it.

The bestowal on any class of a voting power disproportionate to their stake in the country, must infallibly give to that class a power potential of using taxation as an instrument of plunder and legislation as a fountain of gain ... and when universal suffrage was reached, it would be simple despotism.

I think that within certain reasonable limits each party should accept the work of its predecessor and try, so far as it can do consistently with the public interest, would work it out to a satisfactory conclusion. And I do not think that in doing so we can be exposed to the imputation of inconsistency or changing our opinions.

Roger Scruton

Political Philosopher and musicologist

The basic premise of conservatism is that worthwhile institutions are hard to build, and easy to destroy, and that a life without institutions is seriously impoverished.

The *Times*, 1983

The idea of social justice on which the welfare state is founded—where social justice is supposed to be something other than charity, a right of the recipient rather than a virtue of the one who gives—seems to sponsor and condone a corruption of the moral sense.

Conservative Texts, 1991

The welfare state that is built upon this conception seems to move precisely away from the conservative conception of authoritative and personal govern-

ment, towards a labyrinthine, privilege sodden structure of anonymous power, nurturing a citizenship that is increasingly reluctant to answer for itself, increasingly void of personal responsibility, and increasingly parasitic on the dispensations of a bureaucracy towards which it can feel no gratitude.
    Ibid.

The welfare state promises more than it can provide, grows like a cancer in the economic order, and finally threatens the process of wealth-creation itself. If the lot of the poor is changed by the welfare state, it is because something else changes also—namely, the productive capacity upon which the welfare state depends, and which it also threatens to extinguish.
    Ibid.

John Seeley

I believe that the [War Ministry] are entirely wrong in thinking that they can substitute tanks for cavalry ... That seems to me a most extraordinary misreading of the lessons of the war ... It would be the most extraordinary misconception of the truth to imagine that in applying science to war the first thing to get rid of is the horse. On the contrary, every advance in science has made the horse a more and more indispensable weapon of war. Heavy artillery fire, heavy-machine gun fire, gas, aeroplane observation—all these make rapid movement more essential.
    Former Secretary of State for War, 1921

Seneca

1st century; Greek philosopher, dramatist and statesman

The foremost art of the kings is the power to endure hatred.
    Thyestes

If you judge, investigate; if you reign, command.

William Shakespeare

1564–1616; Dramatist

O thoughts of men accurst!
Past, and to come seem best, things
    present worst!
    King Henry IV, Part II

Let them obey that know not how to rule.
    Ibid.

The first thing we do, let's kill all the lawyers.
    Ibid.

Not all the water in the rough rude sea
Can wash the balm off an appointed
    king.
    King Richard II

Give every man your ear, but very few
    your voice,
Take each man's censure but reserve
    your judgement.
    Hamlet

There's hope a great man's memory may outlive his life by half a year.
    Ibid.

Men's evil manners live in brass, their virtues we write in water
    Ibid.

We must not make a scarecrow of the
law,
Setting it up to fear the birds of prey,
And let it keep one shape, till custom
make it
Their perch and not their terror.
Measure for Measure

Some are born great, some achieve
greatness, and some have greatness
thrust upon 'em.
Twelfth Night

When our actions do not, or fears do
make us traitors.
Macbeth

Bernard Shaw

1856–1950; Dramatist and intellectual

Charity deals with symptoms instead of
causes.
Man and Superman

Money ... enables us to get what we
want instead of what other people
think we want.
*The intelligent Woman's Guide to
Socialism*

Michael Shersby

1933–97; Conservative MP 1972–97

The police force in Britain is a reactionary force. It has to respond ...
1990

Edward Shils

Human beings need the help of their
ancestors; and they need the help
which is provided by their own
biological ancestors and they need the
help of the ancestors of their communities and institutions, of the ancestors
and they need the help of the ancestors of their communities and institutions ... The destruction or the
discrediting of these cognitive, moral,
metaphysical, and technical charts is a
step into chaos.
Tradition, 1981

Slogans

Safety First
1929 General Election Slogan

This is the Road
1950 General Election Manifesto

Britain Strong and Free
1951 General Election Manifesto

United for Peace and Progress
1955 General Election Manifesto

Life's Better with the Conservatives.
Don't let Labour ruin it.
1959 General Election Manifesto

Prosperity with a Purpose
1964 General Election Manifesto

Action Not Words
1966 General Election Manifesto

A Better Tomorrow
1970 General Election Manifesto

Who Governs Britain?
1974 General Election

Labour isn't working
1979 General Election Poster

Challenge of Our Times
1983 General Election Manifesto

The Next Moves Forward
1986 Conservative Party Conference

The Best Future for Britain
1992 General Election Manifesto

You can only be sure with the Conservatives

1997 General Election Manifesto

Samuel Smiles

Victorian Moralist

The spirit of self-help is the root of all genuine growth in the individual, and, exhibited in the lives of the many, it constitutes the true source of national vigour and strength.

Help from without is often enfeebling in its effects, but help from within invariably invigorates.

Self Help, 1859

Adam Smith

1723–1790; Moral Philosopher and Political Economist

Every individual is constantly exerting from himself to find out the most advantageous employment for whatever capital he can command. It is his own advantage, indeed, and not that of society, which he has in view. But the study of his own advantage naturally, or rather necessarily leads him to prefer that employment which is most advantageous to society.

Wealth of Nations, 1776

The property which every man has in his own labour, as it is the original foundation of all other property, so it is the most sacred and the most inviolable.

Ibid.

There is no art which one government sooner learns of another than that of draining money from the pockets of the people.

Ibid.

Nobody but a beggar chooses to depend chiefly upon the benevolence of his fellow citizens.

Ibid.

The uniform constant and uninterrupted effort of every man to better his condition, the principle from which public and national, as well as private opulence is originally derived is frequently powerful enough to maintain the natural progress of things towards improvement, in spite of both the extravagance of government and of greater errors of administration.

Ibid.

Great nations are never impoverished by private, though they sometimes are by public prodigality and misconduct. The whole, or almost the whole public revenue, is in most countries employed in maintaining unproductive hands.

Ibid.

Without any intervention of law ... the private interests and passions of men naturally lead them to divide and distribute the stock of every society, among all the different employments carried on in it, as nearly as possible in the proportion which is most agreeable to the interests of the whole society.

Ibid.

Alexander Solzhenitsyn

Russian novelist

I have spent my whole life under a Communist regime, and I will tell you that a society without any objective legal scale is a terrible one indeed. But a society with no other scale than the legal one is not quite worthy of man either.

Commencement Address, Harvard University, 1978

[I]t is time to remember that the first thing we belong to is humanity. And humanity is separated from the animal kingdom by thought and speech and they should naturally be free. If they are fettered we go back to being animals.

Letter to the Writer's Union, Moscow, Quoted in the *New York Times*, November 15, 1969

Thomas Sowell

Compassion is the use of tax money to buy votes. Insensitivity is the objection to the use of tax money to buy votes.

Herbert Spencer

1820–1903; Sociologist

Conservatism defends those coercive arrangements which a still lingering savageness makes requisite. Radicalism endeavours to realise a state more in harmony with the character of the ideal man.

1850

An argument fatal to the communist theory, is suggested by the fact ... that a desire for property is one of the elements of our nature.

Social Statistics, 1851

Liberty of each, limited by the like liberties of all, is the rule in conformity with which society must be organised.

Ibid.

Feudalism, Serfdom, slavery, all tyrannical institutions, are merely the most vigorous kind to rule, springing out of, and necessary to, a bad state of man. The progress from these is the same in all cases—less government.

Ibid.

Society exists for the benefit of its members; not the members for the benefit of society.

Principles on Ethics, 1892, 1893

All socialism involves slavery.

The Man versus the State, 1884

The Republican form of government is the highest form of government: but because of this it requires the highest type of human nature—a type no-where at present existing.

Essays, 1891

A Frenchman who having been three weeks here, proposed to write a book on England, after three months found that he was not quite ready, and after three years concluded that he knew nothing about it.

Study of Sociology

Ivor Stanbrook

1924–; Conservative MP, 1970–92

It is the normal British practice for the wife to go where her husband desires.

1982

Edward Stanley

1789–1869

When I first came into Parliament, Mr Tierney, a great Whig authority, used always to say that the duty of an Opposition was very simple—it was to oppose everything and propose nothing.

Adlai Stevenson

1900—1965; American statesman

Patriotism is not a short and frenzied outburst of emotion but the tranquil and steady dedication of a lifetime.
Speech to American Legion, 1952

A wise man does not try to hurry up history.
Ibid.

Leo Strauss

1899–1973; American Political Philosopher

The difficulty of defining the difference between liberalism and conservatism with the necessary universality is particularly great in the United States, since this country came into being through a revolution, a violent change or break with the past. One of the most conservative groups here calls itself the Daughters of the American Revolution.
Liberalism: Ancient and Modern, 1968

Jonathan Swift

1667–1745; Satirist and writer

Confine the expression of popular feeling within rigid limits, surround it with iron bands, and a spark may cause a terrific explosion. Leave it free and like gunpowder scattered in the open air, even if set alight it will do no damage.

Michael Taylor

I suggest that the more the state intervenes in such situations, the more

'necessary' (on this view) it becomes, because positive altruism and voluntary co-operative behaviour atrophy in the presence of the state and grow in its absence. Thus, again, the state exacerbates the conditions which are supposed to make it necessary. We might say that the state is like an addictive drug: the more of it we have, the more we 'need' it and the more we come to 'depend' on it.
The Possibility of Cooperation, 1987

Norman Tebbit

1931–; Conservative MP, 1970–92, Cabinet Minister 1981–87

I grew up in the thirties, with an unemployed father. He didn't riot. He got on his bike and looked for work.
Conservative Party Conference, Blackpool, October 1981

The Labour Party is not dead, just brain dead.

The trigger of today's outburst of crime and violence … lies in the era and attitudes of post-war funk which gave birth to the permissive society.
The Guardian, 4 November 1985

The word 'conservative' is used by the BBC as a portmanteau word of abuse for anyone whose views differ from the insufferable, smug, sanctimonious, naïve, guilt-ridden, wet, pink orthodoxy of that sunset home of the third-rate minds of that third-rate decade, the 1960s.
The Independent, 24 February 1990

Liberals are Enid Blyton Socialists—a dustbin for undecided votes.

Those who stand outside the town hall and scream and throw rotten eggs are not the real unemployed. If they were really hard up they would be eating them.

Why don't you go and have another heart attack?
> To Labour MP Tom Litterick

Take a sedative.
> To Denis Healey

I'm older than you are sonny, and you can take me on when you grow up.

The cricket test—which side do you cheer for? Are you still looking back to where you came from or where you are?
> On the loyalties of British immigrants

Maastricht is like that famous dead parrot. They may try to nail it on the perch again but nobody will believe it is still alive.
> 1992

I am not impressed by being called anti-European by those who were in short trousers when I began campaigning for Britain to enter the Common Market.
> 1993

That foul abomination, that running sore of Britain's politics, John Major's political tar baby, John Smith's self-imposed political ball and chain, the crumbling altar of the xenophobic paranoiac world of Monsieur Delors.
> On the Maastricht Treaty

I hope Mrs Thatcher will go until the turn of the century looking like Queen Victoria.
> 1987

Alfred Lord Tennyson
1809–92; Poet Laureate

For I dipt into the future, far as human
  eye could see;
Saw the vision of the world, and all the
  wonder that would be …
Yet I doubt not through the ages one
  enduring purpose runs,
And the thoughts of men are widened
  with the process of the suns.
> *Locksley Hall,* 1838

'Forward' rang the voices then, and of
  the many mine was one.
Let us hush this cry of 'Forward' till ten
  thousand years have gone.
> *Locksley Hall Sixty Years After,* 1887

When was age so cramm'd with men-
ace? Madness? written, spoken lies?
> Ibid.

A doubtful throne is ice on summer seas.
> *Idylls of the Kings,* 1869

Tertullian
c.150–c.225 BC; Christian theologian

Prevention of birth is a precipitation of murder.

Carol Thatcher
1953–; Daughter of Margaret Thatcher

After all she's done, I think this is an act of gutless treachery. As far as I'm concerned Tory is now a four-letter word.
> To a journalist outside her home, 22 November 1990

Oh Mum, it's me. I think you're a heroine. [Bursts into tears] I don't know how you made that speech. It's just so awful what they've done—your party are complete shits.

> Speaking to her mother on the evening of 22 November 1990

Being the only girl in the world who can say that her mother was Britain's first woman Prime Minister is honour enough for me.

> 13 June 1992

I now have to spell Thatcher when I make table reservations at restaurants—but I can cope with that.

> The *Independent,* 28 December 1993

Denis Thatcher

1915–; Husband of Margaret Thatcher

For forty years I have been married to one of the greatest women the world has ever produced. All I could produce—small as it may be—was love and loyalty.

Margaret Thatcher, Baroness Thatcher of Kesteven

1925–; Member of Parliament, 1959–93, Cabinet Minister 1970–74, Prime Minister 1979–1990

This woman is headstrong, obstinate and dangerously self-opinionated.

> Report on Margaret Roberts by the ICI Personnel Department, rejecting her job application, 1948

Every Conservative desires peace. The threat to peace comes from Communism which has powerful forces ready to attack anywhere. Communism waits for weakness, it leaves strength alone. Britain must therefore be strong, strong in her arms, strong in her faith, strong in her own way of life.

> Margaret Roberts election leaflet, 1950

It is expensive to be in politics. One has to be mobile, one has to be well groomed, and one has to entertain.

> *Guardian,* March 1962

The legal system we have and the rule of law are far more responsible for our traditional liberties than any system of one man one vote. Any country or Government which wants to proceed towards tyranny starts to undermine legal rights and undermine the law.

> At the Conservative Party Conference, October 1966

Civil servants have not got the expertise at their disposal which a merchant bank has. If they had such expertise, they would probably be working very successfully for a merchant bank.

> 1967

We must recognise certain groups of people who need help, but the rest of us must take responsibility for ourselves, and we must stop being such a subsidised-minded society.

> At the Scottish Conservative Party Conference, May 1969

No woman in my time will be Prime Minister or Foreign Secretary—not the top jobs. Anyway I wouldn't want to be Prime Minister. You have to give yourself one hundred per cent to the job.

> 1969

This business of the working class is on its way out I think. After all, aren't I working class? I work jolly hard, I can tell you.

> *London Evening News,* October 1969

We are not in politics to ignore people's worries; we are in politics to deal with them.

Many of our troubles are due to the fact that our people turn to politicians for everything.

It costs just as much to train a bad teacher as it does to train a good teacher.
1973

Please don't use the word tough. People might get the impression that I don't care. And I do care very deeply. Resilient, I think.
August 1973

I don't want to be leader of the Party—I'm happy to be in the top dozen.
1974

We failed the people.
On the Heath Government, *Daily Telegraph,* February 1974

We should back the workers, not the shirkers.
February 1974

It was then that the iron entered my soul.
On her time in the Heath Cabinet

The charm of Britain has always been the ease with which one can move into the middle class.
London Evening Standard, October 1974

Some Chancellors are micro-economic. Some Chancellors are fiscal. This one is just plain cheap … If this Chancellor can be Chancellor, anyone in the House could be Chancellor.
On Denis Healey, January 1975

Look Keith, if you're not going to stand, I will.
To Sir Keith Joseph after he decided not to stand against Edward Heath for the Party leadership

Forget that I'm a woman. Forget the accusations that I am a Right Winger demanding privilege—I had precious little privilege in my early years.
February 1975

We must build a society in which each citizen can develop his full potential, both for his own benefit and for the community as a whole.
1975

I've got my teeth into him, and I'm not going to let go.
On Edward Heath during the leadership contest, February 1975

To me it is like a dream that the next name in the list after Harold Macmillan, Sir Alec Douglas-Home and Edward Heath is Margaret Thatcher.
February 1975

The better I do, the more is expected of me. I am ready for that. I think I have the strength to do anything that I feel has to be done.
Daily Telegraph, September 1975

You cannot bring about prosperity by
  discouraging thrift
You cannot strengthen the weak by
  weakening the strong
You cannot help strong men by tearing
You cannot help the wage earner by
  pulling down the wage payer
You cannot further the brotherhood by
  encouraging class hatred

You cannot help the poor by destroying the rich

You cannot establish sound security on borrowed money

You cannot keep out of trouble by spending more than you earn

You cannot build character and courage by taking away man's initiative and independence

You cannot help men permanently by doing for them what they could and should do for themselves

> Abraham Lincoln, kept by Mrs Thatcher in her handbag

We must have an ideology. The other side have got an ideology they can test their policies against. We must have one as well.

> 1975

I sometimes think the Labour Party is like a pub where the mild is running out. If someone does not do something soon, all that is left will be bitter and all that is bitter will be left.

> 1975

In a Socialist society, parents should be seen and not heard.

> Conservative Party Conference, 10 October 1975

The first duty of a government is to uphold the law, and if it tries to bob, weave and duck round that duty when it is inconvenient the governed will do exactly the same thing, and then nothing will be safe, not home, not liberty, not life itself.

> 1975

Let our children grow tall, and some grow taller than others.

> Speech in the United States, 1975

I am convinced that Christian, democratic, conservative and centre parties in Europe should now join together in an effective working alliance ... this is a task of historic importance , and one in which we should invest all our energies.

> 1976

The Budget gives away the money the Chancellor has not even borrowed yet.

> On Denis Healey's 1976 Budget

We look to our alliance with NATO as the precise guarantee of our own security and, in the world beyond Europe, the United States is still the prime champion of freedom ... We believe in the Conservative Party that our foreign policy should continue to be based on a close understanding with our traditional ally, America.

> 1976

If your only opportunity is to be equal then it is not opportunity.

> 28 November 1976

For the Conservative Party politics has always been about something more than gaining power. It has been about serving the nation. We are above all a patriotic party ... nothing that's bad for Britain can ever be good for Conservatives.

> 1976.

Ladies & Gentlemen, I stand before you tonight in my green chiffon evening gown, my face softly made up, my hair softly waved ... The Iron Lady of the western world? Me? A cold warrior? Well, yes—if that is how they wish to interpret my defence of the values and freedom fundamental to our way of life.

Referring to the Soviet Magazine *Red Star,* which was the first to call her the Iron Lady, 1976

Sometimes I've heard it said that Conservatives have been associated with unemployment. That's absolutely wrong. We'd have been drummed out of office if we'd had this level of unemployment.

On the Labour Government's employment record, 1977

We want a society in which we are free to make choices, to make mistakes, to be generous and compassionate. That is what we mean by a moral society—not a society in which the State is responsible for everything, and no one is responsible for the State.

At Zurich University, 14 March 1977

My great fear is that when the time comes, I might fail.

April 1977

Let me tell you a little about my extremism. I am extremely careful never to be extreme. I am extremely aware of the dangerous duplicity of Socialism, and extremely determined to turn back the tide before it destroys everything we hold dear. I am extremely disinclined to be deceived by the mask of moderation that Labour adopts whenever an election is in the offing, a mask now being worn by all those who would 'keep the red flag flying here'.

Conservative Party Conference, 14 October 1977

We do not believe that if you cut back what Government does you diminish its authority. On the contrary, a government that did less, and therefore did better, would strengthen its authority.

Conservative Party Conference, 14 October 1977

Europe is the source of history's great endeavour, whereby the spirit of man, restless and ever ambitious, seeks always to renew itself by reaching outwards and upwards. The challenge for the next generation is to use the growing authority that will come from the greater unity of Europe to span the gaps between races and continents, between the rich and the poor, between the free and the unfree of the world. This is a great role and cannot be carried out by winning minds.

Rome, 1977

Choice is the essence of ethics. If there were no choice there would be no ethics, no good, no evil. Good and evil only have meaning in so far as man is free to choose.

1977

We must learn again to be one nation or one day we shall be no nation.

1978

There are still people in my party who believe in consensus politics. I regard them as Quislings, as traitors ... I mean it.

1978

Marxists get up early to further their cause. We must get up even earlier to defend our freedom.

Daily Mail, May 1978

If you wash your hands of Northern Ireland you wash them in blood.
Conservative Party Conference, 13 October 1978

Freedom is not synonymous with an easy life ... There are many difficult things about freedom: It does not give you safety, it creates moral dilemmas for you; it requires self-discipline; it imposes great responsibilities; but such is the destiny of Man and in such consists his glory and salvation.
1978

There are two ways of making a Cabinet. One way is to have in it people representing the different points of view within the party, within the broad philosophy. The other way is to have in it only the people who want to go in the direction which every instinct tells me we have to go: clearly, steadily, firmly, with resolution. As Prime Minister, I could not waste my time having internal arguments.
1979

I am not a consensus politician—I'm a conviction politician.
1979

Let us make this country safe to work in. Let us make this country safe to walk in. Let us make it a country safe to grow up in. Let us make it a country safe to grow old in.
In a Party Political Broadcast, 30 April 1979

Communism never sleeps, never changes its objectives. Nor must we.
Financial Times, May 1979

Where there is discord may we bring harmony. Where there is error, may we bring truth. Where there is doubt, may we bring faith. Where there is despair, may we bring hope.
Quoting St Francis of Assisi on the steps of 10 Downing Street, May 1979

In the age of materialism we stand for value. In an age of selfishness we believe in service. In an age of sectional interests we sill uphold the flag of patriotism, honour, family, courage, integrity and self-sacrifice. We do not equate permissiveness with civilised behaviour. We will neither permit ourselves, nor encourage others to overstep the bounds of conscience, morality and the law. It is because we are the party of freedom that we are also the party of the law.

Unless we change our ways and our direction, our greatness as a nation will soon be a footnote in the history books, a distant memory of an offshore island, lost in the mist of time like Camelot, remembered kindly for its noble past.
2 May 1979

We should not underestimate the enormity of the task which lies ahead. But little can be achieved without sound money. It is the bedrock of sound government.
May 1979

The mission of this government is much more than the promotion of economic progress. It is to renew the spirit and solidarity of the nation.
6 June 1979

When I look at him [Edward Heath] and he looks at me, I don't feel that it is a man looking at a woman. More like a woman being looked at by another woman.

> To Sir John Junor, 1979

If someone is confronting our essential liberties, if someone is inflicting injuries and harm, by God I'll confront them!

> 1979

Any woman who understands the problems of running a home will be nearer to understanding the problems of running a country.

> 1979

Pennies don't fall from heaven, they have to be earned on earth.

> *Sunday Telegraph,* November 1979

Nobody would remember the Good Samaritan if he had only good intentions, he had money as well.

> 1980

Iron entered my soul. You need a touch of steel. Otherwise you become like India rubber.

> BBC Radio, March 1980

I must be absolutely clear about this. Britain cannot accept the present situation on the budget. It is demonstrably unjust. It is politically indefensible. I cannot play Sister Bountiful to the Community while my own electorate are being asked to forego improvements in the fields of health, education, welfare and the rest.

> Winston Churchill Memorial Lecture, Luxembourg, 18 October 1980

To those waiting with baited breath for that favourite media catchphrase, the U Turn, I have only one thing to say. You turn if you want to. The Lady's not for turning.

> Conservative Party Conference, 10 October 1980

I want my money back!

> Dublin EC Summit, November 1980

If a woman like Eva Peron with no ideals can get that far, think how far I can go with all the ideals I have.

> *Sunday Times,* 1980

I don't mind how much my Ministers talk, as long as they do what I say.

> 1980

You belong to the North East, why don't you boost it? Not always standing there as moaning minnies. Now stop it!

> Description of journalists on Tyneside

If you have conviction people are much more likely to come out and support you. Most of the great faiths upon which our own moral values are founded would never have got started if their prophets had gone out to the people and said: 'Brothers, I believe in consensus.'

> *News of the World,* September 1981

Our judgement is that the presence of the Royal Marines garrison … is sufficient deterrent against any possible aggression.

Oh, those poor shopkeepers.

> Visiting Toxteth after the 1981 riots

Competition works. It is thanks to Freddie Laker that you can cross the

Atlantic for so much less than it would have cost in the early 1970s.

Speech to Conference, 1981

The people of the Falkland Islands, like the people of the United Kingdom, are an island race. They are few in number but they have the right to live in peace, to choose their own way of life and to determine their own allegiance. They way of life is British; their allegiance is to the Crown. It is the wish of the British people and the duty of Her Majesty's Government to do everything that we can to uphold that right. That will be our hope and our endeavour, and, I believe, the resolve, of every Member of this House.

In the House of Commons, 3 April 1982

When you stop a dictator there are always risks, but there are great risks in not stopping a dictator. My generation learned that long ago.

1982

Gentlemen, I have spent the night thinking about this Peruvian (peace) initiative and I have to tell you that if it is your decision to accept then you will have to find another Prime Minister.

To the War Cabinet, May 1982

It is exciting to have a real crisis on your hands when you have spent half your life dealing with humdrum issues like the environment.

May 1982

Just rejoice at the news and congratulate our armed forces and the Marines. Rejoice!

To journalists, following the retaking of South Georgia, 1982

We have ceased to be a nation in retreat. We have instead a new found confidence—born in the economic battles at home and tested and found true 8,000 miles away ... And so today, we can rejoice at our success in the Falklands and take pride in the achievement of the men and women of our task force. But we do so, not as some flickering of a flame which must soon be dead. No, we rejoice that Britain has rekindled that spirit which has fired her for generations past and which today has begun to burn as brightly as before. Britain found herself again in the South Atlantic and will not look back from the victory she has won.

3 July 1982

There are forces more powerful and pervasive than the apparatus of war. You may chain a man, but you cannot chain his mind. You may enslave him, but you will not conquer his spirit. In every decade since the war Soviet leaders have been reminded that their pitiless ideology only survives because it is maintained by force. But the day will come when the anger and frustration of the people is so great that force cannot contain it. Then the edifice cracks; the mortar crumbles ... one day, liberty will dawn on the other side of the wall.

In Berlin, 29 October 1982

Most of us have stopped using silver every day.

Successful businessmen do not take jobs in nationalised industries.

1982

The National Health Service is safe with us ... The principle of adequate healthcare should be provided for all regardless of ability to pay must be the function of any arrangements for financing the NHS. We stand by that.
> Conservative Party Conference, October 1982

Oh, Lord, teach me to learn that occasionally I make mistakes.
> Quoting her favourite poem, BBC Radio, 1982

If you want anything said, ask a man; if you want anything done, ask a woman.
> *The Changing Anatomy of Britain,* 1982

Oh, I have got lots of human weaknesses, who hasn't?
> The *Times,* 1983

State socialism is totally alien to the British character.
> 1983

You can strike your way down, but you have to work your way up.
> 1983

Will this thing jerk me off?
> Firing a field gun on the Falkland Islands, January 1983

If you are pronouncing a new law that wherever Communism reigns against the will of the people, even though it's happened internally, there the United States shall enter, then we are going to have really terrible wars in the world.
> Condemning the US invasion of Grenada, 1983

I was brought up by a Victorian Grandmother. We were taught to work jolly hard. We were taught to prove yourself; we were taught self reliance; we were taught to live within our income. You were taught that cleanliness is next to Godliness. You were taught self respect. You were taught always to give a hand to your neighbour. You were taught tremendous pride in your country. All of these things are Victorian values. They are also perennial values. You don't hear so much about these things these days, but they were good values and they led to tremendous improvements in the standard of living.
> LBC Radio, April 1983

I was asked whether I was trying to restore Victorian values. I said straight out I was. And I am.
> 1983

It's a pity about Ronnie (Reagan), he just doesn't understand economics at all.
> 1983

And what a prize we have to fight for: no less than the chance to banish from our land the dark, divisive clouds of Marxist Socialism.
> Scottish Conservative Party Conference, May 1983

It's a result that will reverberate through our history. Its consequences will outlive most of us here tonight.
> On the 1983 election result, 7 June 1983

Socialism and Britain go ill together. It is not the British character.
> *Director Magazine,* September 1983

We got a really good consensus during the last election. Consensus behind my convictions.
> 1984

I love being at the centre of things.
1984

I would feel desperate if I had been without a good regular income for twenty weeks.
1984

I came to office with one deliberate intent—to change Britain from a dependent to a self reliant society, from a give-it-to-me to a do-it-yourself nation, to a get-up-and-go instead of a sit-back-and-wait Britain.
The *Times*, 8 February 1984

What do you think of those two then?
To male advisers, while holding up Page 3 of The *Sun* in front of them

I am always on the job.
Interview on *Aspel & Co,* LWT, 1984

In the Conservative Party we have no truck with outmoded Marxist doctrine about class warfare. For us it is not who you are, who your family is or where you come from that matters, but what you are and what you can do for your country that counts.
1984

What we've got is an attempt to substitute the rule of the mob for the rule of the law. It must not succeed.
On the Miners' Strike, 1984

Scabs? They are lions!
On working miners, Conservative Party Conference, 13 October 1984

Beer and sandwiches at No.10? No, never.
Rejecting idea of negotiations to end Miners' Strike

I am an ally of the United States. We believe the same things, we believe passionately in the same battle of ideas, we will defend them to the hilt. Never try to separate me from them.
To Mikhail Gorbachev at their first meeting in 1984.

The bomb attack on the Grand Hotel early this morning was first and foremost an inhuman, undiscriminating attempt to massacre innocent, unsuspecting men and women staying in Brighton for our Conservative Conference. Our first thoughts must at once be for those who died and for those who are now in hospital recovering from their injuries. But the bomb attack clearly signified more than this. It was an attempt not only to disrupt and terminate our conference; it was an attempt to cripple Her Majesty's democratically elected Government. That is the scale of the outrage we have all shared, and the fact that we are gathered here now, shocked but composed and determined, is a sign not only that this attack has failed but that all attempts to destroy democracy by terrorism will fail.
Conservative Party Conference, 12 October 1984

In church on Sunday morning—it was lovely and we haven't had many lovely days—the sun was coming through the stained glass window and falling on some flowers. It just occurred to me that this was the day I was not meant to see. Then all of a sudden I thought 'there are some of my dearest friends who are not seeing this day'.
Following the IRA bomb attack on the Cabinet in Brighton, October 1984

I wasn't lucky, I deserved it.
On winning a school prize, aged 9

I like Mr Gorbachev. We can do business together.
> On Mikhail Gorbachev, December 1984

We had to fight the enemy without in the Falklands. We always have to be aware of the enemy within, which is more difficult to fight and more dangerous to liberty.
> On the miners' strike, 1984–85

The Labour Party believes in turning workers against owners; we believe in turning workers into owners.
If they do not wish to confer the honour, I am the last person who would wish to receive it.
> On Oxford University's decision not to give her an Honorary Degree, 1985

Yes, unemployment breeds frustration, but it's an insult to the unemployed to suggest that a man who doesn't have a job is likely to break the law.
> Conservative Party Conference, 11 October 1985

They have the usual socialist disease; they have run out of other people's money.

I took a pair of old scissors. I cut the card into pieces and sent it back to them in their prepaid envelope with a letter protesting against a gross invasion of privacy.
> On receiving a credit card.

I may not be Prime Minister at six o'clock.
> To colleagues just before the No Confidence Debate over Westland, 26 January 1986

I know nothing about diplomacy, but I know I want certain things for Britain.
> 1986

Has he resigned or has he gone for a pee?
> To Cabinet colleagues on Michael Heseltine's resignation, January 1986

If you want to cut your own throat, don't come to me for a bandage.
> To Robert Mugabe on South African sanctions, July 1986

There is just one thing I would like to make clear. The rose I am wearing is the rose of England.
> A dig at Labour's red rose logo, Conservative Party Conference, 1986

Dr Johnson could have said: when you know you are going to be privatised, it concentrates the mind wonderfully.
> 1986

What did it ever do for me?
> On feminism

Popular capitalism is on the march ... Of course, there will always be people who, in the name of morality, sneer at this and call it 'materialism'. But isn't it moral that people should want to improve the material standard of living of their families, by their own effort? Isn't it moral that families should work for the means to look after their old folk? Isn't it moral that people should save, so as to be responsible for themselves? ... And it is for Government to work with that grain in human nature to strengthen the strand of responsibility and independence: it benefits the family; it benefits the children; it is the essence of freedom.
> Scottish Conservative Party Conference, May 1987

I feel more genuine affection this time. I think I have become a bit of an institution and, you know, the sort of thing people expect to see around the place.

> At the start of the general election campaign, May 1987

I exercise my right as a free citizen to spend my own money in my own way, so that I can go on the day, the time, to the doctor I choose and get out fast.

> On why she chooses to use private healthcare, causing a political storm during the General Election campaign, June 1987

Margaret Thatcher: If people just drool and drivel they care, then I turn round and say, right, I also look to see what you actually do.

David Dimbleby: Why do you use the words drool and drivel they care, is that what you think saying that you care about people's lives amounts to?

Margaret Thatcher: No, I don't. I'm sorry I used those words.

> Interview on the BBC 9 O'Clock News, 10 June 1987

We've got a big job to do in some of those inner cities, a really big job.

> To Party Workers at Conservative Central Office, 12 June 1987

This is only the third time of asking. I hope to go on and on and on.

> During the General Election campaign, May 1987

There is no such thing as Society. There are individual men and women, and there are families.

> 1987

It would be fatal for us to stand just where we are now. What would be our slogan for the 1990s if we did that? Would 'consolidate' be the word that we stitch on our banners? Whose blood would run faster at the prospect of five years of consolidation?

> Speech to the Conservative Party Conference, 9 October 1987

We are in the fortunate position, in Britain, of being, as it were, the senior person in power.

> To a reporter en route to Moscow, 1987

I've seen and heard so many things on the BBC that infuriate me almost every day of the week—tendentious reporting, unfair comment, unbearable violence and vulgarity—that I hesitate to say yes when any part of the BBC asks me to do anything.

> To George Urban, 29 June 1988

I totally disagree about sanctions as did the previous Labour Government and unlike him [Neil Kinnock] I am not prepared to stand there comfortably in this house and impose starvation and poverty on millions and millions of black South Africans and black children.

> Defending her opposition to sanctions against South Africa, 1988

We have not successfully rolled back the frontiers of the state in Britain to only to see them reimposed at a European level, with a European super-state exercising a new dominance from Brussels.

> 1988

Make all you can, save all you can, give all you can.
>   Quoting John Wesley, 1988

We have become a Grandmother.
>   To reporters outside Number Ten Downing Street, 1989

He is another one of us.
>   On John Major, 1989

Human rights did not begin with the French Revolution ... [they] really stem from a mixture of Judaism and Christianity ... [we English] had 1688, our quiet revolution, where Parliament exerted its will over the King ... it was not the sort of revolution that France's was ... 'Liberty, equality, fraternity'— they forgot obligations and duties, I think. And then, of course the fraternity went missing for a long time.
>   Interview with Le Monde, 1989

It took us a long time to get rid of the effects of the French Revolution 200 years ago. We don't want another one.
>   30 June 1989

You can't buck the market.
>   On Chancellor Nigel Lawson's attempts to shadow the Deutsche Mark, 1989

I went to Oxford University, but I've never let that hold me back.
>   Conservative Party Conference, 13 October 1989

I am staying my own sweet, reasonable self.
>   Following the resignation of Nigel Lawson, October 1989

Advisers advise, Ministers decide.
>   On her relationship with Sir Alan Walters, 26 October 1989

Unassailable, unassailable.
>   Description of Nigel Lawson in an interview with Brian Walden, 29 October 1989

If we let it succeed no small country will feel safe again.
>   On Iraq's invasion of Kuwait, 2 August 1990

All right, George, all right. But this is no time to go wobbly.
>   To George Bush, August 1990

Beneath its contrived self-confidence lies a growing certainty that the world and history has passed it by and that if Britain rejects it as I believe it will, Socialism must return forever to its proper place—the reading room of the British Library where Karl Marx found it—Section: history of ideas. Subsection: nineteenth century. Status: archaic.
>   Speech to the Conservative Party Conference, October 1990

Carol Thatcher: Can you manage the supermarket shopping?
Margaret Thatcher: Good heavens, yes, dear, I've opened enough of them.
>   December 1990

Others bring me problems, David brings me solutions.
>   On David (later Lord) Young, 1990

As leader of the Progressive Conservatives I thought he put too much stress of the adjective and not enough on the noun.
>   On Canadian Premier Brian Mulroney

Yes, the Commission wants to increase its powers, Yes, it is a non-elected body and I do not want the Commission to increase its powers at the expense of the House, so of course we differ. The President of the Commission, Mr Delors, said at a press conference the other day that he wanted the European Parliament to be the democratic body of the Community. He wanted the Commission to be the Executive and he wanted the Council of Ministers to be the Senate. No! No! No!

30 October 1990

Ours is a creed which travels and endures. Its truths are written in the human heart. It is the faith which once more has given life to Britain and offers hope to the world. We pledge in this Party to uphold these principles of freedom and fight for them. We pledge it to our allies overseas, and we pledge it to this country we are proud to serve.

The conclusion of Margaret Thatcher's final speech to a Conservative Party Conference, 12 October 1990

I'm still at the crease, though the bowling's been pretty hostile of late. And, in case anyone doubted it, can I assure you that there will be no ducking the bouncers, no stonewalling, no playing for time? The bowling's going to get hit all round the ground. That's my style.

Lord Mayor's Banquet, 12 November, 1990

Not, I'm afraid, as good as we had hoped.

Peter Morrison, about to give the results of the Leadership election to Mrs Thatcher, 1990

I'm naturally very pleased that I got more than half the parliamentary party and disappointed that it's not enough to win on the first ballot so I confirm it is my intention to let my name go forward for the second ballot.

Outside the Paris Embassy, November 1990

I fight on, I fight to win.

Upon leaving Downing Street for the Commons, 21 November 21 1990

Now look here, you miserable little worm. You are in this Cabinet because I put you there and for no other reason. So I expect your support, and if I don't get it you will be out of my Cabinet when I reshuffle it after all this nonsense is over.

Cecil Parkinson outlining what he thought Margaret Thatcher should have said to errant Ministers

The Labour Party is led by a pigmy and we are led by a giant. We have decided that the answer to our problems is to find a pigmy of our own.

Cecil Parkinson, November 1990

Having consulted widely among colleagues, I have concluded that the unity of the Party and the prospects of victory in a general election would be better served if I stood down to enable Cabinet Colleagues to enter the ballot for the leadership.

1990

Margaret Thatcher: Europe is strongest when it grows through willing co-operation and practical measures, not compulsion or bureaucratic dreams.

Alan Beith: Will the Prime Minister tell us whether she intends to continue her personal fight against a single currency and an independent central bank when she leaves office?

Dennis Skinner: No, she's going to be the governor (laughter)

Margaret Thatcher: What a good idea! I hadn't thought of that. But if I were, there'd be no European Central bank, accountable to no one, not least of all to national Parliaments. Because the point of that kind of Europe with a central bank is no democracy, taking powers away from every single Parliament, and having a single currency, monetary policy and interest rates, which takes all political power away from us. As my Right Honourable Friend [Nigel Lawson] said in his first speech after the proposal for a single currency, a single currency is about the politics of Europe. It is about a federal Europe by the back door. So I'll consider the Honourable Gentleman's [Mr Skinner's] proposal. Now, where were we? I'm enjoying this, I'm enjoying this!

Michael Carttiss: Cancel it. You can wipe the floor with these people!
> No Confidence Debate, 22 November, 1990

It's a funny old world.
> At a Cabinet meeting following her resignation, 27 November 1990

I shan't be pulling the levers, but I shall be a very good back-seat driver.
> On her role following her departure from Number Ten, 1990

Every Prime Minister needs a Willie.
> On William Whitelaw, 1991

One is an ordinary person, and don't you forget it!
> To Eve Pollard, 1991

In my view dictators do not surrender. They have to be well and truly defeated.
> *Independent on Sunday,* 20 January 1991

I have never been defeated by the people. It is my great pride.
> Interview with Barbara Walters, February 1991

If you have a good Thatcher, you keep your home water and wind-proof.
> Interview with Barbara Walters, February 1991

Home is where you come to when you've nothing better to do.
> 11 May 1991

I do not accept the idea that all of a sudden Major is now his own man. There isn't any such thing as Majorism.
> 25 April 1992

People who start things don't often see the end of them—take Moses and the Promised Land.
> On her Premiership, 1992

Given time, it would have been seen as one of the most far-reaching and beneficial reforms ever made in the working of local government.
> On the Community Charge (Poll Tax), 1993

It would be the equivalent of having the Prime Minister of England invite the Oklahoma City bombers to 10

Downing Street, to congratulate them
on a job well done.

> On President Clinton's welcome of
> Gerry Adams

What is this thing called consensus?
Consensus is something you reach
when you cannot agree.

When the time is right.

> The mantra for joining the European
> Exchange Rate Mechanism

They have a new colour. They call it
gold; it looks like yellow to me.

> On the Liberal Democrats.

The sheer professionalism of the
British civil service, which allows
governments to come and go with a
minimum of dislocation and a maximum of efficiency, is something other
countries with different systems have
every cause to envy.

> 1993

It is the people's turn to speak. It is
their powers of which we are the
custodians.

> Calling for a referendum on
> Maastricht, 1993

We have been a little like an accom-
plice in a massacre. We cannot carry on
like that.

> On the West's role in Bosnia, 17 April
> 1993

It was treachery with a smile on his face.
Perhaps that was the worst thing of all.

> Describing her betrayal by the
> Cabinet, BBC TV, 1993

The lesson of this century is that
Europe will only be peaceful if the
Americans are on this continent.

> 18 April 1993

[The] root cause of our contemporary
social problems– to the extent that
these did not reflect the timeless
influence and bottomless resources of
old fashioned human wickedness—was
that the state had been doing too much
… Society was made up of individuals
and communities. If individuals were
discouraged and communities disori-
entated by the state stepping into to
take decisions which should properly
be made by people, families and
neighbourhoods then society's problems would not diminish.

> *The Downing Street Years* (1993)

In my day that would have required
the occasional use of the handbag.
Now it will be a cricket bat. But that's
a good thing because it will be harder.

> On John Major's negotiations on the
> Maastricht Treaty, 1993

I personally could never have signed
this Treaty.

> On the Maastricht Treaty, 12 June 1993

… He is probably the most formidable
leader we have seen since Gaitskell … I
see a lot of Socialism behind their front
bench but not in Mr Blair—I think he
genuinely has moved.

> On Tony Blair, BBC TV, 1994

Your President, President Clinton, is a
great communicator. The trouble is, he
has absolutely nothing to communicate.

> To American political observer,
> Daniel Forrester, March 1994

They have hit at everything I believed in.

> On John Major's government, 1995

I don't think I was unkind to him, I
supported him a lot—I chose him!

> June 1995

We introduced the Community Charge. I still call it that. I like the Poles—I never had any intention of taxing them.
On the Poll Tax, Nicholas Ridley Memorial Lecture, 22 November 1996

Clarence Thomas

US Supreme Court Justice

Conservatives should be no more timid about asserting the responsibilities of the individual than they should be about protecting individual rights.
July 1991

James Thompson

When Britain first, at Heaven's command
Arose from out of the azure main,
This was the charter of the land,
And guardian angels sang this strain,
Rule Britannia, rule the waves,
Britons never will be slaves.
1740

Henry David Thoreau

There will never be a really free and enlightened State until the State comes to recognise the individual as a higher and independent power, from which all its own power and authority are derived, and treats him accordingly.

Anyone in a free society where the laws are unjust has an obligation to break the law.

Alexis de Tocqueville

1805–1859; French writer and statesman

When the religion of a people is destroyed, doubt gets hold of the higher powers of the intellect, and half paralyses all the others. Every man accustoms himself to have only confused and changing notions on the subjects most interesting to his fellow-creatures and himself.
Democracy in America, 1840

I know of no country, indeed, where the love of money has taken stronger hold on the affections of men and where a profounder contempt is expressed for the theory of the permanent equality of property.
Ibid.

In democracies, nothing is more great or brilliant than commerce: it attracts the attention of the public, and fills the imagination of the multitudes; all energetic passions are directed towards it.
Ibid.

Leo Tolstoy

1828–1910; Russian Novelist

Government is an association of men who do violence to the rest of us.

Harry Truman

1884–1972; American President 1944–52

Men make history and not the other way round. In periods where there is no leadership, society stands still. Progress occurs when courageous skilful leaders seize the opportunity to change things for the better.

It is a recession when your neighbour loses his job. It's a depression when you lose your own.

I have found the best way to give advice to your children is to find out what they want and then advise them to do it.

The Republican Party either corrupts its liberals or expels them.

The buck stops here.
Paperweight on Truman's desk

Desmond Tutu

South African Bishop

Freedom and liberty lose out by default because good people are not vigilant.

Mark Twain

American Novelist

It is by the goodness of God that in our country we have those three unspeakable precious things; freedom of speech, freedom of conscience, and the prudence never to practice either of them.
Following the Equator, 1897

Peter Viereck

American Philosopher

Conservatism, which is for politics what classicism is for literature, is in turn the political secularisation of the doctrine of original sin. In contrast, radicalism is Rousseau's 'natural goodness of man, collectivised into a touching political faith in the 'masses.' Nazi radicalism equates Rousseau's Noble Savage with the radical mass (the Volk); Marxist radicalism equates him with the economic mass (the proletariat). But he is not worshipped like this by

the churches. The churches, Protestant, Catholic, or … Jewish, draw the fangs on the noble savage and clip his ignoble claws.
Conservatism Revisited, 1946

Virgil

70–19 BC; Roman Poet

Others, I suppose will more subtly mould the breathing bronze, draw forth the living features from the marble, plead causes better, mark with the rod the wanderings of the sky and foretell the rising stars; Thou, Roman, be mindful to rule the peoples with imperial sway (these shall be they arts) to impose the way of peace, to spare the conquered and put down the proud.
The Aenid

Voltaire

1694–1778; Philosopher

I detest your views, but I am prepared to die for your right to express them.

Liberty was born in England from the quarrels of tyrants.
Lettres philosophiques

David Waddington

1929–; Conservative MP, 1968–74, 1979–91, Cabinet Minister 1987–90

Sentences served should be much closer to sentences passed.
As Home Secretary, 1990

The vast majority of offences are committed not by determined young professionals but by dishonest youngsters left to their own devices.
As Home Secretary, 1990

William Waldegrave

1946–; Conservative MP, 1979–97, Cabinet
Minister, 1989–97

We said zero, and I think any statistician will tell you that when you're
dealing with very big numbers, zero
must mean plus or minus a few.
> On hospital waiting lists, 1992

In exceptional cases it is necessary to
say something that is untrue to the
House of Commons. The House of
Commons understands that and has
always accepted that.
> As Minister for Open Government,
> 1994

Peter Walker

1932–; Conservative MP, 1961–92

Rivers and lakes are polluted past
praying for. Seas are overfished. Forests
are vanishing. Pollution of the air and
the water are threatening the two
previously most predictable and essential elements in man's very existence …
As our cities become more congested,
our lives more merchandised, and our
leisure more pre-packaged, there must
be growing awareness that nature is
now our most precious possession.
> 1970

Dame Irene Ward

Conservative MP

Is my right honourable friend saying
that Wrens' skirts must be held up until
all sailors have been satisfied?
> Responding to Navy Minister's statement
> that new women's uniforms would be
> dealt with as soon as male officers had
> theirs. House of Commons, 1940

George Washington

1732–99; American President 1789–97;

Government is not reason. Government is not eloquence. It is force. And,
like fire, it is a dangerous servant and a
fearful master.

Associate yourself with men of good
quality if you esteem your own reputations; for 'tis better to be alone than in
bad company.
> *Rules of Civility*

To be prepared for war is one of the
most effectual means of preserving
peace.
> First annual address to Congress,
> 1790

The very idea of the power and the
right of the people to establish government, presupposes the duty of every
individual to obey the established
government.
> Farewell Address, 1796

J. C. Watts

US Congressman

If liberals can't beat you, if they're
losing on the issues, they do one of
two things. They either call you a bigot
or a racist. Or they sue you.

My father taught that the only helping
hand you're ever going to be able to
rely on is the one at the end of your
sleeve.

The American dream does not happen
by asking Americans to accept what's
immoral and wrong in the name of
tolerance.
> GOP Radio Response, 4 February 1997

Auberon Waugh
Novelist

... the small troupe of exhibitionists, failed vaudeville artists, juicy young Boy Scouts and degenerate old voluptuaries which is the Liberal Party.

Contradictions between the individualistic, free-market stance and traditional Conservative appeals to authority, patriotism, law and order are two a penny, and have often been remarked on. The electoral calculation has always been that the two opposed camps—the 'individualists' who are trying to make money, and the 'conservatives' who already have it—will make common cause at the end of the day.
The *Spectator*, 1989

It is an alarming thought that if we are ever invaded by monsters from outer space, the man who will be appointed to save us as Minister for Monsters will be this joke yobbo who could easily be mistaken for the traditional plumber with a cleft palate who has lost his dentures down the lavatory.
On Denis Howell MP

Evelyn Waugh
Social Commentator

The trouble with the Conservative Party is that it has never turned the clock back a single second.

I believe that man is, by nature an exile and will never be self sufficient or complete on this earth; that his chances of happiness and virtue, here, remain more or less constant through the centuries and, generally speaking, are not much affected by the political and economic conditions in which he lives...

I believe that inequalities of wealth and position are inevitable and that it is therefore meaningless to discuss the advantages of their elimination; that men naturally arrange themselves into a system of classes; that such a system is necessary for any form of co-operative work, more particularly the work of keeping a nation together.
Mexico: An Object Lesson (1939)

He is not a man for I ever had esteem. Always in the wrong, always surrounded by crooks, a most unsuccessful father—simply 'Radio personality' who outlived his prime.
On Winston Churchill, 1965, Ibid.

Daniel Webster
Let our object be our country, our whole country and nothing but our country.
1825

Duke of Wellington
1769–1852; Prime Minister 1828–1830, 1834–1839

I don't know what effect these men will have upon the enemy, but, by God, they terrify me.
On a new draft of soldiers sent out during the Peninsular War

Nothing except a battle lost can be half so melancholy as a battle won.
Comment after the Battle of Waterloo

Nobody cares a damn about the House of Lords. The House of Commons is everything in England and the House of Lords nothing.
To Thomas Creevy in Brussels

An extraordinary affair, I gave them their orders and they wanted to stay and discuss them.

> As Prime Minister on his first Cabinet, 1828

I never saw so many shocking bad hats in my life.

> 1832, on seeing the first reformed House of Commons

Don't quote Latin. Say what you have to say and then sit down

> Advice to a new MP

I have no small talk and Peel has no manners.

Earl of Wemyss

We grow corn, oats, hay and straw. Motors do not eat oats, they do not eat hay and they do not lie on the straw and when horses are done away with, it will not be worth while our growing these agricultural articles of consumption having lost our best customer.

> 1903

Paul M. Weyrick

… the Old Right tends to be intellectual and upper class. It is an accurate generalisation that the New Right tends to be middle class, blue-collar and ethnic in its origins.

> *Blue Collar or Blue Bird? The New Right Compared with the Old Right,* 1982

Though the upper classes had more intellectual expertise, they tended to become deficient in something that was strong in the working middle classes: values.

> Ibid.

Well-bred, well-heeled youth allowed right and wrong to become blurred, and tradition to become a romantic decoration. Respect among working people was a consciously instilled value.

> Ibid.

R. J. White

Conservatism is less a political doctrine than a habit of mind, a mode of feeling, a way of living. And the human content of the Party is no less amorphous than the so called 'creed'. The Party is, in fact, the perfect secular analogy of its great historical ally, the Church of England. It contains not only the convinced and the converted who think they know what they believe. It contains also the vast residue of politics which would be hard put to describe itself as anything else at all.

> *The Conservative Tradition,* 1970

William Whitelaw

1918–99; Conservative MP, 1955–83, Cabinet Minister 1970–74, Deputy Prime Minister 1983–87

I have always said it is a great mistake ever to pre-judge the past.

> As Northern Ireland Secretary 1972

They are going about the country stirring up complacency.

> On Labour Ministers, 1974

I have the thermometer in my mouth and I am listening to it all the time.

> On party morale, 1974

Those who say that I am not in agreement with the policy are, rightly or wrongly, quite wrong.

> On the party's immigration policy

It is never wise to appear to be more clever than you are. It is sometimes wise to appear slightly less so.
1975

It is both possible and moral, to love one's country and hate its government … In the long run those who shout 'racialist' loudest will do real damage to race relations and the true interests of the ethnic minority groups in our society by their obstinate refusal to face facts and to recognise the genuine worries and fears of so many of our fellow citizens … I do not believe we have any hope of promoting the sort of society which we want unless we are prepared to follow a policy which is clearly designed to work towards the end of immigration.
1976

From 6.45 a.m. to lights out at 9.30 p.m. life will be conducted at a brisk tempo. Much greater emphasis will be put on and constructive activities, on discipline and tidiness, on self-respect and respect for those in authority.
> As Home Secretary, announcing 'short, sharp, shock' treatment for juvenile offenders, 1979

I can assure you that I definitely might take action.
> As Home Secretary, 1981

Ann Widdecombe
1947–; Conservative MP, 1987–

I think the rest of the world will think we're mad, and indeed we are. We've turned out the greatest Prime Minister in the post-war years simply because of short-term nerves.
> BBC TV News, 22 November 1990

He has something of the night about him.
> On Michael Howard, former Home Secretary, 20 May 1997

Oscar Wilde
1854–1900; Writer

The state in the end depends on the vigour of the character of the individuals which make it up; and that character is strengthened by the effort to find a way out of difficulties and hardships, and is weakened by the habit of looking to state help.

If individual gifts and attainments were infallible signs of wisdom and goodness … and the knowing, clever and talented (vile word!) were always rational; if the mere facts of science confined or suppressed the softening humanising influences of the moral world … then indeed, political power might not unwisely be conferred as the honorarium or privilege of having passed through all the forms of the National School.
> *The Soul of Man under Socialism*, 1895

Earl of Wilmington

No Sir, you have a right to speak, but the House will have a right to judge whether they will hear you.
> As Speaker, on whether Members had a right to be heard, Hatsell's Precedents 1818.

Woodrow Wilson

A Conservative is a man who sits and thinks—mostly sits.

Nicholas Winterton

1938–; Conservative MP, 1971–

Certain elements of the British Medical Association leadership have gone over the top and taken fully entrenched positions,

> On health reforms, 1989

Sir Kingsley Wood

Are you aware it is private property? Why, you'll be asking me to bomb Essen next.

> As Secretary of State for the Air, on plans to bomb the Black Forest, 1939.

Lord Young of Graffham

1932–; Businessman & Conservative Politician, Cabinet Minister, 1985–89

The idea of a pilot scheme is to see whether it will fly.

> As Employment Secretary, 1989

Oh look—with hindsight you can always look back.

> As former Trade and Industry Secretary responding to government criticism of the 1985 Harrods/ House of Fraser takeover, 1990

INDEX

A

B

Also available in this series:

The *Dictionary of Labour Quotations*

edited by Stuart Thomson; with forewords by Rt Hon. Neil
Kinnock and Simon Hoggart.

The *Dictionary of Liberal Quotations*

edited by Duncan Brack and Robert Ingham; with forewords
by Charles Kennedy MP and Rt Hon. Robert Maclennan MP.

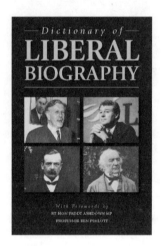

The *Dictionary of Liberal Biography*

edited by Duncan Brack; with forewords by Rt Hon.
Paddy Ashdown MP and Professor Ben Pimlott

*containing the biographies of over 200 individuals who have
made major contributions to the Liberal Party, SDP or Liberal
Democrats, or to the development of British Liberalism*

The *Dictionary of Conservative Biography* and the
Dictionary of Labour Biography will be available in
late 2000.

All available from Politico's Political Bookstore

8 Artillery Row, London SW1P 1RZ

tel: 0171 931 0090; fax: 0171 828 8111

email: politicos@artillery-row.demon.co.uk